Albert Bandura
Stanford University

D0223927

Social
Learning
Theory

PRENTICE-HALL, INC. *Englewood Cliffs, New Jersey 07632*

Library of Congress Cataloging in Publication Data

BANDURA, ALBERT, Date
  Social learning theory.

  Bibliography: p.
  Includes index.
    1. Learning, Psychology of. 2. Socialization.
I. Title.
LB1084.B357 1976   153.1'5   76-43024
ISBN 0-13-816751-6
ISBN 0-13-816744-3 pbk.

To
Ginny
Mary
and
Carol

Printed in the United States of America

10 9 8 7 6 5 4 3 2

Prentice-Hall International, Inc., *London*
Prentice-Hall of Australia Pty. Limited, *Sydney*
Prentice-Hall of Canada, *Toronto*
Prentice-Hall of India Private Limited, *New Delhi*
Prentice-Hall of Japan, Inc., *Tokyo*
Prentice-Hall of Southeast Asia Pte. Ltd., *Singapore*
Whitehall Books Limited, *Wellington, New Zealand*

Prentice-Hall Series in Social Learning Theory

ALBERT BANDURA, *Editor*

AGGRESSION: A SOCIAL LEARNING ANALYSIS
Albert Bandura

BEHAVIOR THERAPY: APPLICATION AND OUTCOME
K. Daniel O'Leary and G. Terence Wilson

BEHAVIOR, SOCIAL PROBLEMS AND CHANGE: A SOCIAL
LEARNING APPROACH
John Kunkel

SCIENCE AND BEHAVIOR: AN INTRODUCTION TO METHODS OF
RESEARCH
John M. Neale and Robert M. Liebert

SOCIAL LEARNING THEORY
Albert Bandura

Contents

Chapter Five
COGNITIVE CONTROL, 159

Chapter Six
RECIPROCAL DETERMINISM, 193

Preface

In this book I have attempted to provide a unified theoretical framework for analyzing human thought and behavior. Views about human nature influence which aspects of psychological functioning are studied most thoroughly and which remain unexamined. Theoretical conceptions similarly determine the paradigms used to collect evidence which, in turn, shapes the particular theory. Thus, for example, theorists who exclude the capacity for self-direction from their view of human potentialities restrict their research to external sources of influence. Detailed analysis of how external influences affect conduct provides confirmatory evidence that behavior is indeed subject to external control. However, limiting the scope of scientific inquiry to certain psychological processes to the neglect of other important ones can reinforce a truncated image of the human potential.

Over the years, the various behavior theories have contributed much to our understanding of how behavior is learned and modified by direct experience. However, the traditional ways of conceptualizing and studying human behavior have been too circumscribed and often hampered by the mechanistic models of an earlier period of development. In recent years substantial progress has been made in our understanding of psychological processes, which calls for a reexamination of some of the fundamental assumptions about how human behavior is acquired and regulated. This book sets forth some of the significant developments within the framework of social learning theory.

Social learning theory emphasizes the prominent roles played by vicarious, symbolic, and self-regulatory processes in psychological functioning. Changes in theoretical perspectives added new paradigms to the standard methods of research. Acknowledgment that human thought, affect, and behavior can be markedly influenced by observation, as well as by direct experience, fostered development of observational paradigms for studying the power of socially mediated experience.

The extraordinary capacity of humans to use symbols enables them to represent events, to analyze their conscious experience, to communicate with others at any distance in time and space, to plan, to create, to imagine, and to engage in foresightful action. Renewal of emphasis on symbolic functions expanded the range of techniques for analyzing thought and the mechanisms by which thought regulates action.

The third distinctive feature of social learning theory is the central role it assigns to self-regulatory processes. People are not simply reactors to external influences. They select, organize, and transform the stimuli that impinge upon them. Through self-generated inducements and consequences they can exercise some influence over their own behavior. An act therefore includes among its determinants self-produced influences. Recognition of people's self-directing capacities provided the impetus for self-regulatory paradigms of research in which individuals themselves serve as the principal agents of their own change.

Social learning theory approaches the explanation of human behavior in terms of a continuous reciprocal interaction between cognitive, behavioral, and environmental determinants. Within the process of reciprocal determinism lies the opportunity for people to influence their destiny as well as the limits of self-direction. This conception of human functioning then neither casts people into the role of powerless objects controlled by environmental forces nor free agents who can become whatever they choose. Both people and their environments are reciprocal determinants of each other.

This book presents a concise overview of the recent theoretical and experimental advances in the field of social learning. Many of the traditional concepts in learning theory are extended and redefined to reflect the changing theoretical emphasis noted above. New findings are presented for psychological processes that have been neglected or only partially investigated in the traditional approaches. Because of the mass and rapid growth of research on social learning, a detailed review of the relevant literature would exceed the scope of this book. A fuller treatment of the conceptual and empirical issues in social learning will be provided in a later volume.

I am most pleased to take this opportunity to acknowledge my indebtedness to those who assisted me in this project. A Fellowship grant from the John Simon Guggenheim Foundation was of considerable help in the early stages of writing this book. I am thankful to Fred Kanfer for his comments on an earlier draft of the manuscript. I also whish to express appreciation to my colleagues and students whose questions have helped to clarify many of the issues discussed in this volume. The revised substance of some of the material that is incorporated in this book was published in the monograph, *Social Learning Theory*, and in the *American Psychologist* (1975) under the title, *Behavior Theory and the Models of Man*. I am grateful for the permission to draw on this material. Finally, I owe a considerable debt of gratitude to Julia Baskett for her invaluable assistance with the manuscript through its various revisions.

Albert Bandura

1

Theoretical Perspective

MANY THEORIES HAVE BEEN PROPOSED OVER THE YEARS to explain human behavior. Until recently, some theorists held that motivational forces in the form of needs, drives, and impulses, frequently operating below the level of consciousness, were the major determinants. Since the proponents of this school of thought consider the principal causes of behavior to be forces within the individual, that is where they look for the explanations of why people behave as they do. Although this view enjoyed widespread popularity and influence, it did not go unchallenged.

Theories of this sort were criticized on both conceptual and empirical grounds. The inner determinants often were inferred from the behavior they supposedly caused, resulting in description in the guise of explanation. A hostile impulse, for example, was derived from a person's irascible behavior, which was then attributed to the action of an underlying hostile impulse. Similarly, the existence of achievement motives were deduced from achievement behavior; dependency motives from dependent behavior; curiosity motives from inquisitive behavior; power motives from domineering behavior, and so on. There is no limit to the number of motives one can find by inferring them from the kinds of behavior they supposedly produce. Indeed, different theories have proposed diverse lists of motivators, some containing a few all-purpose drives, others embracing a varied assortment of specific drives.

The conceptual structure of theories that invoke impulses as the principal motivators of behavior has been further criticized for disregarding the enormous complexity of human responsiveness. An internal motivator cannot possibly account for the marked variation in the frequency and strength of a given behavior in different situations, toward different persons, and at different times. When diverse environmental conditions produce corresponding variations in behavior, the postulated inner cause cannot be less complex than its effects.

It should be noted in passing that it is not the existence of motivated behavior that is being questioned, but whether such behavior is at all explained by ascribing it to the action of impulses. The limitations of this type of analysis can be illustrated by considering a common activity, such as reading, which has the qualities of a highly motivated behavior. People spend large sums of money purchasing reading material; they expend effort obtaining books from libraries; they engage in reading for hours on end; and they can become emotionally upset when deprived of reading material (as when their daily newspaper is not delivered through an oversight).

Following the common practice of inferring the existence of drives from persistent behavior, one could ascribe the activated reading to the force of a "reading drive"—or, more likely, to some higher motive. However, if one wanted to predict what people read, when, how long, and the order in which they choose to read different material, one would look not for drives but for preceding inducements and expected benefits derived from reading and for cognitive factors that influence reading activities. On the antecedent side, one would want to know, among other things, people's reading assignments, their deadlines, and the type of information they require to deal effectively with the demands of everyday life. Knowledge about the reading material people find rewarding or boring as well as the effects of reading or ignoring certain materials are also important consequential determinants. Reading activities are further regulated cognitively by people's anticipations, intentions, and self-evaluations. There is a crucial difference between ascribing motivating potentials to antecedent, incentive, and cognitive inducements, which are verifiable by experimentation, and positing acquired drives, which have been found lacking in explanatory value (Bolles, 1975).

While the conceptual adequacy of the impulse energy theories could be debated at length, their empirical limitations could not be ignored indefinitely. They provide ready interpretations of past events, but they are deficient in predicting future ones (Mischel, 1968; Peterson, 1968). Most any theory can explain things after the fact. The explanatory power of a psychological theory is gauged by its accuracy in specifying the conditions governing psychological phenomena and the mechanisms by which the determinants produce their effects. The approaches under discussion have not fared well when tested for their explanatory capabilities either.

The value of a theory is ultimately judged by the power of the procedures it generates to effect psychological changes. Other sciences are evaluated by their eventual contributions to prediction and technical innovations using that knowledge. Suppose, for example, aeronautical scientists developed certain principles of aerodynamics in wind tunnel tests; if in applying these principles they were never able to design an aircraft that could fly, the value of their theoretical assumptions would be highly questionable. The same judgment would be applied to theorizing in the medical field if certain theories about physiological processes never led to any effective treatments of physical maladies. Psychological approaches which attribute behavior to the operation of internal impulses consider the achievement of insight or self-awareness essential for producing enduring behavioral changes. Through the process of labeling people's impulses, which manifest themselves in many guises, the underlying determinants of their behavior are gradually made conscious. After these impulses are brought into awareness, they presumably cease to function as instigators, or they become more susceptible to conscious control.

However, studies measuring actual changes in behavior have had difficulty demonstrating that the behavior of persons who received psychodynamically-oriented treatment changed any more than that of comparable individuals who had not undergone such procedures (Bandura, 1969; Rachman, 1971). Gaining insight into one's underlying motives, it seems, is more like a belief conversion than a self-discovery process. As Marmor (1962), among others, has noted, each psychodynamic approach has its own favorite set of inner causes and its own preferred brand of insight. The hypothesized determinants can be readily confirmed in self-validating interviews by offering suggestive interpretations and selectively reinforcing clients' observations whenever they are consistent with the therapists' beliefs. Thus, advocates of differing theoretical orientations repeatedly discover their chosen motivators at work but rarely find evidence for the motivators emphasized by the proponents of competing views. In fact, if one wanted to predict the types of insights and unconscious motivators that persons are apt to discover in themselves in the course of such analyses, it would be more helpful to know the therapists' conceptual belief system than the clients' actual psychological status.

Questions about belief conversions in the name of self-awareness would apply equally to behavioral approaches if they mainly taught people to construe their actions in behavioral terms but failed to alter the behavior for which clients sought aid. For this reason, psychological methods are best evaluated on the basis of their effectiveness in changing actual psychological functioning.

It eventually became apparent that in order to make progress in understanding human behavior, more stringent requirements would have to be used in evaluating the adequacy of explanatory systems. Theories must demonstrate predictive power. They must accurately identify the determinants of human behavior as well as the intervening mechanisms responsible for the changes.

Developments in behavior theory shifted the focus of causal analysis from amorphous internal determinants to detailed examination of external influences on human responsiveness. Behavior has been extensively analyzed in terms of the stimulus conditions that evoke it and the reinforcing conditions that maintain it. Researchers have repeatedly demonstrated that response patterns that are generally attributed to inner causes can be induced, eliminated, and reinstated by varying external influences. Results of such investigations have led many psychologists to view the determinants of behavior as residing not within the organism but in environmental forces.

The notion that human behavior is externally regulated, though amply documented, has not been enthusiastically received. To many people it implies a one-way control process which reduces individuals to passive respondents to the vagaries of whatever influences impinge upon them. Popular accounts of the potentials of psychological control conjure up frightening images of societies in which inhabitants are manipulated at will by occult technocrats.

There is another implication of radical behaviorism that raises objections in the minds of many. If the environment controls behavior, it was reasoned, then behavior must vary with changing circumstances. Behaviorists would not entirely agree with this view because whether people behave uniformly or variably depends upon the functional equivalence of the environments. Thus, if acting intelligently in diverse settings has functional value, people will be consistently intelligent in situations that otherwise differ markedly. By contrast, if issuing orders to police officers brings punishment while ordering store clerks brings better service, then people will behave authoritatively with clerks but cautiously with the police. Behavior theory is therefore concerned with the conditions determining both generality and specificity in conduct, rather than championing only variability in behavior. Nevertheless, the notion that behavior may be situationally specific contradicts firmly held beliefs that people possess traits or dispositions which lead them to behave consistently under changing circumstances. The old controversy over situational and dispositional determinants of behavior, which had remained dormant for years, has once again become the subject of attention.

Studies in which such behavior as, for example, aggression or dependency, were measured in different settings revealed limited consistency in conduct from one situation to another (Mischel, 1968). In commenting on the issues, Mischel discusses factors that may possibly lead people to see behavioral consistencies where they do not exist. The factors listed as creating the impression of consistency include physical constancies in appearance, speech, and expressive behavior; regularity of the settings in which a person is repeatedly observed; reliance upon broad and ambiguous trait categories encompassing heterogeneous behavior; internal pressures for consistency to maintain a stable view of people; and researcher's use of personality tests that require people to rate their behavior in "typical" rather than in specific situations. Changeable responsiveness therefore tends to be glossed over, ignored, or reinterpreted.

Efforts to strip traits and motives of their sovereignty have not gone uncontested. Proponents of these theories argue that seemingly different behaviors may be manifestations of the same underlying motive. This type of argument has not been especially persuasive because no reliable criteria have been provided for identifying the behaviors that are expressions of a particular motive and those that are not. Some researchers questioned the assumptions of the traditional methods used to study behavioral consistencies. Bem and Allen (1974) advanced the view that some people are highly consistent in some areas of behavior, but the evidence of cross-situational consistency is obscured when data from consistent and variable responders are combined in behavior dimensions defined in terms of the researcher's frame of reference. In tests of this proposition, Bem and Allen have shown that individuals who describe themselves as consistent on certain behavior dimensions given trait names (e.g., friendliness, conscientiousness) are rated with higher agreement by others in these areas of behavior than are individuals who identify themselves as being highly variable in behavior. However, the implications of this evidence for the issue of behavioral consistency is difficult to assess because most of the findings are reported in terms of inter-rater correlations of summary scores that pool ratings of behavior across situations. In addition to a behavioral measure, subjects were rated by their parents, by a peer, and by themselves for friendliness and conscientiousness on a questionnaire describing many different situations. But the ratings for each trait dimension were summed for each judge across situations into a global score. In testing for consistency one must measure how individuals vary in their behavior under different circumstances rather than how they stand in relation to others, or how well judges agree among themselves in their overall ratings of the individuals selected to study.

The most informative methodology for studying cross-situational consistencies is to record how much people vary in their behavior across situations that differ measurably in the probable consequences for the behavior being examined. Situations chosen for study should be scaled in terms of consequences they customarily provide for the particular behavior rather than selected arbitrarily. Such studies would undoubtedly reveal that all people behave discriminatively most of the time. It is only by including a range of values of the environment that people's responsiveness to situational circumstances can be adequately evaluated. The number of individuals who might be categorized as unchanging responders would fluctuate depending upon the behavior selected for study, the extent to which the situations sampled differ in likely consequences for the given conduct, how much variability is tolerated in the criterion of consistency, and whether one measures verbal reports of behavior or the behavior itself. Acting friendly, just as acting intelligently, is functional in diverse settings and would therefore appear more consistently than behaviors that produce different effects under dissimilar circumstances. It would be difficult to find adolescents, for instance, who are consistently aggressive toward parents, teachers, peers, and police officers, because the consequences for the same conduct vary markedly (Bandura and Walters, 1959). Even in the case of a widely acceptable behavior such as friendliness, the ranks of the consistent responders can be substantially reduced simply by including some situations in which friendliness is less probable, as when individuals are being exploited, or discriminated against. Only those who are grossly undiscerning or who have a poor sense of reality would remain steadfastly amiable.

It is unfortunate that the label "consistency" has been applied to the issue of behavioral variability because the term has misleading connotations. Consistency not only implies virtues of steadfast, principled conduct, but sets up the contrast as "inconsistency" with its implications of instability and expediency. In many instances the opposite is the case. People would have to be highly inattentive to the world around them, obtuse, or indifferent to the personal and social effects of their conduct to act the same irrespective of circumstances. Nevertheless, the inversion of value implications of the term consistency serves to divert attention from the study of the reciprocal interaction between environmental and behavioral determinants to the search for invariant conduct.

Most of the participants in the controversy over the determinants of behavioral variation eventually adopted the view that behavior results from the interaction of persons and situations, rather than from either factor alone (Bowers, 1973, Endler & Magnusson, 1975). The consensus has reduced the level of dispute, but the basic question of how these two sources of influence interact in determining behavior remains to be clarified.

Interaction can be conceptualized in different ways reflecting alternative views of how causal processes operate. In the unidirectional notion of interaction, persons and situations are treated as independent entities that combine to produce behavior. This approach is usually represented as $B = f(P,E)$, where B signifies behavior, P the person, and E the environment. As will be shown later, the validity of this commonly held view is questionable on several grounds. Personal and environmental factors do not function as independent determinants, rather they determine each other. Nor can "persons" be considered causes independent of their behavior. It is largely through their actions that people produce the environmental conditions that affect their behavior in a reciprocal fashion. The experiences generated by behavior also partly determine what a person becomes and can do which, in turn, affects subsequent behavior.

A second conception of interaction acknowledges that personal and environmental influences are bidirectional, but retains a unidirectional view of behavior. In this analysis, persons and situations are depicted as interdependent causes of behavior as though it were only a product that does not figure at all in the causal process $[B = f(P \rightleftharpoons E)]$. As we have already seen, behavior is an interacting determinant, not simply an outcome of a "person-situation interaction."

In the social learning view of interaction, analyzed fully later as a process of reciprocal determinism, behavior, other personal factors, and environmental factors all operate as interlocking determinants of each other [B $\overset{P}{\underset{}{\longleftrightarrow}}$ E]. The relative influences exerted by these interdependent factors differ in various settings and for different behaviors. There are times when environmental factors exercise powerful constraints on behavior, and other times when personal factors are the overriding regulators of the course of environmental events.

A valid criticism of extreme behaviorism is that, in a vigorous effort to avoid spurious inner causes, it has neglected determinants of behavior arising from cognitive functioning. Proponents of this approach marshalled numerous reasons why cognitive events are inadmissible in causal analyses. It was, and still is, argued that cognitions are inaccessible except through untrustworthy self-reports, that they are inferences from effects, that they are epiphenomenal, or that they are simply fictional.

Because some of the inner causes invoked by theorists over the years have been ill-founded does not justify excluding all internal determinants from scientific inquiry. A large body of research now exists in which cognitions are activated instructionally, their presence is assessed indirectly, and their functional relationship to behavior is carefully examined. Results of such studies reveal that people learn and retain behavior much better by using cognitive aids that they generate than by reinforced repetitive performance. With growing evidence that cognition has causal influence on behavior, the arguments against the influence of internal determinants began to lose their force.

A theory that denies that thoughts can regulate actions does not lend itself readily to the explanation of complex human behavior. Although cognitive activities are disavowed in the operant conditioning framework, their role in causal sequences simply cannot be eliminated. Therefore, adherents of operant theory translate cognitive operations into behavioristic terms, and ascribe their effects to the direct action of external events. Let us consider a few examples of this externalization process. When informative cues affect behavior through the intervening influence of thought, the process is portrayed as one of stimulus control; that is, stimuli are seen as prompting behavior directly, without reference to the judgmental link. When people act protectively in the presence of stimuli previously associated with painful experiences, the stimuli are presumed to have become aversive rather than that the individuals have learned to anticipate aversive consequences. In fact, it is people's knowledge of their environment, not the stimuli, that are changed by correlated experience. Thus, for example, if a given word foreshadows physically painful stimulation the word assumes predictive significance for the individual not the painful properties of the physical stimuli.

The issue of the locus at which behavioral determinants actually operate applies to reinforcement influences as well as to environmental stimuli. It has always been the cardinal rule of operant theory that behavior is controlled by its immediate consequences. If momentary response effects determined performance, organisms should rapidly cease responding when only occasionally reinforced whereas, in fact, their behavior is most persistent under such conditions. Thus, if only every 50th response is reinforced, 98 percent of the outcomes are extinctive and only 2 percent are reinforcing. Because behavior continues to be performed despite predominantly dissuading effects, one must look beyond immediate environmental consequences for the determinants.

Some operant researchers have recently developed the proposition that behavior is regulated by integrated feedback rather than through its immediate effects (Baum, 1973). According to this view, organisms integrate data on how often their responses are reinforced over a substantial period of time and regulate their behavior according to the aggregate consequences. This type of analysis comes close to linking the effect of consequences on action through the integrating influence of thought. People have to remember the circumstances and how often their behavior is reinforced and to extract the pattern of outcomes from sequences of events over time. Cognitive skills represent the integrating capability.

In the social learning view, people are neither driven by inner forces nor buffeted by environmental stimuli. Rather, psychological functioning is explained in terms of a continuous reciprocal interaction of personal and environmental determinants. Within this approach, symbolic, vicarious, and self-regulatory processes assume a prominent role.

Psychological theories have traditionally assumed that learning can occur only by performing responses and experiencing their effects. In actuality, virtually all learning phenomena resulting from direct experience occur on a vicarious basis by observing other people's behavior and its consequences for them. The capacity to learn by observation enables people to acquire large, integrated patterns of behavior without having to form them gradually by tedious trial and error.

The abbreviation of the acquisition process through observational learning is vital for both development and survival. Because mistakes can produce costly, or even fatal consequences, the prospects for survival would be slim indeed if one could learn only by suffering the consequences of trial and error. For this reason, one does not teach children to swim, adolescents to drive automobiles, and novice medical students to perform surgery by having them discover the appropriate behavior through the consequences of their successes and failures. The more costly and hazardous the possible mistakes, the heavier is the reliance on observational learning from competent examples. Apart from the question of survival, it is difficult to imagine a social transmission process in which the language, lifestyles, and institutional practices of a culture are taught to each new member by selective reinforcement of fortuitous behaviors, without the benefit of models who exemplify the cultural patterns.

Some complex behaviors can be produced only through the aid of modeling. If children had no opportunity to hear the utterances of models, it would be virtually impossible to teach them the linguistic skills that constitute a language. It is doubtful that one could ever shape intricate words, let alone create grammatical speech, by selective reinforcement of random vocalization. In other behaviors that are formed by unique combinations of elements selected from numerous possibilities, the chances of producing spontaneously the response patterns, or something resembling them, is quite remote. Where novel forms of behavior can be conveyed effectively only by social cues, modeling is an indispensable aspect of learning. Even when it is possible to establish new behaviors through other means, the process of acquisition can be considerably shortened through modeling.

The capacity to use symbols provides humans with a powerful means of dealing with their environment. Through verbal and imagined symbols people process and preserve experiences in representational forms that serve as guides for future behavior. The capability for intentional action is rooted in symbolic activity. Images of desirable futures foster courses of action designed to lead toward more distant goals. Through the medium of symbols people can solve problems without having to enact all the various alternative solutions; and they can foresee the probable consequences of different actions and alter their behavior accordingly. Without symbolizing powers, humans would be incapable of reflective thought. A theory of human behavior therefore cannot afford to neglect symbolic activities.

Another distinguishing feature of social learning theory is the prominent role it assigns to self-regulatory capacities. By arranging environmental inducements, generating cognitive supports, and producing consequences for their own actions, people are able to exercise some measure of control over their own behavior. To be sure, the self-regulatory functions are created and occasionally supported by external influences. Having external origins, however, does not refute the fact that, once established, self-influence partly determines which actions one performs.

A comprehensive theory of behavior must explain how patterns of behavior are acquired and how their expression is continuously regulated by the interplay of self-generated and external sources of influence. From a social learning perspective, human nature is characterized as a vast potentiality that can be fashioned by direct and vicarious experience into a variety of forms within biological limits. The level of psychological and physiological development, of course, restricts what can be acquired at any given time. These issues are discussed at length in the following chapters.

2

Origins
of
Behavior

EXCEPT FOR ELEMENTARY REFLEXES, people are not equipped with inborn repertoires of behavior. They must learn them. New response patterns can be acquired either by direct experience or by observation. Biological factors, of course, play a role in the acquisition process. Genetics and hormones affect physical development which in turn can influence behavioral potentialities. The dichotomy of behavior as either learned or innate has a declining number of proponents as knowledge of behavioral processes increases.

Though extreme hereditarians and environmentalists still exist, it is now widely acknowledged that experiential and physiological influences interact in subtle ways to determine behavior and therefore are not easily separable.

Even when new responses are formed entirely on the basis of learning experiences, physiological factors serve as contributing influences. While the organization of behavioral components into new patterns results from experience, the rudimentary elements are present as part of natural endowment. To cite an example, children are born with a set of rudimentary sounds that they eventually learn to combine into a large variety of words and sentences. These basic phonetic elements may appear trivial compared to the complicated patterns learned later on, but they are nevertheless essential. It would be misleading, however, to call behavior instinctual simply because it employed a few innate elements. Many so-called instinctual behaviors, even in lower species, contain a large learning component.

Complex behaviors do not emerge as unitary patterns, but are formed through integration of many constituent activities of differing origins. For this reason, it is more fruitful to analyze the determinants of behavioral processes than to categorize behaviors as learned or innate or to try to apportion relative weights to these factors.

Learning By Response Consequences

The more rudimentary mode of learning, rooted in direct experience, results from the positive and negative effects that actions produce. When people deal with everyday events, some of their responses prove successful, while others have no effect or result in punishing outcomes. Through this process of differential reinforcement, successful forms of behavior are eventually selected and ineffectual ones are discarded.

Learning by reinforcement is commonly portrayed as a mechanistic process in which responses are shaped automatically and unconsciously by their immediate consequences. Simple actions can be altered by their effects without awareness of the relationship between actions and outcomes. However, the cognitive capacities of humans enable them to profit more extensively from experience than if they were unthinking organisms.

Response consequences have several functions. First, they impart information. Second, they serve as motivators through their incentive value. The third, and most controversial, function concerns their capacity to strengthen responses automatically. A full understanding of learning by response consequences therefore requires detailed consideration of these functions.

INFORMATIVE FUNCTION

In the course of learning, people not only perform responses but also notice the effects they produce. By observing the different outcomes of their actions, they develop hypotheses about which responses are most appropriate in which settings. This acquired information then serves as a guide for future action. Accurate hypotheses give rise to successful performances, whereas erroneous ones lead to ineffective courses of action. Cognitions are thus selectively strengthened or disconfirmed by the differential consequences accompanying the more remotely occurring responses (Dulany & O'Connell, 1963).

Contrary to the mechanistic view, outcomes change behavior in humans largely through the intervening influence of thought. Reinforcing consequences serve as an unarticulated way of informing performers of what they must do to gain beneficial outcomes and to avoid punishing ones. Because learning by response consequences is largely a cognitive process, consequences generally produce little change in complex behavior when there is no awareness of what is being reinforced. Even if certain responses have been positively reinforced, they will not increase if individuals believe, from other information, that the same actions will not be rewarded on future occasions (Estes, 1972).

MOTIVATIONAL FUNCTION

Anticipatory capacities enable humans to be motivated by prospective consequences. Past experiences create expectations that certain actions will bring valued benefits, that others will have no appreciable effects, and that still others will avert future trouble. By representing foreseeable outcomes symbolically, people can convert future consequences into current motivators of behavior. Most actions are thus largely under anticipatory control. Homeowners, for instance, do not wait until they experience the distress of a burning house to purchase fire insurance; people venturing outdoors do not ordinarily depend on the discomfort of a torrential rain or a biting snowstorm to prompt them to dress appropriately; nor do motorists usually wait until inconvenienced by a stalled automobile to replenish gasoline.

The capacity to bring remote consequences to bear on current behavior by anticipatory thought encourages foresightful behavior. It does so by providing both the stimulus for appropriate action and the sustaining inducements. Because anticipatory incentives increase the likelihood of the kind of behavior that is ultimately reinforced time and time again, this type of incentive function has great utility.

REINFORCING FUNCTION

Explanation of reinforcement originally assumed that consequences increase behavior automatically without conscious involvement. This view was challenged by the results of verbal learning experiments in which experimenters reinforced certain classes of words verbalized by participants and ignored all others. Changes in how frequently subjects produced reinforced verbalizations was then examined as a function of whether the participants recognized which types of words produced rewards. Spielberger and De Nike (1966) measured awareness at periodic intervals throughout the session. They found that reinforcing consequences were ineffective in modifying behavior as long as participants were unaware of the reinforcement contingency; but participants suddenly increased the appropriate behavior when they discovered which responses would be rewarded. Other investigators (Dulany, 1968), using different tasks and reinforcers, likewise found that behavior is not much affected by its consequences without awareness of what is being reinforced. Neither these findings nor generalizations based on them went unquestioned.

Earlier studies by Postman and Sassenrath (1961) examined the temporal relation between emergence of awareness and changes in responsiveness. In these experiments, reinforcement produced small improvements in performance prior to awareness, but participants markedly increased appropriate responses after they hit upon the correct solution. Learning, they concluded, can occur without awareness, albeit slowly and quite inefficiently. The subsequent increase in correct responses makes it easier to discern what is favored; once the discovery has been made, the appropriate behavior is readily performed, given valued incentives.

Discrepant findings concerning the relationship between awareness and behavior change are largely due to how adequately awareness is measured. If awareness is assessed after many trials have elapsed, participants may figure out the correct responses late in the series after they have increased noticeably by reinforcement in the absence of awareness. Indeed, some evidence seems to suggest just this, for when recognition of reinforcement contingencies is measured at long intervals, awareness appears to precede behavior change, but when measurements are made at short intervals, performance gains seem to precede awareness for subjects who later recognize the correct responses (Kennedy, 1970, 1971). Whether they were partially aware before altering their behavior, but did not express their provisional thoughts, remains to be demonstrated.

The procedures used in the preceding studies are adequate for demonstrating that awareness can facilitate change in behavior, but they are ill-suited for resolving the basic issue of whether awareness is necessary for learning or performance change. Because the responses and their outcomes are observable, one must rely on participants' verbal reports to determine whether and when awareness has been gained.

The question of whether learning must be consciously mediated is answered decisively by using tasks that prevent awareness because the action-outcome relationship cannot be observed. Awareness is precluded when the appropriate responses are unobservable but their consequences are not, or the correct responses are noticeable but their reinforcing consequences are not.

Hefferline and his associates (Hefferline, Bruno & Davidowitz, 1970) have successfully modified unobservable responses by reinforcement. In these studies, the occurrence of visibly imperceptible muscular contractions, detected by the experimenter through electronic amplification, are reinforced either by monetary reward or by termination of unpleasant stimulation. The unseen responses increased during reinforcement and decreased after reinforcement was withdrawn. None of the participants could identify the response that produced the reinforcing consequences, although they generated hypotheses about the relevant activities.

Awareness is not an all-or-none phenomenon. It is possible to achieve increases in performance on the basis of misleading hypotheses if these are partially correlated with the correct solution to the task. If the participants in a verbal learning study believe that comments about household items are the rewardable responses, when actually references to kitchen utensils is the correct response class, they are likely to generate some appropriate responses. Similarly, in studies of nonverbal tasks some observable activity that itself is not

entirely appropriate may at times activate the relevant unseen responses. Awareness can thus exist in degree of accuracy, depending on how closely the chosen hypotheses are
correlated with the correct one. Small changes occurring without awareness may well be attributable to partially correlated
hypotheses.

Although the issue is not yet completely resolved, there
is little evidence that reinforcers function as automatic
shapers of human conduct. Even if improved methodologies
established that elementary responses can be learned without
awareness of what is being reinforced, this would not mean
that complex behavior can be similarly acquired. As an illustration, consider a task involving rule-governed behavior.
Suppose subjects are presented with words of varying length,
and told that their task is to respond by providing a correct
number corresponding to each word. Let us select an arbitrary rule that gives the "correct number" by subtracting the
number of letters in a given word from 100, dividing the
remainder by 2, and then multiplying this result by 5. Correct
responses are derived from a high-order rule requiring a
three-step transformation of the external stimulus. To create
accurate responses one must perform several mental operations in a particular sequence. An unthinking organism is
unlikely to show any gains in accurate performance, however
long its responses are reinforced.

A vast amount of evidence lends validity to the view that
reinforcement serves principally as an informative and motivational operation rather than as a mechanical response
strengthener. The notion of "response strengthening" is, at
best, a metaphor. After responses are acquired the likelihood
that they will be used in a given situation can be readily
altered by varying the effects they produce, but the responses
cannot be strengthened any further. For example, people will
drive automobiles for the resulting benefits, but the benefits
do not add increments of strength to the driving responses.
The dubious status of both automaticity and response
strengthening, and the vestigial connotations of the term reinforcement, make it more fitting to speak of *regulation* than
reinforcement of behavior by its consequences. It is in the
former sense that the concept of reinforcement is being used
in this book.

It is fortunate that consequences do not automatically enhance every response they follow. If behavior were reinforced by every momentary effect it produced, people would be overburdened with so many competing response tendencies that they would become immobilized. Limiting learning to events that are sufficiently salient to gain recognition has adaptive value. For lower organisms possessing limited symbolizing capacities there are evolutionary advantages to being biologically structured so that response consequences produce lasting effects mechanically without requiring symbolic processing of ongoing experiences.

Reinforcement provides an effective means of regulating behaviors that have already been learned, but it is a relatively inefficient way of creating them. It might be noted in passing that rarely do people learn behaviors under natural conditions that they have never seen performed by others. Because reinforcement influences ordinarily occur together with numerous behavioral examples to draw upon, it is difficult to determine whether reinforcement creates the new behavior or activates what was already partly learned by observation.

Learning Through Modeling

Learning would be exceedingly laborious, not to mention hazardous, if people had to rely solely on the effects of their own actions to inform them what to do. Fortunately, most human behavior is learned observationally through modeling: from observing others one forms an idea of how new behaviors are performed, and on later occasions this coded information serves as a guide for action. Because people can learn from example what to do, at least in approximate form, before performing any behavior, they are spared needless errors.

PROCESSES OF OBSERVATIONAL
LEARNING

According to social learning theory, modeling influences produce learning principally through their informative func-

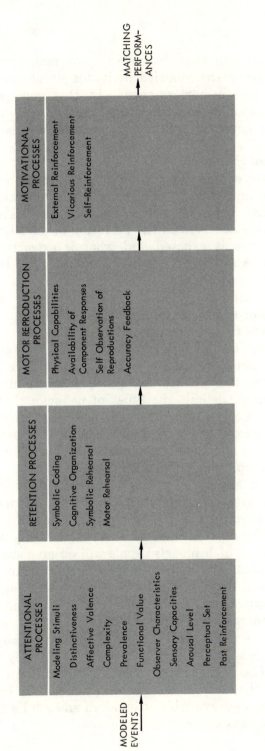

Figure 1 Component processes governing observational learning in the social learning analysis.

tion. During exposure observers acquire mainly symbolic representations of the modeled activities which serve as guides for appropriate performances. In this conceptualization, which is summarized schematically in Figure 1, observational learning is governed by four component processes.

Attentional Processes

People cannot learn much by observation unless they attend to, and perceive accurately, the significant features of the modeled behavior. Attentional processes determine what is selectively observed in the profusion of modeling influences to which one is exposed and what is extracted from such exposures. A number of factors, some involving the observers' characteristics, others involving the features of the modeled activities themselves, and still others involving the structural arrangement of human interactions, regulate the amount and types of observational experiences.

Among the various attentional determinants, associational patterns are clearly of major importance. The people with whom one regularly associates, either through preference or imposition, delimit the types of behavior that will be repeatedly observed and hence learned most thoroughly. Opportunities for learning aggressive conduct, for example, differ markedly for members of assaultive gangs and for members of groups exemplifying pacific lifestyles.

Within any social group some individuals are likely to command greater attention than others. Modeled conduct varies in effectiveness. The functional value of the behaviors displayed by different models is therefore highly influential in determining which models people will observe and which they will disregard. Attention to models is also channeled by their interpersonal attraction. Models who possess engaging qualities are sought out, while those lacking pleasing characteristics are generally ignored or rejected.

Some forms of modeling are so intrinsically rewarding that they hold the attention of people of all ages for extended periods. This is nowhere better illustrated than in televised modeling. The advent of television has greatly expanded the range of models available to children and adults alike. Unlike their predecessors, who were limited largely to familial and subcultural sources of modeling, people today can observe and learn diverse styles of conduct within the comfort of their homes through the abundant symbolic modeling provided by the mass media. Models presented in televised form are so effective in capturing attention that viewers learn much of what they see without requiring any special incentives to do so (Bandura, Grusec, & Menlove, 1966).

The rate and level of observational learning is also partially determined by the nature of the modeled behaviors themselves as, for example, their salience and complexity. In addition, observers' capacities to process information govern how much they will benefit from observed experiences. People's perceptual sets, deriving from past experience and situational requirements, affect what features they extract from observations and how they interpret what they see and hear.

Retention Processes

People cannot be much influenced by observation of modeled behavior if they do not remember it. A second major process involved in observational learning concerns retention of activities that have been modeled at one time or another. In order for observers to profit from the behavior of models when they are no longer present to provide direction, the response patterns must be represented in memory in symbolic form. Through the medium of symbols, transitory modeling experiences can be maintained in permanent memory. It is the advanced capacity for symbolization that enables humans to learn much of their behavior by observation.

Observational learning relies mainly upon two representational systems—imaginal and verbal. Some behavior is retained in imagery. Sensory stimulation activates sensations that give rise to perceptions of the external events. As a result of repeated exposure, modeling stimuli eventually produce enduring, retrievable images of modeled performances. On later occasions, images (centrally aroused perceptions) can be summoned up of events that are physically absent. Indeed, when things are highly correlated, as when a name is consistently associated with a given person, it is virtually impossible to hear the name without experiencing an image of that person. Similarly, mere reference to an activity that has been repeatedly observed (e.g., driving an automobile) usually arouses its imaginal counterpart. Visual imagery plays an especially important role in observational learning during early periods of development when verbal skills are lacking, as well as in learning behavior patterns that do not lend themselves readily to verbal coding.

The second representational system, which probably accounts for the notable speed of observational learning and retention in humans, involves verbal coding of modeled events. Most of the cognitive processes that regulate behavior are primarily verbal rather than visual. Details of the route traveled by a model, for example, can be acquired, retained, and later reproduced more accurately by converting the visual information into a verbal code describing a series of right and left turns (e.g., RLRRL) than by reliance upon visual imagery of the route. Observational learning and retention are facilitated by such symbolic codes because they carry a great deal of information in an easily stored form.

After modeled activities have been transformed into images and readily utilizable verbal symbols, these memory codes serve as guides for performance. The importance of symbolic coding in observational learning is revealed in studies conducted both with children (Bandura, Grusec, & Menlove, 1966; Coates & Hartup, 1969) and with adults (Bandura & Jeffery, 1973; Bandura, Jeffery, & Bachicha, 1974; Gerst, 1971). Observers who code modeled activities into either words, concise labels, or vivid imagery learn and retain behavior better than those who simply observe or are mentally preoccupied with other matters while watching.

In addition to symbolic coding, rehearsal serves as an important memory aid. When people mentally rehearse or actually perform modeled response patterns, they are less likely to forget them than if they neither think about them nor practice what they have seen. Many behaviors that are learned observationally cannot be easily established by overt enactment because of either social prohibitions or lack of opportunity. It is therefore of considerable interest that mental rehearsal, in which individuals visualize themselves performing the appropriate behavior, increases proficiency and retention (Bandura & Jeffery, 1973; Michael & Maccoby, 1961). The highest level of observational learning is achieved by first organizing and rehearsing the modeled behavior symbolically and then enacting it overtly (Jeffery, 1976).

Some researchers (Gewirtz & Stingle, 1968) have been especially concerned with conditions that produce initial imitative responses on the assumption that they help to explain observational learning at later development. There is some reason to question, however, whether developmentally early and later imitations have equivalent determinants. In early years, the child's imitative responses are evoked directly and immediately by models' actions. Later on, imitative responses are usually performed without the models present, long after the behavior has been observed. Immediate imitation does not require much in the way of cognitive functioning because the behavioral reproduction is externally guided by the model's actions. By contrast, in delayed modeling, the absent events must be internally represented so that the difference between physically prompted and delayed modeling is like the difference between drawing a picture of one's automobile when it is at hand, and drawing it from memory. In the latter situation, the hand does not automatically sketch the car; rather, one must rely on memory guides, mainly imaginal representations.

Motor Reproduction Processes

The third component of modeling involves converting symbolic representations into appropriate actions. To understand this response guidance function requires analysis of the ideomotor mechanisms of performance. Behavioral reproduction is achieved by organizing one's responses spatially and temporally in accordance with the modeled patterns. For purposes of analysis, behavioral enactment can be separated into cognitive organization of responses, their initiation, monitoring, and refinement on the basis of informative feedback.

In the initial phase of behavioral enactment, responses are selected and organized at the cognitive level. The amount of observational learning that will be exhibited behaviorally partly depends on the availability of component skills. Learners who possess the constituent elements can easily integrate them to produce the new patterns; but if some of these response components are lacking, behavioral reproduction will be faulty. When deficits exist, then the basic sub-skills required for complex performances must first be developed by modeling and practice.

There are other impediments at the behavioral level to doing what one has learned observationally. Ideas are rarely transformed into correct actions without error on first attempt. Accurate matches are usually achieved by corrective adjustments of preliminary efforts. Discrepancies between the symbolic representation and execution serve as cues for corrective action. A common problem in learning complex skills, such as golf or swimming, is that performers cannot fully observe their responses, and must therefore rely upon vague kinesthetic cues or verbal reports of onlookers. It is difficult to guide actions that are only partially observable or to identify the corrections needed to achieve a close match between representation and performance.

Skills are not perfected through observation alone, nor are they developed solely by trial-and-error fumbling. A golf instructor, for example, does not provide beginners with golf balls and clubs and wait for them to discover the golf swing. In most everyday learning, people usually achieve a close approximation of the new behavior by modeling, and they refine it through self-corrective adjustments on the basis of informative feedback from performance and from focused demonstrations of segments that have been only partially learned.

Motivational Processes

Social learning theory distinguishes between acquisition and performance because people do not enact everything they learn. They are more likely to adopt modeled behavior if it results in outcomes they value than if it has unrewarding or punishing effects. Observed consequences influence modeled conduct in much the same way. Among the countless responses acquired observationally, those behaviors that seem to be effective for others are favored over behaviors that are seen to have negative consequences. The evaluative reactions that people generate toward their own behavior also regulate which observationally learned responses will be performed. They express what they find self-satisfying and reject what they personally disapprove (Hicks, 1971).

Because of the numerous factors governing observational learning, the provision of models, even prominent ones, will not automatically create similar behavior in others. One can produce imitative behavior without considering the underlying processes. A model who repeatedly demonstrates desired responses, instructs others to reproduce the behavior, prompts them physically when they fail, and then rewards them when they succeed, may eventually produce matching responses in most people. If, on the other hand, one seeks to explain the occurrence of modeling and to achieve its effects predictably, one has to consider the various determining factors discussed above. In any given instance, then, the failure of an observer to match the behavior of a model may result from any of the following: not observing the relevant activities, inadequately coding modeled events for memory representation, failing to retain what was learned, physical inability to perform, or experiencing insufficient incentives.

DEVELOPMENTAL ANALYSIS OF
MODELING

Because observational learning entails several subfunctions that evolve with maturation and experience, it depends upon prior development. Modeling can be increased by reinforcing matching behavior, but such demonstrations are not of much help in explaining imitation failures, or in identifying what exactly is being acquired during the process. Facility in observational learning is increased by acquiring and improving skills in selective observation, in memory encoding, in coordinating sensorimotor and ideomotor systems, and by the ability to foresee probable consequences of matching another's behavior. Observational learning is hindered by deficits, and increased by improvements, in its component functions.

In studying the origin and determinants of modeling it is essential to distinguish between instantaneous and delayed reproduction. In the earliest years of development, children's modeling is largely confined to instantaneous imitation. As children develop skill in symbolizing experience and translating it to motor modalities, their capacity for delayed modeling of intricate patterns of behavior increases.

In developmental studies, chronological age is widely used as an index of cognitive development. Although performances requiring cognitive functioning generally increase with age, the relationships are not always orderly ones. Some discrepancies arise because many things other than cognitive competency also change as children grow older. Relating changes in functioning to age has normative value but it tells us little about the subprocesses governing the altered performances. One can better understand how developmental factors affect the capacity for observational learning by measuring the degree to which component functions have evolved than by relying on age as the index of development.

Developmental studies need not be confined solely to changes in functioning under natural circumstances. Another procedure is to study proficiency in observational learning by children who have received different amounts of pretraining in component functions over a period of time. This is an especially effective way of identifying the developmental determinants of observational learning because the critical factors are created directly.

Piaget (1951) presents a developmental account of imitation, in which symbolic representation plays an important role, especially in higher forms of modeling. At the earlier sensorimotor stages of development, imitative responses can be evoked in children only by having the model repeat the child's immediately preceding responses in alternating imitative sequences. During this period, according to Piaget, the children are unable to imitate responses they have not previously performed spontaneously, because actions cannot be assimilated unless they correspond to already existing schemata. Piaget reports that when new elements are introduced, or even when familiar responses that children have acquired but are not exhibiting at the moment occur, they do not respond imitatively. Imitation is thus restricted to reproduction of activities that children have already developed, that they can see themselves make, and that they have performed immediately before the model's repetition.

The limitations in infant imitativeness observed by Piaget in the longitudinal study of three children are not entirely corroborated by other investigators. Infants can acquire by observation new skills and transfer them to different situations (Kaye, 1971). It is assumed by Piaget that during initial stages children do not differentiate between self-imitation and imitation of the actions of others. If they cannot distinguish modeled activities from their own, the theory must include additional assumptions to explain why a child's own behavior can originally induce matching responses but identical actions initiated by others cannot.

In a detailed longitudinal study, Valentine (1930) shows that infants do imitate modeled acts within their capabilities even though they are not performing them beforehand. Moreover, matching performances, from which imitative capabilities are inferred, vary markedly depending on who the models are, what they select to model, and how they do it. Infants imitate their mothers much more than they do other people. They sometimes fail to respond to initial demonstrations but imitate the actions if repeated a number of times. Repeated modeling will thus reveal higher infant imitative capacities than brief modeling.

In Piaget's view, schemata, which refer to schematic plans of action, determine what behaviors a person can or cannot imitate. The critical issue in observational learning is not how input is matched to preformed plans but how input creates the plans. Schema formation, according to Piaget, is determined by maturation and by experiences that are moderately incongruent with existing mental structures. Modeled events that are highly novel presumably cannot be incorporated.

There are commonalities between social learning and Piaget's theory in their emphasis on the development of plans of action. Both recognize the importance of sensorimotor and ideomotor learning; that is, young children must develop ability to translate what they perceive to corresponding actions, and to convert thought into organized sequences of actions.

They differ, however, in how representations are abstracted from exemplars and in the limiting conditions of modeling. In the social learning view, observational learning is not confined to the moderately unfamiliar. Nor is self-discovery through behavioral manipulation the only source of information, as emphasized in Piagetian theory. Information about new responses can be extracted from observing modeled examples as well as from the consequences of one's own behavior. If sensory and motor systems are sufficiently developed, and the component skills exist, there is no reason why children cannot learn novel responses by watching others, though obviously the moderately familiar would be easier to learn than the markedly different. From the perspective of the multiprocess theory presented earlier, deficiencies in imitative performance, which are usually attributed by Piaget to insufficiently differentiated schemata, may also result from inadequate attention to modeled activities, from inadequate retention, from motor difficulties in executing learned patterns, or from insufficient incentives. The incentive determinant deserves further comment because it bears importantly on the evaluation of findings from naturalistic studies.

The level and accuracy of children's imitations of what they see and hear is partly influenced by how models respond to their behavior. Young children imitate accurately when they have incentives to do so, but their imitations deteriorate rapidly if others do not care how they behave (Lovaas, 1967). When only children's responses are observed and recorded, imitative deficiencies arising from faulty incentives may be incorrectly attributed to shortcomings within the children. Because most observational studies with infants involve a two-way influence process, imitative performances reflect not only the competency of the child but the reactions of the participating models. If models respond alike to performances that differ in quality, children do not imitate too well, whereas they accurately reproduce behavior within their capacity if models show appropriate interest.

The discussion thus far has been concerned with early

stages in the development of imitation as depicted by Piaget. As children's intellectual development progresses, they become capable of delayed imitation of modeled performances which they cannot see themselves make. These changes presumably come about through coordination of visual and sensorimotor schemata and through differentiation of the children's own actions from those of others. They now begin systematic trial-and-error performance of responses until they achieve good matches to new modeled patterns.

At the final stages of development, which generally begin in the second year of life, children attain representational imitation. Schemata are coordinated internally through imaginal representation to form new patterns of modeled behavior without requiring overt provisional trials of actions. The change that could be produced by modeling would be limited if coded representations were confined to imaginal replicas of modeled activities. Most modeled behavior is acquired and retained through the medium of verbal symbols. Had Piaget extended his studies of imitation into later childhood years, verbal representations would doubtless have emerged as an important functional mediator in delayed modeling.

A comprehensive theory of modeling must explain not only how patterned behavior is acquired observationally, but also how frequently and when imitative behavior will be performed, the persons toward whom it is expressed and the social setting in which it is most likely to be exhibited. Piaget's account of imitation contains only a few general statements about the motivational factors regulating performance of matching behavior. Imitation is variously attributed to an intrinsic need for acting and knowing, to a desire to reproduce actions that differ partially from existing schemata, and to the esteem in which the model is held. Such factors are must too general to account satisfactorily for selective imitation of different models, of the same models at different times and places, and of different responses exhibited by the same models (Bandura & Barab, 1971). In view of the abundant evidence that imitative performances are extensively

regulated by their consequences, the influence of reinforcement determinants must be included in explanatory schemes,
whatever their orientation may be.

COMPARATIVE ANALYSIS OF
MODELING

The role of symbolic processes in observational learning
can be evaluated through comparative studies. If species
higher in the phylogenetic scale have increasing capability to
symbolize experience, then one would expect differences between species in their potentialities for delayed modeling.
Systematic comparisons have not been conducted between
different species in observational learning on tasks varying in
complexity and need for memory representation. Findings of
various studies that happen to use different species nevertheless have suggestive value.

Lower species will learn simple acts through modeling if
they can perform the behavior concurrently or shortly after it
is exemplified by a model. Observational learning is less reliable, however, if there is an appreciable lapse of time between watching and performing.

With higher species the superiority of observational
learning over learning by reinforcement is more striking.
Higher animals can by watching acquire complicated sequences of responses even though they do not perform them
until some time after the original demonstrations. The most
impressive evidence for delayed modeling of novel patterns of
behavior comes from chimpanzees reared in human families
(Hayes & Hayes, 1952). They sit at typewriters striking key-
boards, apply lipstick to their faces before mirrors, open cans
with screwdrivers, and engage in other human activities,
without prior tutoring, which they have seen performed from
time to time. The success of Gardner and Gardner (1969) in
teaching sign language to a chimpanzee reveals the advanced
capacity of primates to acquire observationally a generalized
communicative skill that is used on future occasions in different settings for a variety of purposes. After being taught by
demonstration a large vocabulary of signs, the animal spontaneously used gestural communication by combining signs to
get adults to do the things it wanted.

LOCUS OF RESPONSE INTEGRATION IN
OBSERVATIONAL LEARNING

New patterns of behavior are created by organizing responses into certain patterns and sequences. Theories of modeling differ on whether component responses are integrated into new forms mainly at central or peripheral levels. Reinforcement theories (Baer & Sherman, 1964; Gewirtz & Stingle, 1968) assume that response elements are selected from overt performance by providing modeling cues and rewarding actions that resemble the modeled behavior and ignoring those that do not. The response components thus extracted are sequentially chained by reinforcement to form more complex units of behavior. Since, in this view, behavior is organized into new patterns in the course of performance, learning requires overt responding and immediate reinforcement.

According to social learning theory, behavior is learned symbolically through central processing of response information before it is performed. By observing a model of the desired behavior, an individual forms an idea of how response components must be combined and sequenced to produce the new behavior. In other words, people guide their actions by prior notions rather than by relying on outcomes to tell them what they must do. Observational learning without performance is amply documented in modeling studies using a non-response acquisition procedure (Bandura, 1971a; Flanders, 1968). After watching models perform novel behavior, observers can later describe the behavior with considerable accuracy, and given appropriate inducements, they often achieve errorless enactments on the first trial.

It is commonly believed that controversies about the locus of learning cannot be satisfactorily resolved because learning must be inferred from performance. This may well be the case in experimentation with animals. To determine whether animals have mastered a maze one must run them through it. With humans, indices of learning exist that are independent of performance. To measure whether humans have learned a maze by observing successful models, one need only ask them to describe the correct pattern of right and left turns. In addition to verbal indices, formation of representations can be assessed by measures of recognition and understanding not requiring motor reproduction. Results of experiments using multiple measures of acquisition show that people learn by watching before they perform (Bandura, Jeffery, & Bachicha, 1974; Brown, 1976).

ROLE OF REINFORCEMENT IN
OBSERVATIONAL LEARNING

Another issue of contention in observational learning concerns the role of reinforcement. Reinforcement-oriented theories assume that matching responses must be reinforced in order to be learned (Baer & Sherman, 1964; Miller & Dollard, 1941; Gewirtz & Stingle, 1968). The operant conditioning analysis relies entirely upon the standard three-component paradigm $S^d \rightarrow R \rightarrow S^r$, where S^d denotes the modeled stimulus, R represents an overt matching response, and S^r designates the reinforcing stimulus. Observational learning presumably is achieved through differential reinforcement. When responses corresponding to the model's actions are positively reinforced and divergent responses are either unrewarded or punished, the behavior of others comes to function as a cue for matching responses.

This scheme does not appear to be applicable to observational learning where observers do not perform the model's responses in the setting in which they are exemplified, where neither the model nor the observers are reinforced, and whatever responses have been acquired observationally are first performed days, weeks, or months later. Under this set of conditions, which represents the most prevalent form of observational learning, two of the factors ($R \rightarrow S^r$) in the three-element paradigm are absent during acquisition, and the third factor (S^d, the modeling cue) is typically absent from the situation in which the observationally learned response is first performed. The operant analysis clarifies how imitative behavior that a person has previously learned can be prompted by the actions of others and the prospect of reward. However, it does not explain how a new response is acquired observationally.

According to the social learning view, observational learning occurs through symbolic processes during exposure to modeled activities before any responses have been performed and does not necessarily require extrinsic reinforcement. This is not to say that mere exposure to modeled activities is, in itself, suffficient to produce observational learning. Not all stimulation that impinges on individuals is necessarily observed by them, and even if noticed, what is registered may not be retained for any length of time.

Reinforcement does play a role in observational learning, but mainly as an antecedent rather than a consequent influence. Anticipation of reinforcement is one of several factors that can influence what is observed and what goes unnoticed. Knowing that a given model's behavior is effective in producing valued outcomes or in averting punishing ones can improve observational learning by increasing observers' attentiveness to the model's actions. Moreover, anticipated benefits can strengthen retention of what has been learned observationally by motivating people to code and rehearse modeled behavior that they value highly.

Theories of modeling differ primarily in the manner in which reinforcement affects observational learning rather than in whether reinforcement may play a role in the acquisition process. As shown in the schematization in Figure 2, the issue in dispute is whether reinforcement acts backward to strengthen preceding imitative responses and their connection to stimuli, or whether it facilitates learning anticipatorily through its effects on attentional, organizational, and rehearsal processes. It follows from social learning theory that observational learning can be achieved more effectively by informing observers in advance about the benefits of adopting modeled behavior than by waiting until they happen to imitate a model and then rewarding them for it.

In social learning theory, reinforcement is considered a facilitative rather than a necessary condition because factors other than response consequences can influence what people attend to. One does not have to be reinforced, for example, to hear compelling sounds or to look at captivating visual displays. When attention is drawn to modeled activities by the

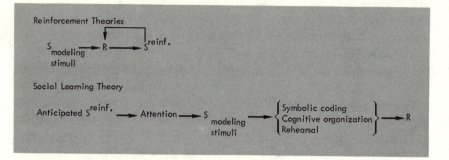

Figure 2   Schematic representations of how reinforcement influences observational learning according to instrumental conditioning theory and social learning theory.

events themselves, the addition of positive incentives does not increase observational learning. Observers display the same amount of observational learning regardless of whether they are informed in advance that correct imitations will be rewarded or are given no prior incentives to learn the modeled performances (Bandura, Grusec, & Menlove, 1966; Rosenthal & Zimmerman, 1977). After the capacity for observational learning has fully developed, one cannot keep people from learning what they have seen.

Because of the traditional assumption that responses must be performed before they can be learned, operant researchers have attempted to reduce observational learning to operant conditioning. As far as learning is concerned, it might be more appropriate to reverse the direction of the reductive analysis. If people learn which behavior is appropriate by observing the effects of their actions, acquisition through operant conditioning becomes a special case of observational learning. Symbolic representations of behavior can be constructed from observing examples or from the informative effects of one's performances.

Both reinforcement and social learning theories assume that whether or not people choose to perform what they have learned observationally is strongly influenced by the consequences of such actions. Social learning theory, however, encompasses a broader range of reinforcement influences including external, vicarious, and self-generated consequences.

THE MODELING PROCESS AND
TRANSMISSION OF RESPONSE
INFORMATION

A major function of modeling influences is to transmit information to observers on how responses can be synthesized into new patterns. This response information can be conveyed by physical demonstration, pictorial representation, or verbal description.

Much social learning occurs on the basis of casual or directed observation of behavior as it is performed by others in everyday situations. As linguistic skills are developed, verbal modeling is gradually substituted for behavioral modeling as the preferred mode of response guidance. People are aided in acquiring social, vocational, and recreational skills by following written descriptions of how to behave. Verbal modeling is used extensively because one can convey with words an almost infinite variety of behaviors that would be inconvenient and time consuming to portray behaviorally.

Another influential source of social learning is the abundant and varied symbolic modeling provided by television, films, and other visual media. It has been shown that both children and adults acquire attitudes, emotional responses, and new styles of conduct through filmed and televised modeling (Bandura, 1973; Liebert, Neale, & Davidson, 1973). In view of the efficacy of, and extensive public exposure to, televised modeling, the mass media play an influential role in shaping behavior and social attitudes. Further developments in communication technology will enable people to observe on request almost any desired activity at any time on computer-linked television consoles (Parker, 1970). With increasing use of symbolic modeling, parents, teachers, and other traditional role models may occupy less prominent roles in social learning.

A major significance of symbolic modeling lies in its tremendous multiplicative power. Unlike learning by doing, which requires shaping the actions of each individual by repeated experience, in observational learning a single model can transmit new behavior patterns simultaneously to vast numbers of people in widely dispersed locations. There is another aspect of symbolic modeling that magnifies its effects. During the course of their daily lives, people have direct contact with only a small sector of the environment. Consequently, their perceptions of social reality are heavily influenced by vicarious experiences—what they see, hear, and read in the mass media. The more peoples' images of reality derive from the media's symbolic environment, the greater is its social impact.

The basic modeling process is the same regardless of whether behavior is conveyed through words, pictures, or live actions. Different forms of modeling, however, are not always equally effective. It is often difficult to convey through words the same amount of information contained in pictorial or live demonstrations. In addition, some forms of modeling may be more powerful than others in commanding attention. Children—or adults, for that matter—rarely have to be compelled to watch television, whereas oral or written reports of the same activities would not hold their attention for long. Furthermore, the symbolic modes rely more heavily upon cognitive prerequisites for their effects. Observers whose conceptual and verbal skills are underdeveloped are likely to benefit more from behavioral demonstrations than from verbal modeling.

SCOPE OF MODELING INFLUENCES

Much of the conduct being modeled at any given time is socially prescribed or highly functional; hence, it is adopted in essentially the same form as it is portrayed. For example, there is little leeway permitted in the proper way to drive an automobile or perform a surgical operation. Modeling influences, however, can create generative and innovative behavior as well. Through a process of abstract modeling, observers derive the principles underlying specific performances for generating behavior that goes beyond what they have seen or heard (Bandura, 1971b; Zimmerman & Rosenthal, 1974).

Abstract Modeling

In studying abstract modeling people observe others performing various responses embodying a certain rule or principle. Observers are later tested under conditions where they can behave in a way that is stylistically similar to the model's disposition, but they cannot mimic the specific responses observed because they must apply what they have learned to new or unfamiliar situations. To take an example, a model generates from a set of nouns sentences containing the passive construction ("The dog *is being* petted," "The window *was* opened," etc.). The sentence examplars vary in content and other features, but their structural property—the passive voice—is the same. Children later are instructed to create sentences from a different set of nouns with the model absent, and their production of passive constructions is recorded.

In abstract modeling, observers extract the common attributes exemplified in diverse modeled responses and formulate rules for generating behavior with similar structural characteristics. Responses embodying the observationally derived rule resemble the behavior the model would be inclined to exhibit under similar circumstances, even though observers have never seen the model behaving in these new situations.

General features can be extracted through repeated exposure to individual exemplars which share common properties. Exposure alone, however, does not ensure that the relevant aspects will be noticed. Factors that increase the salience and significance of the common features greatly facilitate abstract modeling. The effects accompanying the model's responses is one such factor. When only the responses embodying the rule produce positive effects for the model, the aspects common to the positive exemplars can be more easily singled out by observers.

In observational learning of difficult concepts, abstract modeling is aided by providing concrete referents in conjunction with the conceptual responses. Young children, for example, learn a language rule with greater ease when the grammatical expressions occur along with corresponding activities that depict the relationships represented in the speech than if the utterances are modeled alone (Brown, 1976). Referential modeling, which presents actual events together with their abstract counterparts, plays an especially influential role in early phases of cognitive development.

Modeling has been shown to be a highly effective means of establishing abstract or rule-governed behavior. On the basis of observationally derived rules, people learn, among other things, judgmental orientations, linguistic styles, conceptual schemes, information-processing strategies, cognitive operations, and standards of conduct (Bandura, 1971a; Rosenthal & Zimmerman, 1977). Evidence that generalizable rules of thought and conduct can be induced through abstract modeling reveals the broad scope of observational learning.

Later, the role of abstract modeling in language learning will be analyzed in some detail. Development of moral judgments is another area in which the abstract modeling paradigm has been extensively applied to test predictions from alternative theories of conceptual learning. It has been repeatedly shown that children tend to alter their standards of moral evaluation in the direction of models' judgments. Proponents of different theories agree that moral reasoning is modifiable through exposure to divergent views, but they differ on how and when such modeling achieves changes.

Workers within the Piagetian developmental tradition assume that moral judgments appear as integrated wholes in distinct stages forming an invariant sequence. Piaget (1948) favors a two-stage order progressing from moral realism, in which rules are seen as unchangeable and punishments are administered in terms of amount of damage done, to relativistic morality that embraces motivational considerations. Kohlberg (1969) postulates a six-stage sequential typology beginning with punishment based obedience and evolving through instrumental hedonism, approval-seeking conformity, respect for authority, contractual legalistic observance, and culminating in private conscience. Since the stages constitute a fixed developmental sequence, individuals cannot learn a given form of moral judgment without first acquiring each of the preceding modes in order. The presumption is that modeling of moral standards that are too discrepant from one's dominant stage have little impact because they cannot be assimilated. Judgmental standards of lesser complexity are similarly rejected because they have already been displaced in attaining succeeding levels. Divergent modeling supposedly creates cognitive disequilibrium in observers which is reduced by adopting a higher stage of moral reasoning. Innate motivators are posited to explain why people do not preserve their equilibrium simply by adhering to their own opinions and rejecting conflicting ones (Rest, Turiel, & Kohlberg, 1969).

A major problem with typologies is that it is hard to find people who fit them. This is because different circumstances call for different decisions and conduct. A given person's moral judgments take many forms rather than being uniformly layered. Eventually further subtypes must be created to handle the diversity people show in their judgments. Personal experiences and changing societal demands produce increasingly differentiated functioning with age. As in any activity that involves increasing complexity, age differences in moral judgment can be found. But individuals at any given level of development usually express different moral judgments depending on circumstances (Bandura & McDonald, 1963). Stage theorists are able to classify people into types only by applying arbitrary rules to coexisting mixtures of judgments spanning several "stages" and by categorizing most people as being in transition between stages (Turiel, 1966).

According to the social learning view, people vary in what they teach, model, and reinforce with children of differing ages. At first, control is necessarily external. In attempting to discourage hazardous conduct in children who have not yet learned to talk, parents must resort to physical intervention. As children mature, social sanctions increasingly replace physical ones. Parents cannot always be present to guide their children's behavior. Successful socialization requires gradual substitution of symbolic and internal controls for external sanctions and demands. After moral standards of conduct are established by tuition and modeling, self-evaluative consequences serve as deterrents to transgressive acts. As the nature and seriousness of possible transgressions by children change with age, parents alter their moral reasoning. For example, they do not appeal to legal arguments in handling misconduct of preschoolers, but they explain legal codes and penalties to preadolescents in efforts to influence future behavior that can have serious consequences.

During the course of development, children also learn

how to get around moral consequences. They discover that
they can avoid, or reduce, reprimands by invoking extenuating circumstances for their conduct. As a result, different
types of vindications become salient cues for moral judgments. Later they learn to attentuate self-condemning consequences for reprehensible conduct by self-exonerating justifications. A theory of moral reasoning must therefore be
equally concerned with the cognitive processes by which the
immoral can be made moral.

Parents of course are not the exclusive source of
children's moral judgments and conduct. Other adults, peers,
and symbolic models play influential roles as well. Children
exposed to conflicting standards exemplified by adult and
peer models adopt different standards of conduct than if
adults alone set the example (Bandura, Grusec, & Menlove,
1967). To complicate matters further, the standards acquired
through modeling are affected by inconsistencies in the behavior of the same model over time, and by discrepancies
between what models practice and what they preach (Bryan
& Walbek, 1970). To the developing child, televised modeling, which dramatizes a vast range of moral conflicts, constitutes another intregral part of social learning. Symbolic modeling influences the development of moral judgments by what
it portrays as acceptable or reprehensible conduct and by the
sanctions and justifications applied to it.

Although developmental trends obviously exist in moral
judgments, the conditions of social learning are much too
varied to produce uniform moral types. Even at the more
advanced levels, some behaviors come under the rule of law,
others under social sanctions, and still others under personal
sanctions. Evidence of age trends, which most every theory
predicts, is often accepted as validating stage theories of
morality. Stage propositions, however, demand much more
than age trends: they assume (1) that there is uniformity of
judgment at any given level; (2) that a person cannot evaluate conduct in terms of a given moral standard without first
adopting a series of preceding standards; and (3) that attainment of a given evaluative standard replaces preceding modes
of thought by transforming them. Empirical findings provide
little support for these presumptions.

Some efforts have been made to test the modifiability of moral judgments within the Kohlberg framework by exposing children to divergent levels of reasoning (Rest, Turiel, & Kohlberg, 1969; Turiel, 1966). The investigators report that children reject opinions below their predominant mode of thinking, have difficulty comprehending opinions that are too advanced for them, and are most likely to adopt views immediately above their own level. Certain methodological shortcomings, however, detract from the generality of these findings. Measures of moral reasoning should include a wide range of factors that are relevant to the formation of moral judgments. In the research cited above, responses are elicited for only a few morally relevant dimensions.

Apparent deficiences in moral reasoning, often attributed to cognitive limitations or insensitivites to certain moral issues, have been shown to be partly artifacts of the assessment procedure used (Chandler, Greenspan, & Barenboim, 1973; Gutkin, 1972; Hatano, 1970). The same individuals express different moral opinions depending upon the number of moral dimensions included in the depicted events, the types of alternatives presented, whether they judge verbal accounts or behavioral portrayals of transgressions, and whether they reveal their moral orientations in abstract opinions or in the severity of sanctions they apply to different acts.

The procedures used to change moral reasoning in research conducted within the stage framework are even more limited than the assessment of effects. Children hear conflicting opinions expressed for only two or three hypothetical situations depicting a moral dilemma remote from their experiences, such as stealing a drug from a pharmacist to save a woman dying of cancer. One can easily fail to achieve changes by using weak influences. Theories claiming the negative (i.e., certain influences cannot produce change) should apply the influences extensively rather than briefly in testing the validity of the theory. Evidence that there are some age trends in moral judgment, that children fail to adopt opinions they do not fully comprehend, and that they are reluctant to express views considered immature for their age can be adequately explained without requiring elaborate stage propositions.

Social learning theory treats moral judgments as social decisions made on the basis of many factors that serve to mitigate or to justify the wrongness of conduct. Among the multidimensional evaluative criteria are included the characteristics of the wrongdoer, the nature of the act, its long-range as well as immediate consequences, the setting in which it occurs, the motivating conditions, the remorse of the transgressor, the number and type of people who are victimized, and a host of other extenuating circumstances. Standards of evaluation are acquired by precept, by example, and by experiencing directly and vicariously the consequences of transgressive acts. Through such diverse experiences people learn which dimensions are morally relevant and how much weight to attach to them.

The moral situations encountered in everyday life contain many decisional ingredients that vary in relative importance, depending upon the particular configuration of events. Hence, factors that are weighed heavily under some combinations of circumstances may be disregarded or considered of lesser import under a different set of conditions. With increasing development, moral judgments change from single-dimensional rules to multidimensional and configural rules of conduct.

Exposure to divergent modeling can alter moral judgments in several ways. By favoring certain judgmental standards, models increase the salience of morally relevant dimensions. The views they express additionally provide justifications for reweighing various factors in making decisions about the wrongness of given acts. In areas of morality, for which society places a premium on acceptable attitudes, public opinions may differ substantially from those that are privately held. Expression of moral convictions provides social sanctions for others to voice similar opinions. Divergent modeling can thus effect changes in moral judgments through attentional, cognitive, and disinhibitory mechanisms.

As in other areas of functioning, modeling influences do not invariably produce changes in moral reasoning. The lack of effects can result from either comprehension deficits or performance preferences. People cannot be much influenced by modeled opinions if they do not understand them. Cognitive skills place limits on what can be acquired through brief exposure to opposing opinions. There is substantial difference, however, between positing prerequisite cognitive functions and fixed sequences of unitary thought. Greater progress can be achieved in identifying the developmental determinants of complex abilities by analyzing the prior competencies needed to master them, than by categorizing people into ill-fitting types.

In voicing opinions, models transmit ideas and preferences. But modeling does not itself guarantee that views which have been learned will be articulated. In the case of performance preferences, modeled judgments are learned but not expressed because they are personally or socially disfavored. The ease with which judgmental standards can be shifted in one direction or another depends upon the conceptual skills they require and the consequences they generate. In addition, judgmental standards vary in discriminability, which affects the facility with which they can be learned. It is much easier to recognize damage then to infer the antecedents or intentions of actions. The claim attributed to learning theory that different moral judgments are equally modifiable has no foundation. Some judgmental changes are obviously more difficult to achieve than others.

An issue that has received surprisingly little attention is the relationship between moral reasoning and moral conduct. The extent to which moral judgments govern conduct will vary depending upon social circumstances. People are ordinarily deterred by anticipatory self-censure from engaging in behavior that violates their moral principles. When transgressive behavior is not easily self-excusable, actions are likely to be consonant with moral standards. But exonerative moral reasoning can be used to weaken internal restraints. Because almost any conduct can be morally justified, the same moral principles can support different actions, and the same actions can be championed on the basis of different moral principles (Bandura, 1973; Kurtines & Greif, 1974). People will behave in reprehensible ways for reciprocal obligations, for social approval, as duty to the social order, or for reasons of principle. Level of moral development may indicate the types of exonerative justifications needed to get a person to transgress, but it does not ensure any particular kind of conduct. The various conditions that are conducive to exonerative moral reasoning will be discussed later in greater detail.

Creative Modeling

Contrary to common belief, innovative patterns can emerge through the modeling process. When exposed to diverse models, observers rarely pattern their behavior exclusively after a single source, nor do they adopt all the attributes even of preferred models. Rather, observers combine aspects of various models into new amalgams that differ from the individual sources (Bandura, Ross, & Ross, 1963). Different observers adopt different combinations of characteristics.

In the case of social behavior, children within the same family may develop dissimilar personality characteristics by drawing upon different parental and sibling attributes. Successive modeling, in which observers later serve as sources of behavior for new members, would most likely produce a gradual imitative evolution of new patterns bearing little resemblance to those exhibited by the original models. In homogeneous cultures, where all models display similar styles of behavior, behavior may undergo little or no change throughout a series of successive models. It is diversity in modeling that fosters behavioral innovation.

Modeling probably contributes most to creative development in the inception of new styles. Once initiated, experiences with the new forms create further evolutionary changes. A partial departure from tradition thus eventually becomes a new direction. The progression of creative careers through distinct periods provides notable examples of this process. In his earliest works, Beethoven adopted the classical forms of Haydn and Mozart, though with greater emotional expressiveness which foreshadowed the direction of his artistic development. Wagner fused Beethoven's symphonic mode with Weber's naturalistic enchantment and Meyerbeer's dramatic virtuosity to evolve a new operatic form. Innovators in other endeavors in the same manner initially draw upon the contributions of others and build from their experiences something new.

The discussion thus far has analyzed creativity through

the innovative synthesis of different sources of influence. While existing practices furnish some of the ingredients for the new, they also impede innovation. As long as familiar routines serve adequately, there is little incentive to consider alternatives. The unconventional is not only unexplored, but is usually negatively received when introduced by the more venturesome. Modeling influences can weaken conventional inclinations by exemplifying novel responses to common situations. People exposed to divergently thinking models are indeed more innovative than those exposed to models who behave in a stereotyped conventional fashion (Harris & Evans, 1973). Although innovative modeling generally enhances creative ideas in others, there are some limits to this influence. When models are unusually productive and observers possess limited skills, their creative efforts may be self-devalued by the unfavorable comparison. Prolific creative modeling can thus dissuade the less talented.

Other Modeling Effects

Models do more than teach novel styles of thought and conduct. Modeling influences can strengthen or weaken inhibitions over behavior that observers have previously learned (Bandura, 1971b). Behavioral restraints are most strongly developed by observing the consequences experienced by models. Seeing models punished tends to inhibit similar behavior in others. Conversely, seeing others engage in threatening or prohibited activities without adverse consequences can reduce inhibitions in observers. Such disinhibitory effects are most strikingly revealed in therapeutic applications of modeling principles (Bandura, 1976a; Rachman, 1972). Exposure to models performing feared activities without any harmful effects weakens defensive behavior, reduces fears, and creates favorable changes in attitudes.

The actions of others can also serve as social cues for eliciting preexisting behavior. Response facilitation is distinguished from observational learning in that nothing new is learned, and from disinhibition, because the behavior is socially acceptable and therefore is unencumbered by restraints. In response facilitation, the modeled actions function simply as social prompts. Inhibitory and disinhibitory effects of modeling are analyzed later in the context of vicarious reinforcement, and social facilitation is examined in the discussion of situational antecedents of behavior.

Modeling influences can have additional effects, though these may be less important. The behavior of models draws attention to the particular objects chosen from the available alternatives. As a result, observers may subsequently use the same objects to a greater extent, though not necessarily in the same way. In one study, for example, children who had observed a model pummel a doll with a mallet not only imitated this specific action, but also used the mallet more in other activities than children who did not see this particular instrument used by others. Finally, observing affective expressions produces emotional arousal, which tends to increase responsiveness. The overall evidence thus reveals that modeling influences can serve as instructors, inhibitors, disinhibitors, facilitators, stimulus enhancers, and emotion arousers.

DIFFUSION OF INNOVATION

The discussion thus far has been concerned mainly with observational learning at the individual level. Modeling also plays a prime role in spreading new ideas and social practices within a society, or from one society to another. Successful diffusion of innovation follows a common pattern: new behavior is introduced by prominent examples, it is adopted at a rapidly accelerating rate, and it then either stabilizes or declines depending upon its functional value. The general pattern of diffusion is similar, but the mode of transmission, the speed and extent of adoption, and the lifespan of innovations varies for different forms of behavior.

Social learning theory distinguishes between two processes in the social diffusion of innovation. These are the acquisition of innovative behaviors and their adoption in practice. With regard to acquisition, modeling serves as the major vehicle for transmitting new styles of behavior. The numerous factors that determine observational learning, discussed earlier, apply equally to the rapid promulgation of innovations.

Symbolic modeling usually functions as the principal conveyance of innovations to widely dispersed areas. This is especially true in the early stages of diffusion. Newspapers, magazines, radio, and television inform people of new practices and their likely benefits or risks. Early adopters therefore come from among those who have had greater exposure to media sources of information about the innovation (Robertson, 1971). After novelties have been introduced symbolically, they are disseminated further to group members through personal contact with local adopters (Rogers & Shoemaker, 1971). When the influence operates through direct modeling, adoptive behavior tends to spread along existing networks of interpersonal communication. If the behavior is highly conspicuous, however, it can be learned from public displays by people who are unacquainted with one another.

Modeling affects adoption of innovations in several different ways. It instructs people in new styles of behavior through social, pictorial, or verbal display. Observers are initially reluctant to embark on new undertakings that involve risks until they see the advantages gained by early adopters. Modeled benefits accelerate diffusion by weakening the restraints of the more cautious potential adopters. As acceptance spreads, the new gains further social support. Models not only exemplify and legitimate innovations, they also serve as advocates by encouraging others to adopt them.

The acquisition of innovations is necessary but not sufficient for their adoption in practice. Social learning theory recognizes a number of factors that determine whether people will act on what they have learned. Stimulus inducements serve as one set of activators. In the consumer field, for example, advertising appeals are used extensively to stimulate consumers to purchase new products. Fashion industries saturate the market with new styles and reduce the availability of the fashions they wish to supplant. Different sources of mass communication furnish prompts from time to time for new technologies, ideologies, and social practices. The more pervasive the stimulus inducements, the greater the likelihood that learned innovations will be tried.

Adoptive behavior is highly susceptible to reinforcement influences. People will espouse innovations that produce tangible advantages. However, because benefits cannot be experienced until the new practices are tried, the promotion of innovations draws heavily upon anticipated and vicarious reinforcement. Advocates of new technologies and ideologies create expectations that they offer better solutions than do established ways. Promoters rely on vicarious reinforcement to increase the likelihood that observers will respond in the recommended manner. In positive appeals, adoptive behavior is depicted as resulting in a host of rewarding effects. Commercials promise that drinking certain beverages or using a particular hair lotion will win the admiration of attractive people, enhance job performance, bolster positive self-images, actualize individualism and authenticity, tranquilize irritable nerves, and arouse the affections of spouses. Negative appeals portray the adverse consequences of failure to pursue the recommended practices. Vicarious punishment, however, is a less reliable means of promoting adoptive behavior. Showing distressing outcomes tends to arouse unpleasant affect which may inadvertently become associated with the publicized items or cause avoidance of the communication itself (Leventhal, 1970).

Many innovations serve as a means of gaining attention and status. People who strive to distinguish themselves from the common and the ordinary adopt new styles in clothing, grooming, recreational activities, and conduct, thereby achieving distinctive status. As the popularity of the new behavior grows, it loses its status-conferring value until eventually it, too, becomes commonplace. Widespread imitation thus instigates further inventiveness to preserve status differentiations.

Fads can be distinguished from fashions largely in terms of the reinforcement supporting the adoptive behavior. When innovations serve primarily to gain social recognition and standing, as is typical of fads, they show a quick rise in popularity and an abrupt decline as their novelty is destroyed by overuse. Fashions, in contrast, enjoy a longer lifespan because they have more enduring benefits. The automobile is an example of a novelty that eventually became a permanent fixture. Innovations that have intrinsic functional value survive as part of common practices until something better comes along.

Adoptive behavior is also partly governed by self-generated consequences to one's own conduct. People readily espouse what they regard as praiseworthy but resist accepting innovations that violate their social and moral convictions. Self-reinforcing reactions are not insulated from the pressures of social influence, however. People are often led to behave in otherwise personally devalued ways through diffusion strategies that circumvent negative self-sanctions. In the marketing field, for example, new products are presented in ways that appear compatible with prevailing values. Energy consuming devices are advertised in the name of conservation; consumer conformity is promoted in the name of individualism. Similar processes operate in the promulgation of behavior having moral implications. People who are ordinarily considerate will engage in reprehensible conduct after it has been redefined in acceptable terms.

Innovations spread at different rates and patterns because they have different requirements for adoption. These serve as additional factors controlling the diffusion process. People will not adopt innovations even though they are favorably disposed toward them if they lack the money, the skills, or the accessory resources that may be needed. Some innovations are more subject to social prohibitions, which wield additional influence over what is adopted.

Among innovative behaviors, none have been scrutinized more intensively than those in the consumer field. Because of the critical role played by initial adopters in the diffusion process, much of the research is aimed at determining whether those who are quick to try new things possess distinguishing characteristics. If certain identifiable types of individuals are the first to adopt new ideas and products, the initiation of the diffusion process could be regulated by directing promotional appeals at them. These early adopters would, in turn, influence others through their trend-setting example.

In more sophisticated investigations, the rate of adoption is plotted over time and the diffusion curve is segmented into innovators, first adopters, later adopters, and finally the laggards. Researchers then examine whether people at the successive stages of adoption differ in any way. It is easy to section diffusion curves but difficult to interpret them. Differences between early and late adopters are generally assumed to arise from their personal characteristics or their social and economic circumstances. Late adopters and laggards presumably wait to see the benefits gained by innovators before trying new things themselves. In fact, some of the variations in time of adoption partly result from differences in when people are first exposed to new products or fashions. Temporal analysis of diffusion may therefore yield misleading results if individuals are not equated for the time and the amount of initial exposure.

As we have already seen, the primary determinants of adoptive behavior are the influences closely tied to it—the stimulus inducements, the anticipated satisfactions, the observed benefits, the experienced functional value, the perceived risks, the self-evaluative derivatives, and the various social barriers and economic constraints. The influential ingredients will vary across products. Those that are publicly conspicuous, as in the case of clothing one wears, will be under greater social control than products that are used privately. In the case of highly expensive items economic factors may outweigh social ones. For this reason, adoption determinants are not generalizable across products, unless they fall in the same class. There is little reason to expect that someone who is innovative in Paris fashions will also be innovative in dishwashing detergents. Adoptive behavior, then, is best analyzed in terms of controlling conditions rather than in terms of types of people. Specificity of innovation is by no means confined to products. It applies equally to the spread of new ideas, as in the innovation and diffusion of public policies across states (Gray, 1973).

In sum, modeling serves as the principal mode of transmitting new forms of behavior, but those who have access to instruments of influence can exercise only partial control over the diffusion process. Not everything that is modeled becomes popular. Dispositional characteristics are of limited value in predicting who, from among the vast assortment of potential adopters, will be most receptive. Social and economic factors, which partly regulate adoptive behavior, set limits on the power of persuasion. Nevertheless, by operating on the determinants they can control, marketers help shape the public tastes and lifestyles.

Many of the preceding illustrations involve diffusion of behavior that is not only allowed socially but is commercially promoted. The adoption process, as revealed by incidence rates, is similar for activities that are socially prohibited. Spread of new styles of collective protest and aggression, for example, conforms to the generalized diffusion pattern (Bandura, 1973). As a rule, however, there is a greater time lag in widespread adoption of dissocial than of prosocial styles of behavior.

The differential consequences and social inducements associated with various forms of conduct most likely account for the temporal variations between exemplification and subsequent adoptions. As we have seen, early adoption of prosocial novelties usually gains the user status. In contrast, behavior that is forbidden by law or by custom carries risk of punishment. It therefore requires the cumulative impact of salient examples to reduce restraints sufficiently to initiate a rise in the modeled behavior. Even under weakened inhibitions, antisocial conduct requires the coexistence of strong aversive inducements or anticipated benefits before the behavior will be adopted.

The analysis of diffusion so far has been largely concerned with the spread of behavior within a society. Revolutionary advances in communications technology, which vastly expand the range of influence, have transformed the social diffusion process. Through the medium of satellite television systems, ideas, values, and styles of conduct are now modeled on a worldwide scale. In the coming years, the electronic media will play an increasingly influential role in the process of intercultural change.

3

Antecedent Determinants

THERE ARE CERTAIN REGULARITIES in the succession or coexistence of most environmental events. Such uniformities create expectations about what leads to what. Knowledge of conditional relationships thus enables one to predict with varying accuracy, what is likely to happen under given antecedent conditions. If people are to function effectively, they must anticipate the probable consequences of different events and courses of action and regulate their behavior accordingly. Without anticipatory capacities people would be forced to act blindly in ways that might prove to be unproductive, if not hazardous. Information about the probable effects of specific actions or events is conveyed by environmental stimuli. One can be informed on what to expect by the distinctive features of places, persons, or things, or by social signals in the language, gestures, and actions of others.

In the earliest period of child development, environmental stimuli, except for those that are inherently aversive or rewarding, have no influence. Through learning experiences, however, a vast array of stimuli eventually acquire the capacity to activate and guide behavior. Environmental cues can either signify events to come or indicate which outcomes particular actions are likely to produce. As a result of correlated experiences over time, events that were formerly neutral gain predictive value. After people discern the relationships between situations, actions, and outcomes, they can regulate their behavior on the basis of such predictive antecedent events. They fear and avoid things that have been associated with aversive experiences, but like and seek those that have had pleasant associations. They inhibit conduct under circumstances that threaten punishing response consequences, but respond readily in contexts signifying rewardable outcomes.

Humans do not simply respond to stimuli; they interpret them. Stimuli influence the likelihood of particular behaviors through their predictive function, not because they are automatically linked to responses by occurring together. In the social learning view, contingent experiences create expectations rather than stimulus-response connections. Environmental events can predict either other environmental occurrences, or serve as predictors of the relation between actions and outcomes. These variant forms of contingency learning will be discussed separately.

Antecedent Determinants of Physiological and Emotional Responsiveness

Physiological responses are brought most readily under the influence of environmental stimuli when events occur closely in time in a highly predictable relationship. If a formerly neutral stimulus is reliably associated with one that is capable of eliciting a given physiological response, the neutral stimulus alone eventually acquires the power to evoke the physiological response or a component of it. Although some types of physiological responses are more susceptible to expectancy learning than others, almost every form of somatic reaction can be brought under the control of environmental stimuli by contingent experiences. As a result, environmental events can affect heart rate, breathing, sweating, muscular tension, gastrointestinal secretions, vascular reactions, and the level of brain activity.

Results of a series of studies by Rescorla (1972) reveal that it is the degree of correlation between events rather than their pairing that is important in the development of antecedent determinants. As a rule, anything that reduces the predictive value of environmental events by lowering their correlations with outcomes diminishes the activating potential of the antecedents. However, in human expectancy learning thought complicates the process. People can develop anticipatory responses to signaling stimuli on the basis of what they are told without actually experiencing the likelihood that given stimuli predict certain environmental outcomes (Grings, 1973). Even when learning results from direct encounters with the environment, people do not always extract the correct probablistic information from their experiences. Moreover, accurate recognition that events occur contingently can produce different anticipatory reactions depending upon accompanying thoughts, a point to which we shall return later.

This process of expectancy learning has important implications for the understanding of behavior involving physiological arousal, such as physiological dysfunctions and defensive behavior. In the psychosomatic field, Dekker, Pelser, and Groen (1957) established asthmatic attacks in patients by pairing formerly ineffective stimuli with allergens that evoked respiratory dysfunctions. Detailed study of other patients, who regularly experienced asthmatic attacks, revealed that a diverse array of environmental events had become elicitors; these included, among other things, political speeches, children's choirs, the national anthem, elevators, goldfish, caged birds, perfume, waterfalls, bicycle races, police vans, and horses. Once the eliciting events had been identified in a particular case, Dekker and Groen (1956) were able to induce asthmatic attacks by presenting the evocative stimuli in actual or pictorial form.

ANXIETY AND DEFENSIVE BEHAVIOR

A great deal of human behavior is activated by events which become threatening through association with painful experiences. A prime function of most anticipatory behavior is to provide protection against potential hazards.

Until recently, defensive behavior was explained in terms of a dual-process theory. According to this view, paired association of neutral and aversive stimuli creates an anxiety drive that motivates defensive behavior; the defensive behavior, in turn, is reinforced by reducing the anxiety aroused by the conditioned aversive stimuli. To eliminate defensive behavior, it was considered necessary to eradicate its underlying anxiety. Therapeutic efforts therefore were keyed to extinguishing anxiety arousal.

This theory, though still widely accepted, has been found wanting (Bolles, 1972; Herrnstein, 1969; Rescorla & Solomon, 1967). Autonomic arousal, which constitutes the principal index of anxiety, is not required for defensive learning. Indeed, the view that defensive behavior is under autonomic control is disputed by several lines of evidence. Since autonomic reactions take much longer to activate than do avoidance responses, the latter cannot be caused by the former. Studies in which autonomic and avoidance responses are measured concurrently indicate that these two modes of activity are partially correlated but not causally related. Avoidance behavior, for example, can persist long after autonomic reactions to learned threats have been extinguished. Surgical removal of autonomic feedback capability in animals has little effect on the acquisition of avoidance responses. Maintenance of avoidance behavior is even less dependent upon autonomic feedback. Depriving animals of autonomic functioning after defensive behavior is learned does not increase the speed with which such activities are extinguished.

Research has cast doubts on the presumed reinforcing sources, as well as the activating sources, of defensive behavior. In the dual-process theory, the anxiety reduction occasioned by escape from the feared stimulus reinforces the defensive behavior. However, the evidence reveals that whether or not defensive behavior removes the feared stimulus has variable effects on the maintenance of the behavior. Moreover, defensive behavior can be acquired and maintained by its success in reducing the frequency of aversive stimulation, even in the absence of feared stimuli to arouse anxiety and to provide a source of negative reinforcement.

The overall evidence indicates that anxiety and defensive behavior are coeffects rather than causally linked. Aversive experiences, either of a personal or vicarious sort, create expectations of injury that can activate both fear and defensive conduct. Because they are coeffects, there is no fixed relationship between autonomic arousal and action. Until effective coping behaviors are developed, threats produce high emotional arousal and various defensive maneuvers. But after people become adept at self-protective behaviors they perform them in potentially threatening situations without having to be frightened. Should their habitual devices fail, they experience heightened arousal until new defensive learning reduces their vulnerability.

Acquired threats activate defensive behavior because of their predictive rather than their aversive qualities. They signal the likelihood of painful outcomes unless protective measures are taken. Defensive behavior, in turn, is maintained by its success in forestalling or reducing the occurrence of aversive events. Once established, defensive behavior is difficult to eliminate even when the hazards no longer exist. This is because consistent avoidance prevents the organism from learning that the real circumstances have changed. Hence, the failure of anticipated hazards to materialize reinforces the expectation that the defensive maneuvers forestalled them. This process of subjective confirmation is captured in the apocryphal case of a compulsive who, when asked by his therapist why he snapped his fingers ritualistically, replied that it kept ferocious lions away. When informed that obviously there were no lions in the vicinity to ward off, the compulsive replied, "See, it works!"

Expectations that have little basis in reality would ordinarily be amenable to change through accurate information. But fearful expectations are not entirely groundless. Some animals do bite, airplanes crash from time to time, and assertiveness is sometimes punished. When injurious consequences occur irregularly and unpredictably, expectations are not easily altered. If apprehensive individuals do not fully trust what they are told, as happens in severe cases, they continue to behave in accordance with their expectations rather than risk painful consequences, however improbable they may be. What such individuals need in order to relinquish their fearful expectations are powerful disconfirming experiences, which verbal assurances alone do not provide. Procedures derived from social learning principles have proven highly effective in promoting rapid reality testing (Bandura, 1976a).

DEVELOPMENT OF AGGRESSION
ELICITORS

The development of aggression elicitors provides another
good example of the learning process under discussion (Bandura, 1973). Results of animal experimentation reveal that,
after a number of paired experiences in which a neutral event
foreshadows provoked assault between animals, the predictive
event alone tends to produce fighting. Toch's (1969) study of
chronic assaulters documents the same process in the development of aggression elicitors in humans through combative
experience. In one of the cases cited the person suffered a
humiliating beating as a youngster at the hands of a larger
opponent, a painful incident that determined his selection of
future victims. Thereafter, he would become violent at the
slightest provocation by a large person. These characteristics
acquired such powerful control over his aggressive behavior
that they often overrode the hazard of attacking powerfully
built opponents. In more formal tests, aggression elicitors
have been found to be especially effective when they appear
concurrently with other aggression inducements such as anger
arousal, aggressive modeling, and disinhibitory justifications
for assaultive conduct (Berkowitz, 1973).

Research will be reviewed shortly on how antecedent
determinants are created through paired experiences that
render stimuli predictive of response consequences. The influential role of antecedent events in regulating aggressive behavior is most clearly revealed in experiments that arrange
the necessary learning conditions. When aggression is rewarded in certain contexts but not in others, the level of
aggressive responding can be altered simply by changing the
contextual events that signal probable outcomes.

SYMBOLIC EXPECTANCY LEARNING

Learning principles would have limited explanatory
value if antecedent determinants could be established only
through first-hand experiences. It is not uncommon, however,
for individuals to react emotionally toward things and people

cast into stereotypes without having had any personal contact with them. Such tendencies are frequently developed through cognitive processes wherein positive and negative symbols of primary experiences serve as the basis for further learning.

Words that arouse emotion often function as vehicles for expectancy learning. Words that conjure up feelings of revulsion and dread can create new fears and hatreds; conversely, words arousing positive reactions can be used to impart pleasing value to associated events. In one laboratory investigation of this process (Gale & Jacobson, 1970), insulting comments were repeatedly paired with a neutral tone. Before long, the tone itself began to elicit emotional reactions as measured physiologically.

Affective learning can also be promoted by pictorial stimuli that have arousal potential. Geer (1968), for example, established autonomic reactions to formerly neutral sounds by pairing them with frightening photographs. The role of learning processes is perhaps nowhere more dramatically evident than in the marked cross-cultural variations in the physical attributes and adornments that become sexual arousers. What arouses people in one society—corpulence or skinniness, upright hemispheric breasts or long pendulous ones, shiny white teeth or black pointed ones, distorted ears, noses, or lips, wide hips or slim ones, light skin color or dark—may be neutral or aversive to members of another social group.

A bold experiment by Rachman (1966) on how fetishes may be acquired throws some light on symbolic learning of sexual arousal. After a photograph of women's boots was regularly associated with slides of sexually stimulating women, men exhibited sexual arousal (as measured by penile volume increases) to the boots alone and generalized the sexual responses to other types of shoes. (Needless to say, these unusual sexual reactions were thoroughly eliminated at the conclusion of the study.) Consistent with these findings, McGuire, Carlisle, and Young (1965) present clinical evidence that deviant sexuality often develops through masturbatory conditioning in which aberrant sexual fantasies develop strong erotic significance by repeated association with the pleasurable experiences of masturbation.

VICARIOUS EXPECTANCY LEARNING

Although emotional responses often are learned from direct experience, they also are frequently acquired observationally. Many intractable fears arise not from personally injurious experiences, but from seeing others respond fearfully toward, or be hurt by, threatening objects. Similarly, evaluations of places, persons, or things often originate from exposure to modeled attitudes.

In vicarious expectancy learning, events become evocative through association with emotions aroused in observers by the affective expression of others. Displays of emotion conveyed through vocal, facial, and postural cues of the model are emotionally arousing to observers. Such affective social cues most likely acquire arousal value as a result of correlated interpersonal experiences. That is, when individuals are in high spirits they treat others amiably, which produces pleasurable effects; conversely, when they are dejected, ailing, distressed, or angry, those around them are likely to suffer in one way or another. Results of a study by Church (1959) support the view that correlated experiences facilitate vicarious arousal. He found that while expressions of pain by an animal evoked strong emotional arousal in animals that had suffered pain together, it had less impact on animals that had undergone equally painful experiences but never in conjunction with suffering of another member of their species, and it left unmoved animals that had never been subjected to any distress.

After the capacity for vicarious arousal is developed, emotional responses can be established toward environmental correlates by observing the affective experiences of others. In laboratory studies of this process (Berger, 1962), observers hear a neutral tone and shortly thereafter see another person exhibit pain reactions (ostensibly to being shocked, though actually feigned). Observers who repeatedly witness this sequence of events begin to respond emotionally to the tone alone, even though they themselves have never experienced any pain in conjunction with it. In everyday life, distresses arise from diverse sources. For instance, the sight of others failing at tasks or reacting anxiously to subjective threats, serve as arousers for vicarious emotional learning (Bandura, Blanchard, & Ritter, 1969; Craig and Weinstein, 1965).

Defensive behavior as well as emotional arousal can be created by vicariously mediated correlation of events. Crooks (1967) measured how long monkeys handled different play objects. Later the monkeys heard tape-recorded distress vocalizations whenever a model monkey touched a particular object, and they heard the same vocalizations played backward (which did not sound like distress reactions) each time the model touched control objects. In subsequent tests, the observer monkeys played freely with the control items but carefully avoided the objects that appeared to hurt another animal. Vicarious avoidance learning has considerable survival value when the dangers are realistic. But since learning mechanisms do not operate selectively, many needless fears can be and are transmitted by the inappropriate apprehensiveness of models.

Similarity of experiences among people make consequences to others predictive of one's own outcomes, and is an especially influential factor in vicarious emotional learning. People who often experience similar outcomes are likely to be affected more strongly by adversities befalling one another than they are by troubles affecting people whose outcomes are unrelated to their own. This partly explains why injuries or rewards to strangers are less vicariously arousing than the suffering and joy of close associates upon whom one is dependent.

In some conceptualizations of empathy, vicarious arousal is presumed to result from intuiting the experiences and emotional states of another person. According to social learning theory, modeled affect generates vicarious arousal through an intervening self-arousal process in which the observed consequences are imagined mainly as occurring to oneself in similar situations. This would suggest that one is more easily aroused by personalizing observed effects than by taking the perspective of another. Consistent with this view, Stotland (1969) found that observers reacted more emotionally to the sight of a person undergoing painful stimulation if they imagined how they themselves would feel than if they imagined how the other person felt.

Exposure to the emotional experiences of others does not invariably produce vicarious learning. Observers can attenuate the emotional impact of modeled anguish through their thoughts and attention. The practice of neutralizing experiences is revealed in a study of vicarious learning as a function of the observers' level of emotional arousal (Bandura & Rosenthal, 1966). Observers who were moderately aroused displayed the most rapid and enduring acquisition of autonomic responses, whereas those who were either minimally or markedly aroused achieved the weakest vicarious learning. Modeled pain reactions proved so upsetting to those observers who were beset by high arousal that they diverted their attention from the sufferer and took refuge in distracting thoughts to escape the unpleasant social situation.

Cognitive Functions in Expectancy Learning

In behavior theory, learning through paired experience, labeled classical conditioning, is commonly viewed as a process wherein conditioned stimuli are directly and automatically connected to responses evoked by unconditioned stimuli. Conditioning is simply a descriptive term for learning resulting from paired stimulation, not an explanation of how the changes come about. Originally, conditioning was assumed to result automatically from events occurring together in time. Closer examination revealed that it is in fact cognitively mediated.

People do not learn much, if anything, from repeated paired experiences unless they recognize that events are correlated (Dawson & Furedy, 1976; Grings, 1973). That awareness is a determinant of conditioning rather than vice versa is shown in an experiment conducted by Chatterjee and Eriksen (1962). Participants who were informed that shock would follow a particular word in a chain of associations quickly developed anticipatory heart-rate responses. In contrast, those who were led to believe that the occurrence of shock was not related in any consistent way to their verbalizations evidenced no autonomic conditioning even though they experienced the same paired stimulation as their aware counterparts.

The most striking evidence of cognitive control of anticipatory responses is provided by studies of the extinction of emotional reactions as a function of induced awareness. Affective reactions of people who are informed that predictive stimuli will no longer be followed by painful events are compared with those of people who are not told that the threat no longer exists. Induced awareness promptly eliminates fear arousal and avoidance behavior in the informed participants, while the uninformed lose their fear only gradually (Bandura, 1969; Grings, 1973).

SELF-AROUSAL FUNCTIONS

The power to arouse emotional responses is by no means confined to external physical stimuli. Affective reactions can be stimulated cognitively. People can easily make themselves nauseated by imagining sickening experiences. They can become sexually aroused by conjuring up erotic fantasies. They can frighten themselves by fear-provoking thoughts. And they can work themselves into a state of anger by ruminating about mistreatment at the hands of offensive provocateurs. Indeed, Barber and Hahn (1964) found that imagined painful stimulation produced subjective discomfort and physiological responses similar to those induced by the actual painful stimulation. The incomparable Satchel Paige, whose extended baseball career provided many opportunities for anxious self-arousal, vividly described the power that thoughts can exert over visceral functioning when he advised, "If your stomach disputes you lie down and pacify it with cool thoughts."

In the social learning analysis, so-called conditioned reactions are considered to be largely self-activated on the basis of learned expectations rather than evoked automatically. The critical factor, therefore, is not that events occur together in time, but that people learn to foresee them from predictive stimuli and to summon up appropriate anticipatory reactions. Several lines of evidence, some of which have already been reviewed, lend validity to the self-arousal interpretation of conditioning.

For individuals who are aware that certain events forebode distress, such events activate fear arousing thoughts, which in turn produce emotional responses. Those who fail to notice, for one reason or another, that the antecedent stimulus foreshadows pain do not conjure up arousing cognitions. As a result, the predictive stimulus rarely evokes emotional responses even when repeatedly paired with unpleasant experiences. When contingency awareness and conditioning are measured concurrently, predictive stimuli do not elicit anticipatory reactions until the point at which awareness is achieved (Dawson & Furedy, 1976). The sudden disappearance of conditioned emotional responses following awareness that the threat has ceased is also explainable in terms of self-arousal processes. When individuals have such knowledge, antecedent stimuli no longer activate frightening thoughts, thus removing the cognitive source of emotional responses.

It follows from self-arousal theory that emotional responses can be developed toward formerly neutral events on a cognitive basis in the absence of physically painful experiences. Grings and others (Bridger & Mandel, 1964; Grings, 1973) report findings bearing on this topic. In these experiments, individuals are told that a given stimulus will sometimes be followed by shock but, except for a sample experience, this never happens. As the trials progress, formerly neutral stimuli become arousing through association with thought produced emotional responses.

The role of contingency recognition in anticipatory learning has been examined extensively, but the self-arousal component has received comparatively little attention. Although it is difficult to establish anticipatory reactions to predictive stimuli without contingency awareness, the presence of awareness alone does not guarantee such learning (Dawson & Furedy, 1976). People can be aware of events without acting on that knowledge. The types of cognitions they generate will determine the strength and persistence of the anticipatory reactions. The more they believe that past contingencies remain in effect, and the more severe the effects they expect, the stronger the anticipatory reactions will be (Dawson, 1966).

Classical conditioning is generally portrayed as a form of learning that occurs through paired stimulation independent of the subject's behavior. This may be true for the occurrence of motor responses during learning. However, internal responding, as measured by cognitive activities, is an essential ingredient in the process. Therefore, in predicting the level of anticipatory reactions one must consider not only awareness of environmental contingencies but self-arousal factors as well.

The extent to which anticipatory behavior is subject to cognitive control may vary depending upon whether it is established symbolically or through direct experience. Bridger and Mandel (1964) found that fear learning was similar regardless of whether neutral stimuli were associated only with threat of painful stimulation or with the threat combined with actual painful experiences. Fear responses that developed through actual painful experiences, however, were less susceptible to change by cognitive means. Thought-induced fear promptly disappeared with the knowledge that the physical threat would no longer be forthcoming. By contrast, fear responses originating in painful experiences persisted for some time despite awareness that the physical threat no longer existed.

These findings may be explained in several ways. One possibility is that emotional responses contain dual components, as Bridger and Mandel suggest. One of the components—created by self-arousal—is readily modifiable by altering one's thoughts. The second component may be a nonmediated one that is directly evoked by external stimuli and hence requires disconfirming experiences for its extinction. Snake phobics, for example, will instantaneously respond with fear at the sight of a snake before they even have time to think about the potential dangers of reptiles.

An alternative interpretation is that when people have undergone painful experiences and there is even a remote chance they may get hurt, external stimuli become such powerful elicitors of fear arousing thoughts that they are not easily subject to voluntary control. Acrophobics, who are told that they can look down safely from the rooftop of a tall building because of protective railings, may be unable to turn off thoughts about the horrendous things that could conceivably happen. Here fearfulness is still cognitively mediated, but individuals are unable to control their thoughts, however safe the situation might appear.

The powerful cognitive control over fearful responding demonstrated under laboratory conditions contrasts with the tenacity of defensive behavior. The difference is probably explainable in terms of the severity and predictability of aversive consequences. In experimental situations, relatively weak threats are completely removed by experimenters who exercise full control over the occurrence of painful outcomes. By contrast, the things people fear excessively in everyday life are ordinarily innocuous but can occasionally be seriously hurtful, despite assurances to the contrary. Laboratory-produced fears likewise persist under uncertain outcomes. Hence, the probability of injury, however remote, can negate the potential influence of factual knowledge on action. For this reason, intense fears are rarely eliminated by reassuring information alone. Rather, frightening expectations must be extinguished by repeated disconfirming experiences.

Nonmediational theories of anticipatory learning assume that associated events must be registered in the nervous system of the organism. It is conceivable that in studies that reduce awareness by diverting subjects' attention to irrelevant events to reduce awareness, the predictive stimuli may not be registered sufficiently to produce learning. Neural responses to afferent input can be substantially reduced by focusing attention on competing events. In neurophysiological studies (Hernandez-Peon, Scherrer, and Jouvet, 1956), for instance, auditory neural responses to a loud sound were virtually eliminated in cats when they gazed at mice, attentively sniffed fish odors, or received shocks that disrupted their attentiveness. Horn (1960) noted a similar weakening of neural responses to a light flashed during active attention to other sights and sounds.

When people direct their attention to extraneous features

or irrelevant events, they may neither experience nor recognize the predictive stimulus. Absence of anticipatory learning in such circumstances may be wrongly attributed to lack of conscious recognition when, in fact, it reflects deficient sensory registration of stimulus events. Proof that awareness is necessary for learning would require evidence that, despite adequate neural registration of paired stimulation, anticipatory responses are not learned unless the relationship between the events is recognized.

Developmental theories often draw sharp distinctions between associative and cognitive processes, with the implication that young children learn by association, and older ones by cognitive processing of input information. As we have seen, cognitive factors markedly affect learning that is widely regarded as purely associative. And associative factors, such as the regularity and contiguity of stimulus conjunction, affect how easily correlation between events can be extracted.

It is evident from the preceding discussion that anticipatory learning is much more complex than is commonly believed. Emotional responses can be brought under the control of intricate combinations of internal and external stimuli that may be either closely related to, or temporally remote from physical experiences. Predictive stimuli can acquire evocative potential on a vicarious basis, or by association with thought-produced arousal, further adding to the complexity of the learning process. Once stimuli become evocative, this function transfers to other classes of stimuli that are similar physically, to semantically related cues, and even to highly dissimilar stimuli that happen to be associated in people's past experiences.

Inborn Mechanisms of Learning

It is a truism that differences exist in the ease with which different responses and environmental contingencies can be learned. Some of these variations are due to the physiological limitations of the sensorimotor and cortical structures with which organisms are innately endowed. They cannot be influenced by sensory information if they lack the appropriate receptors, nor can they learn repertoires of behavior that exceed their physical capacities. Moreover, the neural systems with which organisms are equipped limit how much central processing of information and central organization of behavior they can achieve.

Seligman and Hager (1972) put forth the interesting notion that genetic endowment also provides specialized associative apparatus that determine how an organism is influenced by experience. According to this principle of preparedness, organisms are biologically constructed through evolutionary selection to associate certain events more easily than others. They learn biologically primed associations with minimal input, but the unprepared ones painstakingly, if at all. The ease of association varies for different species and is, presumably, highly specific to events.

Substantial evidence can be marshalled to support specialized biological preprogramming in subhuman species (Hinde & Hinde-Stevenson, 1973; Seligman & Hager, 1972). Thus, for example, illness will readily create taste aversions in many animals, but painful shocks will not; shocks will establish avoidance of audiovisual stimuli, where illness will not. Arbitrary responses, which compete with ones that are more natural to a species, are difficult to establish or to modify by reinforcement. Moreover, animals may persist in performing natural responses even when they prevent reinforcement. Based on these findings, Seligman and Hager argue against general mechanisms of learning, which serve diverse purposes, in favor of event-specific associative mechanisms.

Evidence that learning in lower species operates under severe biological constraints does not mean that human learning is also governed by event-specific mechanisms. Because of both the advanced human capacity to symbolize experience and limited inborn programming, humans are capable of learning an extraordinary variety of behaviors. They learn to play tennis, to build automobiles, to fly airplanes, to create social systems and bureaucracies, and to espouse ideologies without requiring specific associative mechanisms for each class of activity. The innate preprogramming that enables animals to deal in a stereotyped fashion with the recurring demands of a limited habitat would not be evolutionarily advantageous for humans, who must often cope with exceedingly complex and rapidly changing circumstances. Under such diverse and highly variable conditions of living, generalizable mechanisms of learning, that rely heavily upon experiential organization of behavior, have greater evolutionary value than do fixed inborn mechanisms, except in the regulation of rudimentary biological functions. Humankind cannot wait for survivors of atomic holocausts to evolve a specific preparedness for avoidance of nuclear weapons.

Generalizing from phylogenetically simpler organisms to humans will yield misleading explanations when the conditions governing a given behavior differ across species. Consider the findings that taste aversions are readily induced in animals by association with illness but not with immediate shock (Revusky & Garcia, 1970). Numerous applications of aversion therapy with alcoholics show that shocks, or even negative imagery, are just as effective in inducing temporary avoidance of alcohol as when the sight, smell, and taste of alcholic beverages are repeatedly associated with drug-induced nausea. Neither method has lasting effects.

Recent evidence suggests that, even in animals, variations in ease of learning may have been prematurely ascribed to selective biological preparedness. In the studies creating taste aversions, food flavors were associated either immediately with shock or, after appreciable delays, with nausea. The type of paired experience thus varied with the time interval of pairing. It now appears that differences in the ease with which aversions are learned is due more to variations in time delays and to stimulus characteristics than to differential associability of gustatory cues with stomach upset. Krane and Wagner (1975) show that delayed shocks produce aversion to sweetened water while immediate shocks do not. By contrast, immediate shocks produce aversion to water accompanied by bright noisy cues but delayed shocks prove ineffective. The authors attribute the variations in aversive learning to the fact that the flavor trace of food is more persistent than the stimulus trace of exteroceptive (auditory-visual) cues.

In the aversion experiments, the duration, course of

development, and intensity of unpleasant experiences are un-controlled as is the temporal contiguity. Such variations in the properties of the aversive events significantly affect how easily aversions can be acquired. If it were found that illness created stronger aversions than did externally-produced pain under similar temporal conditions, explanations in terms of innate associability should be viewed with reservation in the absence of adequate controls for intensity and duration of the aversive events.

Researchers who are concerned with biological determi-nants of learning sometimes question traditional animal ex-perimentation on the grounds that arbitrary responses and contingencies are selected for study. In a thoughtful review of the preparedness concept, Schwartz (1974) argues that it is precisely because of this arbitrariness that analysis of animal learning has any relevance to human learning. People orga-nize and regulate their behavior largely on the basis of indi-vidualized experience. Analysis of how behavior is fashioned from experience and brought under arbitrary contingencies can therefore be more informative about how influences might operate on human conduct than is the study of actions that lower organisms are genetically predisposed to make.

Variations in ease of learning do not necessarily reflect inborn preparedness. Some contingencies are learned more readily than others because the events covary in time and space in ways that facilitate recognition of causal relation-ships (Testa, 1974). The influential factor here is the recog-nizability of external covariation rather than selective inter-nal associability. Rate of learning is also markedly affected by experiential preparedness. Experience makes predictive stim-uli more distinctive, furnishes prerequisite competencies, creates incentives, and instills habits that may either facili-tate or retard learning of new behavior patterns.

Some of the interpretative problems that arise when var-iations in human learning are attributed to innate prepared-ness are illustrated in speculations about the origin of human fears. According to Seligman (1971), people are biologically disposed to fear things that have threatened human survival through the ages. It remains to be demonstrated whether the events people fear are better predicted from their threat to survival or from the degree to which they are correlated with direct, vicarious, and symbolic aversive experiences.

Among the various human anxieties, those related to sexual activities rank high. It would be difficult to find evolutionary advantages to impotence or frigidity. In the course of evolution more people have probably drowned than died of snake bites, but snake phobias are more prevalent than fear of water. Snakes acquire threat value through a combination of experiences, involving fearful parental modeling reinforced by frightening personal experiences, grisly folklore, and illustrations of reptiles as menacing animals (Bandura, Blanchard, & Ritter, 1969).

Among the things that are correlated with aversive experiences, animate ones are more apt to give rise to phobias than are inanimate things. This is because animate threats, by virtue of their ability to act and be mobile, can appear at unpredictable times and places and inflict injury despite self-protective efforts. Active unpredictable threats over which one has only partial control give more cause for generalized anxiety than equally aversive threats that are predictable, immobile, and safe as long as one chooses to stay away from them. It is in the properties of events, then, rather than in the experiences of one's ancestors that answers to the selectivity of human phobias are most likely to be found.

In a laboratory test of innate preparedness, Olman, Erixon, and Lofberg (1975) found that adults developed fear reactions through paired shock as readily to pictures of faces and houses as to pictures of snakes, but that reactions to the faces and houses were extinguished more rapidly. Since preparedness is defined in terms of rate of acquisition, the expected predisposition to learn to fear snakes was not supported by the findings. In everyday life, houses and faces are repeatedly correlated with neutral and positive experiences as well as with negative ones, whereas references to snakes are almost uniformly negative. Differential rates of extinction are more likely due to differential correlates here and now than to snakes bites suffered by a few ancestors generations ago.

Dysfunctional Expectancy Learning

Contingency learning has considerable adaptive value. Unfortunately, as was alluded to earlier, it can also produce needless distress and self-limiting defensiveness. Dysfunctions of this sort can arise in several different ways.

COINCIDENTIAL ASSOCIATION

Of the numerous contextual events that occur in conjunction with aversive outcomes, some are actually related to the effects, while others are only coincidental. Because of one's selective attention or the distinctiveness of events, it is sometimes the coincidential correlates that assume predictive value. The following letter, taken from an advice column in a newspaper, provides a striking illustration of such inappropriate expectancy learning:

Dear Abby:

My friend fixed me up with a blind date and I should have known the minute he showed up in a bow tie that he couldn't be trusted. I fell for him like a rock. He got me to love him on purpose and then lied to me and cheated on me. Every time I go with a man who wears a bow tie, the same thing happens. I think girls should be warned about men who wear them.

Against Bow Ties

In the above example, the letter writer had generalized strong reactions to bow ties, a stimulus one would not expect to be routinely correlated with deceitfulness. To the extent that her anticipatory distrust evokes negative counterreactions from bow-tied men, her defensive behavior is perpetuated by the unpleasant experiences it creates. Coincidential association is thereby converted to a genuine correlation. In this process, the inappropriate behavior is maintained by self-produced reality rather than by conditions that have existed in the past but are no longer in effect.

INAPPROPRIATE GENERALIZATION

Irrational defensive behavior often arises when one over-generalizes from events associated with aversive experiences to innocuous events that are similar either physically or semantically. In the often quoted study by Watson and Rayner (1920), for example, in the course of several pairings of a rat with sudden noise, a young boy not only learned to fear the rat, but also generalized the fear widely to other furry objects such as rabbits, dogs, fur coats, cotton, wool, and even human hair. As a rule, the more similar innocuous stimuli are to those originally associated with aversiveness, the stronger are the generalized reactions.

Innocuous events can acquire aversive potential through generalization on the basis of semantic similarity. To cite a clinical example, Walton and Mather (1963) report the case of a woman who suffered from obsessions about being dirty and spent much of her time performing incapacitating hygiene rituals. This obsessive-compulsive behavior began with her severe guilt feelings of "dirtiness" because of a love affair with a married man. Eventually, a wide range of stimuli related to urogenital activities and all forms of dirt became disturbing to her.

Corrective Learning

Until recently, efforts to eliminate defensive behavior relied heavily upon the interview as the vehicle of change. Eventually it became apparent from results of such applications that conversation is not an especially effective way of altering human behavior. In order to change, people need corrective learning experiences.

Developments in the field of behavioral change reveal two major divergent trends. This difference is especially evident in the modification of dysfunctional inhibitions and defensive behavior. On the one hand, explanations of change processes are becoming more cognitive. On the other hand, it is performance based treatments that are proving most powerful in effecting psychological changes. Regardless of the method involved, treatments implemented through actual performance achieve results consistently superior to those in which fears are eliminated to cognitive representations of threats (Bandura, 1977). Symbolic procedures have much to contribute as components of a multiform performance-oriented approach, but they are usually insufficient by themselves.

In the social learning view, psychological changes, regardless of the method used to achieve them, derive from a common mechanism. The apparent divergence of theory and practice is reconciled by recognizing that change is mediated through cognitive processes, but the cognitive events are induced and altered most readily by experiences of mastery arising from successful performance.

Psychological procedures, whatever their form, alter expectations of personal efficacy. Within this analysis, efficacy and outcome expectations are distinguished, as shown schematically in Figure 3. An outcome expectancy is defined here as a person's estimate that a given behavior will lead to certain outcomes. An efficacy expectation is the conviction that one can successfully execute the behavior required to produce the outcomes. Outcome and efficacy expectations are differentiated because individuals can come to believe that a particular course of action will produce certain outcomes, but question whether they can perform those actions.

The strength of people's convictions in their own effectiveness determines whether they will even try to cope with difficult situations. People fear and avoid threatening situa-

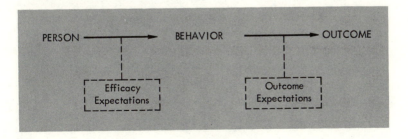

Figure 3 Diagrammatic representation of the difference between efficacy expectations and outcome expectations.

tions they believe themselves unable to handle, whereas they behave affirmatively when they judge themselves capable of handling successfully situations that would otherwise intimidate them.

Perceived self-efficacy not only reduces anticipatory fears and inhibitions but, through expectations of eventual success, it affects coping efforts once they are initiated. Efficacy expectations determine how much effort people will expend, and how long they will persist in the face of obstacles and aversive experiences. The stronger the efficacy or mastery expectations, the more active the efforts. Those who persist in performing activities that are subjectively threatening but relatively safe objectively will gain corrective experiences that further reinforce their sense of efficacy thereby eventually eliminating their fears and defensive behavior. Those who give up prematurely will retain their self-debilitating expectations and fears for a long time.

Expectations of personal efficacy are based on several sources of information. Figure 4 presents the diverse influence

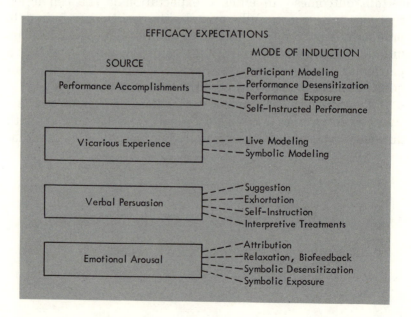

Figure 4 Major sources of efficacy expectations and the sources through which different modes of influence operate.

procedures commonly used to reduce defensive behavior and the source through which each treatment operates to create expectations of mastery. Any given method, depending on how it is applied, may of course draw on one or more sources of efficacy information. By postulating a common mechanism of operation, this conceptual scheme is designed to account for behavioral changes achieved by different modes of treatment.

Performance accomplishments provide the most dependable source of efficacy expectations because they are based on one's own personal experiences. Successes raise mastery expectations; repeated failures lower them, especially if the mishaps occur early in the course of events. After strong efficacy expectations are developed through repeated success, the negative impact of occasional failures is likely to be reduced. Indeed occasional failures that are later overcome by determined effort can strengthen self-motivated persistence through experience that even the most difficult of obstacles can be mastered by sustained effort. The effects of failure on personal efficacy therefore partly depend upon the timing and the total pattern of experiences in which they occur. Once established, efficacy expectancies tend to generalize to related situations.

Many expectations are derived from *vicarious experience.* Seeing others perform threatening activities without adverse consequences can create expectations in observers that they too will eventually succeed if they intensify and persist in their efforts. They persuade themselves that if others can do it, they should be able to achieve at least some improvements in performance.

A number of modeling variables likely to affect mastery expectations have been shown to enhance the disinhibiting power of modeling procedures. Phobics benefit more from seeing fearful models gradually overcome their difficulties by determined effort than from observing facile performances by adept models (Kazdin, 1974a; Meichenbaum, 1971). Similarity to the model in regard to other characteristics can likewise increase the effectiveness of symbolic modeling. Observing a model perform disinhibited behavior that results in beneficial consequences produces greater improvements than witnessing the same performances without any evident consequences (Kazdin, 1974c, 1975). Diversified modeling, in which the activities observers regard as hazardous are repeatedly shown to be safe by a variety of models, is more effective than the same performances by a single model (Bandura & Menlove, 1968; Kazdin, 1974b). If people of widely differing characteristics can succeed, then observers have a reasonable basis for increasing their own sense of self-efficacy.

In attempts to influence human behavior, *verbal persuasion* is widely used because of its ease and ready availability. People are led, through persuasive suggestion, into believing they can cope successfully with what has overwhelmed them in the past. Efficacy expectations induced in this manner are likely to be weak and shortlived. In the face of distressing threats and a long history of failure in coping with them, whatever success expectations are induced by suggestion will be rapidly extinguished by disconfirming experiences. Results of several lines of research attest to the weakness of verbal persuasion that creates expectations without providing an authentic experiential base for them.

Emotional arousal can influence efficacy expectations in threatening situations. People rely partly upon their state of physiological arousal in judging their anxiety and vulnerability to stress. Because high arousal usually debilitates performance, individuals are more likely to expect success when they are not beset by aversive arousal than when they are tense, shaking, and viscerally agitated. Fear reactions generate further fear.

Researchers working within the attributional framework (Valins & Nisbett, 1971) have attempted to modify avoidance behavior by directly manipulating the cognitive labeling of emotional arousal. The presumption is that if phobics are led to believe that the things they have previously feared no longer affect them internally, the cognitive reevaluation alone will reduce avoidance behavior. Misattribution of emotional arousal is another variant of the attributional approach to modification of fearful behavior. In this procedure, fearful people are led into believing that their emotional arousal is caused by a nonemotional source. To the extent that they no longer label their agitated state as anxiety, they will behave more boldly. It may be possible to reduce mild fears by this means, but mislabeling arousal or attributing it to erroneous sources is not of much help to the highly anxious (Bandura, 1977; Borkovec, 1973). Severe acrophobics, for example, may be temporarily misled into believing that they are no longer fearful, but they will reexperience unnerving internal feedback when confronted with dreaded heights.

In addition to the expectancy determinants analyzed thus far, *situational circumstances* affect efficacy expectations. Some situations require more arduous performances and present a higher risk of feared consequences than do others. Success expectations will vary accordingly. The level and strength of preceived self-efficacy in public speaking, for example, will differ depending upon the subject matter, the format of the presentation, and the types of audiences that will be addressed. Discrepancies between success expectations and performance are most likely to arise under situational uncertainty.

Treatments combining modeling with guided participation have proved most effective in eliminating dysfunctional fears and inhibitions (Bandura, 1977). Participant modeling favors successful performance as the principle vehicle of psychological change. Avoidance of subjectively real, but objectively unwarranted, threats keeps behavior out of touch with existing conditions of reinforcement. Through participant modeling it is possible to achieve rapid reality testing, which provides the corrective experiences for change.

People suffering from intractable fears and inhibitions are not about to do what they dread. In implementing participant modeling, therapists therefore structure the environment so that clients can perform successfully despite their incapacities. This is achieved by enlisting a variety of response induction aids. The therapist first models threatening activities in easily mastered steps. Clients then enact the modeled conduct with appropriate guidance until they can perform it skillfully and fearlessly. If they are unable to do so, the therapist introduces performance aids that eventually ensure success. Joint performance with the therapist, who offers physical assistance if necessary, enables fearful clients to engage in threatening activities which they refuse to do on their own. Graduated subtasks and performances for increasingly longer periods can be used to ensure continuous progress should difficulties arise. Arranging protective conditions to reduce the likelihood of feared consequences is a further means of weakening dysfunctional restraints that retard change. If such environmental arrangements prove insufficient to induce desired behavior, incapacitating restraints can be overcome by reducing the severity of the threat itself.

As treatment progresses, the supplementary aids are withdrawn so that clients cope effectively unassisted. Self-directed mastery experiences are then arranged to reinforce a sense of personal efficacy. Through this form of treatment, incapacitated clients lose their fears, become able to engage in activities they formerly inhibited, and develop more favorable attitudes toward the things they abhorred. Chronic phobics who suffer from recurrent nightmares no longer experience disturbing dreams after their phobias are eliminated.

Empirical tests of the relationship between expectancy and performance have generally yielded weak results because the measures of expectancy are mainly concerned with people's hopes rather than with their sense of mastery. Moreover, expectation is typically measured in terms of a global self-rating as though it were a static, unidimensional factor. Efficacy expectations differ from the outcome expectations commonly measured in expectancy analyses of behavioral change. In the latter instances, participants simply judge how much they expect to benefit from a given procedure. These global measures reflect a mixture of, among other things, hope, wishful thinking, belief in the potency of the procedures, and faith in the therapist. It comes as no surprise that such measures have little relationship to magnitude of behavioral change.

Efficacy expectancies vary on several dimensions that have important performance implications. They differ in *magnitude*. Thus, when tasks are ordered according to level of difficulty, the efficacy expectations of different individuals may be limited to the simpler tasks, extend to moderately difficult ones, or include even the most taxing performances. Efficacy expectations also differ in *generality*. Some kinds of experiences create only limited mastery expectations, while others instill a more generalized sense of efficacy that extends well beyond the specific treatment situation. In addition, expectancies vary in *strength*. Weak expectations are easily extinguishable by disconfirming experiences, whereas individuals who possess strong expectations of personal mastery will persevere in their coping efforts despite dissuading experiences.

A meaningful expectancy analysis, therefore, requires detailed assessment of the magnitude, generality, and strength of efficacy expectations with the same precision that changes in behavior are measured. Results of such an analysis reveal that treatments based on performance accomplishments produce higher and stronger efficacy expectations than do vicarious experiences alone (Bandura, Adams, & Beyer, 1977). Behavioral changes correspond closely to the magnitude of expectancy change. The stronger the efficacy expectations, the higher the likelihood that threatening tasks will be dealt with successfully.

Antecedent Determinants of Action

The same behavior often has different effects depending upon, among other factors, the time, the place, and the persons toward whom it is directed. Driving through a busy intersection on a red light, for example, will have painfully different consequences than crossing on a green light. When variations in certain situational, symbolic, and social cues are regularly associated with differential response outcomes, the cues come to serve as activators and guides for action. People therefore pay close attention to the aspects of their environment that predict reinforcement but ignore those that do not. The capacity to regulate one's responsiveness on the basis of antecedent events predictive of response consequences provides the mechanism for foresightful behavior.

Stimuli acquire predictive value by being correlated with differential response consequences. Traditional accounts of this process focus mainly on unarticulated modes of influence in which responses are rewarded or punished only in the presence of certain cues but never in other contexts. The predictive value of stimuli is undoubtedly established and maintained in many instances through actual correlation with response effects. However, people's symbolic capacity enables them to gain such information without having to enact responses in all the different circumstances to discover the probable outcomes that each stimulus signifies. Much contingency learning is, in fact, achieved by verbal explanations that describe the circumstances under which particular actions are rewardable and punishable. One does not have to suffer legal consequences, for instance, in order to learn the conditions under which given types of conduct are forbidden by law.

People often behave appropriately without either personal experience or explanation of probable response consequences. This is because information about predictive stimuli is derived vicariously by observing how the behavior of others is reinforced in different situations. Although actions are frequently guided by judgments based on what one has observed or been told, the maintenance of antecedent determinants that have been established verbally or vicariously ordinarily requires periodic confirmation through direct experience.

The effects of actions are in large part socially mediated. Predictive social cues, therefore, play an especially significant role in the regulation of human conduct. Children often behave quite differently in the presence of either parent in accordance with the particular parent's disciplinary practices. A telling illustration of this process is given in the following report of an autistic boy who expressed destructive behavior freely with his lenient mother, but rarely did so in the presence of his father, who would not tolerate aggression:

> Whenever her husband was home, Billy was a model youngster. He knew that his father would punish him quickly and dispassionately for misbehaving. But when his father left the house, Billy would go to the window and watch until the car pulled out. As soon as it did, he was suddenly transformed. . . . "He'd go into my closet and tear up my evening dresses and urinate on my clothes. He'd smash furniture and run around biting the walls until the house was destruction from one end to the other. He knew that I liked to dress him in nice clothes, so he used to rip the buttons off his shirts, and used to go in his pants [Moser, 1965, p. 96].

In a formal study of how behavior is socially cued, Redd and Birnbrauer (1969) had one adult reward a group of seclusive children for playing cooperatively, while a second adult rewarded them equally regardless of how they behaved. Later, the mere appearance of the contingently rewarding adult evoked cooperative play, whereas the noncontingent adult had no influence on the children's social behavior. When the adults reversed their reinforcement practices, their power to elicit play behavior changed accordingly.

People generally regulate their behavior on the basis of more subtle social cues. Consider the common example of parents who are quick to issue commands to their children but do not always see to it that their requests are heeded. Eventually children learn to ignore demands voiced in mild or moderate tones. The parents' mounting anger becomes a predictive cue that compliance will be enforced, so that only shouts produce results. As a result, many households are run on a fairly high decibel level.

MODELING DETERMINANTS

Of the numerous predictive cues that influence behavior at any given moment, none is more common or effective than the actions of others. People applaud when others clap, they laugh when others laugh, they exit from social events when they see others leaving, and on countless other occasions their behavior is prompted and channeled by modeling influences.

The actions of others acquire predictive value through correlated consequences in much the same way as do nonsocial physical and symbolic stimuli. Modeling cues prompt similar conduct when behaving like others produces rewarding outcomes, but they elicit divergent behavior when actions dissimilar to the model are reinforced. Because people usually display behavior of proven value, following good examples is much more efficacious than tedious trial and error. Thus, by relying on the actions of knowledgeable models, novices can act appropriately in diverse settings and at different events without having to discover what constitutes acceptable conduct from the shocked or pleased reactions of witnesses to their groping performances. The dictum "When in Rome do as the Romans do'' underscores the functional value of modeling cues.

The power of example in eliciting and channeling behavior is well documented by both laboratory and field studies. One can get people to behave altruistically, to volunteer their services, to delay or to seek gratification, to show affection, to behave punitively, to prefer certain foods and apparel, to converse on particular topics, to be inquisitive or passive, and to engage in most any course of action by having such conduct exemplified. The types of models that prevail within a given social setting affect which human qualities, from among many alternatives, will be selectively activated.

People differ in the degree to which their behavior is guided by modeling influences, and not all models are equally effective in eliciting the types of behavior they themselves exemplify. Responsiveness to modeling cues is largely determined by three factors, which in turn derive their activating power largely from correlative relationships to response outcomes. These include the characteristics of models, the attributes of observers, and the response consequences associated with matching behavior.

With regard to the characteristics of models, those who have high status, competence, and power are more effective in prompting others to behave similarly than are models of lower standing. The force of prestigeful modeling is shown in a field study of behavioral contagion among children at summer camps (Lippitt, Polansky, & Rosen, 1952). Observers recorded how often children imitated the actions of peers when they made no effort to get others to follow their example. A few boys who possessed high power served as the major sources of social behavior. Their actions set the style for others. The influence of prestigeful models is even more convincingly demonstrated by Lefkowitz, Blake, and Mouton (1955). Pedestrians were more likely to cross a street on a red light when they saw a presumably high-status person in executive attire do so, than when the same transgression was performed by the same person dressed in patched trousers, scuffed shoes, and a blue denim shirt.

It is not difficult to explain why status enhances the cueing function of modeled conduct. The behavior of models who have gained distinction is more likely to be successful, and hence to have greater functional value for observers, than that of models who are relatively low in vocational, intellectual, or social competence. When following different models produces divergent effects, the models' characteristics and symbols of status assume informative value in signifying the probable consequences of behavior exemplified by the different models.

In situations in which people are uncertain about the wisdom of modeled courses of action, they must rely on such cues as general appearances, speech, style, age, symbols of socioeconomic success, and signs of expertise as indicators of past successes. The effects of a model's status tend to generalize from one area of behavior to another, as when prominent athletes express preferences for breakfast cereals as though they were nutrition experts. Unfamiliar persons likewise gain influence by their similarity to models whose behavior proved successful in the past.

Some attention has been devoted to identifying the types of people who are most responsive to modeling influences. Those who lack confidence and self-esteem, who are dependent, and who have been frequently rewarded for imitativeness are especially prone to adopt the behavior of successful models. But these are not the only people who profit greatly by example. These prosaic correlates are based mainly on results of studies in which unfamiliar models exhibit responses that have little or no functional value for observers beyond the immediate situation. General observation indicates that perceptive and confident people readily emulate both idealized models and those whose behavior is highly useful. It is exceedingly unlikely that dull, dependent students who lack self-confidence would profit more from observing skillful performances by instructors, brain surgeons, airline pilots, or inventive researchers than would understudies who are bright and self-assured. When modeling is explicitly used to develop competencies, the more talented and venturesome are apt to derive the greater benefits from observation of exemplary models.

Generalizations about the correlates of modeling must be accepted with reservation because the functional value of modeled behavior overrides the influence of either model or observer characteristics. The attributes of models exert greatest influence when it is unclear what consequences their behavior is likely to have. The probable value of modeled conduct must therefore be judged from appearances and signs of achievement. A prestigious or attractive model may induce a person to try a given course of action, but if the behavior should prove unsatisfactory, it will be discarded and the model's future influence diminished. Studies conducted under conditions in which response consequences are not evident may, therefore, exaggerate the role played by model characteristics in the continuing guidance of behavior.

EXTRACTION OF CONTINGENCY RULES

Environmental features that predict the effects of different courses of action are usually part of a bewildering variety of irrelevant events. To complicate matters further, many of the contingencies governing reinforcement combine multiple factors into configural rules of conduct. To illustrate this point, consider a task in which individuals are asked to judge the appropriateness of drinking alcohol at different times, in different settings, and under different social circumstances. These three factors, as well as many irrelevant cues (e.g., the type of liquor being drunk, the sex of the drinker), are portrayed in varying combinations in a set of pictures. Let us arbitrarily designate "acceptable" those pictures showing an adult drinking liquor at home or in a bar in the evening with others, and call solitary daytime drinking at home or in work settings as "inappropriate." As the individuals try to judge which factors are relevant on the basis of provisional suppositions, they receive feedback as to whether or not they are correct.

At first they select certain aspects as the basis for responding. Most of their initial judgments will be inappropriate because they would not have hit upon the classificatory rule immediately. A few of their judgments, however, are likely to prove successful because the factors selected as relevant will appear as part of the correct configuration in some of the situations pictured. By comparing how the features of the situations differ in the positive and negative instances, other aspects common to the positive instances will be selected and tested. On the basis of further informative feedback, individuals will continue to revise their suppositions until they eventually extract the essential features and combine them into a multidimensional contingency. In this example, the predictive configuration includes the joint presence of temporal, social, and situational features.

In regulating their behavior on the basis of multidimensional contingencies, individuals must discern the predictive factors, weight them appropriately, and combine them into generalizable rules of action. The component functions considered earlier in observational learning operate in the acquisition of rules by direct or vicarious experience. Individuals select certain cues for attention on the basis of preparatory set, learned biases, or the inherent salience of the features. They then seek behavioral verification of their suppositions through informative feedback to overt responses. By selecting, testing, and revising their suppositions they eventually combine the relevant factors into the correct configural rule. Thus, attentional processes, cognitive processing, behavioral reproduction, and response consequences all play a role in rule learning.

It should be emphasized again that most rules of action are conveyed by instruction rather than discovered by direct experience. This is easy to lose sight of, because despite its prevalance, such preceptive learning receives little attention in psychological theorizing and research. Behavior theories tend to stress learning through one's own successes and failures. The Piagetian approach emphasizes gradual development on the basis of one's own improvised experiences. In actuality, learning is fostered by modeling and instruction as well as by informative feedback from one's own transactions with the environment.

DEFECTIVE CONTINGENCY LEARNING

Competent functioning requires discriminative responsiveness, often to subtle variations in circumstances. Some behavior disorders primarily reflect inadequate contingency learning due to faulty reinforcement practices or to the loss of such functions under stress. People are less able to distinguish critical from irrelevant features of the environment under strong than mild threat, and those prone to emotional arousal are most adversely affected in this regard (Rosenbaum, 1956).

Because of the importance of symbolic communication in human relationships, deficient or inappropriate responsiveness to verbal cues can have serious consequences. As part of a program to develop procedures for modifying psychotic behavior, Ayllon and his associates provide many illustrations of how the function of language can be undermined and restored by its outcome correlates (Ayllon & Haughton, 1962). In one study, a group of schizophrenics with severe chronic eating problems were totally unresponsive to meal announcements or to persuasive appeals. Because of concern for their health, they were escorted by nurses to the dining room, spoon-fed, tube-fed, and subjected to other infantalizing treatments. It appeared that the nurses' coaxing, persuading, and feeding inadvertently reinforced the eating problems. By rewarding nonresponsiveness to verbal requests, language lost its function. All social rewards for ignoring the announcement of mealtime and for refusals to eat were therefore withdrawn; following meal call, the dining room remained open for thirty minutes and any patient who failed to appear during that time simply missed the meal. After these consequences were instituted, patients responded in a socially appropriate manner to meal calls and fed themselves.

Bizarre contingencies can produce idiosyncratic behavior that would be inexplicable without knowing the conditions of social learning. Lidz, Cornelison, Terry, and Fleck (1958) report a case in which sibling schizophrenics believed, among other strange things, that the word disagreement meant constipation. This peculiar conceptual behavior is quite understandable considering the contingencies that prevailed in this household. Whenever the sons disagreed with their mother she informed them that they were constipated and required an enema. The boys were then undressed and given enemas, a procedure that endowed disagreement with a most unusual meaning.

Without attentiveness to modeling influences, competencies cannot be easily developed because of limited opportunities for observational learning. In his studies of language learning in autistic children, Lovaas (1967) shows how the benefits of example are negated by faulty reinforcement practices. Autistic children who lacked communicative speech modeled therapists' verbalizations with a high degree of accuracy when rewards were made contingent upon appropriate reproductions of speech. When the same children were equally generously rewarded but without regard to the quality of their verbalizations, their utterances progressively deteriorated until they bore little resemblance to the linguistic behavior modeled for them by the therapists. Reinstating appropriate contingencies restored the function of modeling influences. Autistic children evidentally are not insensitive to environmental events when they are predictive of reinforcing outcomes.

4

Consequent Determinants

IF PEOPLE ACTED WITH FORESIGHT on the basis of informative environmental cues but remained unaffected by the results of their actions they would be too insensible to survive for long. Behavior is, in fact, extensively regulated by its consequences. Responses that result in unrewarding or punishing effects tend to be discarded, whereas those that produce rewarding outcomes are retained. Human behavior, therefore, cannot be fully understood without considering the regulatory influence of response consequences.

Behavior theories have traditionally differentiated between antecedent and consequent regulation of actions. This distinction is based on the assumption that behavior is directly strengthened and weakened by its immediate consequences. Because the likelihood of behavior is affected by the events following it does not mean its control resides at that locus. It will be recalled from the earlier discussion that consequences determine behavior largely through their informative and incentive value. For the most part, response consequences influence behavior antecedently by creating expectations of similar outcomes on future occasions. The likelihood of particular actions is increased by anticipated reward and reduced by anticipated punishment.

As mentioned briefly earlier, behavior is related to its reinforcing outcomes at the level of aggregate rather than momentary consequences (Baum, 1973). That is, people do not respond to each momentary item of feedback as an isolated experience. Rather, they process and synthesize feedback information from sequences of events over long periods of time regarding the conditions necessary for reinforcement, and the pattern and rate with which actions produce the outcomes. It is for this reason that vast amounts of behavior can be maintained with only infrequent immediate reinforcement. Because outcomes affect behavior through integrative thought, knowledge about schedules of reinforcement can exert greater influence upon behavior than does the reinforcement itself (Baron, Kaufman, & Stauber, 1969; Kaufman, Baron, & Kopp, 1966).

Research on how outcomes regulate behavior has been predominantly concerned with immediately occurring external consequences. In theories that recognize only the role of external consequences and contend that they shape behavior automatically, people are viewed mainly as reactors to environmental influences. But external consequences, as influential as they often are, are not the only kind of outcomes that determine human behavior. People partly guide their actions on the basis of observed consequences and on the basis of consequences they create for themselves. These three regulatory systems, based on external, vicarious, and self-produced consequences, are treated in detail next.

External Reinforcement

The most impressive demonstrations of how behavior is influenced by its effects are provided by studies using a reversal design. In this procedure, the incidence of a selected behavior is recorded during natural baseline conditions. Then changes in the behavior are measured when reinforcement influences are successfively introduced and withdrawn.

Applications of reinforcement procedures to the modification of many different refractory behaviors typify this approach. One case, selected from a large number reported by Harris, Wolf, and Baer (1964), illustrates the successive reversals. First, the person who is having difficulties is observed for a time to determine the frequency of the dysfunctional behavior, the contexts in which it occurs, and the reactions it elicits from others. In the case under discussion, an extremely withdrawn boy was spending about 80% of his time secluded in isolated areas of the nursery school. Observation revealed that the teachers unwittingly reinforced his seclusiveness by paying a great deal of attention to him when he was withdrawn, reflecting his feelings of loneliness, consoling him, and urging him to play with his peers. On the infrequent occasions when the child happened to join other children, the teachers took no special notice.

In the second phase of the program, a new set of reinforcement practices is instituted. Continuing with the above case, the teachers stopped rewarding seclusiveness with attention and support. Instead, whenever the boy sought out other children, a teacher joined the group and gave it her full attention. In a short time, the boy's withdrawal declined markedly, and he was spending about 60% of his time playing with other children.

After the desired changes have been achieved, the original reinforcement practices are reinstated to determine whether the dysfunctional behavior was, in fact, maintained by its social consequences. In this third phase, the teachers behaved in their customary way, being inattentive to the boy's sociability but responding with comforting ministrations whenever he withdrew. The effect of this well meaning-approach was to drive the child back into seclusiveness. Findings such as these underscore the need to evaluate social practices by their effects on recipients rather than by the humanitarian intent of the practitioners.

In the final phase, the beneficial contingencies are reintroduced, the dysfunctional patterns are eliminated, and the adaptive ones are rewarded until they are adequately supported by their natural consequences. In the present case, the teachers gradually reduced their rewarding attentiveness as the boy derived increasing enjoyment from play activities with his peers. In follow-up observations, he continued to enjoy his social relationships, which contrasted markedly with his original seclusiveness.

In numerous other studies employing incentive procedures with both children and adults, a wide variety of deleterious behaviors—including self-injurious actions, assaultiveness, psychosomatic malfunctions, delusional preoccupations, autistic behavior, chronic anorexia, psychogenic seizures, asthmatic attacks, psychotic expressions, and other disorders of long standing—have been successfully eliminated, reinstated, and again removed by altering their reinforcing consequences.

Behavioral changes that prove effective in securing valued rewards are not always that readily reversible (Baer & Wolf, 1967). And in the case of conduct that may have adverse effects, concern arises over the ethics of reinstating it after it has been eliminated. Therefore, multiple baseline procedures are often used in studying reinforcement processes as an alternative to the reversal design. This involves measuring baselines of several behaviors all at once and then applying reinforcement successively first to one of the behaviors, then to the second, and so on. The various behaviors generally change substantially at the point at which reinforcement is introduced.

The regulatory influence of reinforcement has been demonstrated with virtually all forms of behavioral functioning. Until recently it was commonly believed that physiological states could be externally aroused but were not subject to influence by consequences. It is now well documented that bodily functions can be regulated to some extent through external feedback. Learning of visceral control is facilitated by biofeedback procedures wherein subjects alter their internal states on the basis of feedback signals from a device that measures and signals the level of the biological activity. By these means, people have been taught to change their heart rate, raise or lower their blood pressure, eliminate tension headaches, reduce gastric acid secretions, increase impaired blood circulation, and modify other internal functions (Blanchard & Young, 1973; Miller, 1969; Shapiro & Schwartz, 1972). There is little evidence, however, to support the early claims that people could attain internal serenity by producing large amounts of alpha brain waves with biofeedback.

The fact that bodily control can be gained with the aid of artificial feedback does not mean that people will be able to exercise that control under natural conditions. Success depends on learning helpful techniques for altering biological functions. Indeed, some preliminary findings suggest that people can exercise better bodily control by developing other ways of regulating biological processes than by relying on biofeedback devices without being instructed on how to do it (Blanchard & Young, 1973). Feedback is most helpful when people already possess the means for producing internal changes.

There are several mechanisms through which control can be gained over bodily functions. One means operates through muscular mechanisms. Visceral reactions are modifiable by self-induced relaxation. Budzynski, Stoyva, and Adler (1970) successfully applied biofeedback and relaxation procedures in treating tension headaches resulting from sustained contraction of scalp and neck muscles. Patients heard a tone with a frequency proportional to the electromyographic (EMG) activity in the monitored forehead muscles. They were instructed to keep the tone low by relaxing their facial muscles. As they became more adept at muscular relaxation, the criterion was raised in graded steps requiring progressively deeper relaxation to achieve low-pitched tones. By this method, patients who had experienced daily headaches for years stopped tensing their facial muscles and eventually eliminated their headaches. Results of other studies reveal that training in self-relaxation is as effective as biofeedback in reducing migraine headaches, insomnia, and blood pressure levels. These findings suggest that biofeedback may be a cumbersome way of getting people to relax their musculature.

Somatic control is possible without the mediation of muscular activities. Another regulatory mode works through attentional mechanisms. The activity levels of biological functions can be altered by focusing attention on neutral events and excluding viscerally arousing ones. Meditation techniques, which can produce measurable changes in somatic reactions, involve restricting the content of one's thought by selective attention to a Sanskrit word or mantra. Nonmeditative procedures, in which persons sit comfortably in a quiet setting with eyes closed and focus their attention on nonarousing events, can work as well.

A third mode of regulating bodily processes operates via cognitive mechanisms. Cognitive activity generates visceral reactions; people can raise their blood pressure, accelerate their heart rate, increase their gastric secretions, and heighten their muscle tension by arousing thoughts. Conversely, they can reduce these somatic functions by tranquilizing thoughts. In studies measuring momentary fluctuations in physiological activation triggered by different thought sequences, arousal is heightened by emotional self-induced thoughts and lowered by neutral thoughts (Schwartz, 1971). When people are left to their own devices in training with biofeedback, as is usually the case, many hit upon cognitive strategies for controlling their physiology.

A question that merits some attention is whether physiological self-regulation involves a reinforcement process. The answer is "no" if reinforcement is viewed as an automatic response strengthener. If reinforcement is considered in terms of its motivating function, then feedback serves as a source of self-motivation for corrective responding. Informative monitoring of one's level of physiological activity provides the basis for setting goals that increase efforts to meet them.

HIERARCHICAL DEVELOPMENT OF
INCENTIVES

What people find reinforcing changes as a result of developmental experiences. At the earliest levels, infants and young children are primarily responsive to immediate physical consequences involving food, painful stimulation, and physical contact. Parents cannot rely on self-actualizing tendencies or joy of learning to keep children out of fires or off busy streets. These early, primary incentives are important not only in their own right; they also provide the basis for symbolic incentives.

In the course of development, rewarding physical experiences are repeatedly associated with expressions of the interest and approval of others, and unpleasant experiences with disapproval. Through correlation of events, these social reactions themselves become predictors of primary consequences and thereby become incentives. The effectiveness of social reactions as incentives derives from their predictive value rather than inhering in the reactions themselves. For this reason, the approval or disapproval of people who exercise rewarding and punishing power is more influential than similar expressions by individuals who cannot affect one's life.

Several factors contribute to the power of interpersonal reinforcers. Similar social expressions can be predictive of a vast array of rewarding or punishing experiences. Disapproval, for example, may result in such unpleasant effects as physical punishment, deprivation of privileges, penalties, withdrawal of interest and attention, and ostracism. An event that signifies various possible consequences will have greater influence than if it portends only a single effect. Moreover, social reactions are not invariably accompanied by primary experiences: praise does not always bring rewards, and reprimands do not always result in punishment. Unpredictability reduces the susceptibility of expectations to extinction.

Because of the intermittency and diversity of correlates, social reinforcers retain their incentive function even under minimal primary support. The development of social incentives has important implications for social learning and successful human relationships. Such incentives provide a convenient way for people to influence each other without having to resort continuously to physical consequences.

Some child-rearing authorities have popularized the view that healthy personality development is built on "unconditional love." If this principle were, in fact, unfailingly applied, parents would respond affectionately regardless of how their children behaved—whether or not they mistreated others, stole whatever they wanted, disregarded the wishes and rights of others, or demanded instant gratification. Unconditional love, were it possible, would make children directionless and quite unlovable. Most readers are undoubtedly acquainted with families where parents who attempted to approximate this condition succeeded in producing "self-actualized" tyrants.

Guideless interest is clearly not enough. Fortunately, the vast majority of parents are not such indiscriminate dispensers of affection. Nor do they confuse authentic responses to the conduct of their children with devaluing them as persons. Children in turn experience greater security in knowing what their parents really value than in feigned unconditional regard. While much parental affection is expressed unconditionally, being human and having some standards, parents are pleased with behavior they value and displeased with reprehensible conduct. It should come as no surprise that even staunch advocates of "unconditional regard" are quite selective in their own social responsiveness, approving the things they like and disapproving those they do not (Murray, 1956; Truax, 1966).

Theories that subscribe to the automaticity view of reinforcement assume that consequences have to be made instantly contingent upon behavior in order to affect it. Immediacy of effects is undoubtedly important for young children who have difficulty linking outcomes to actions when a delay or other activities are interposed. After symbolic skills are developed, however, people can cognitively bridge delays between behavior and subsequent outcomes without mistaking what is being reinforced. Behavior can therefore be effectively maintained by making preferred activities available on later occasions contingent upon engaging in or completing a given task. As Premack (1965) has shown, almost any activity can serve as an incentive for performing a less preferred activity. Money, which can be exchanged for countless things that people desire, is also widely used on a deferred basis as a powerful generalized incentive.

The reinforcement practices described above essentially involve a process of social contracting. Positive arrangements affirm that if individuals do certain things, they are entitled to specified rewards and privileges. In the case of negative sanctions, censurable conduct carries punishment costs. The process is portrayed in reinforcement terms, but the practice is that of social exchange. Most social interactions are, of course, governed by such conditional agreements, although they usually are not couched in the language of reinforcement. Describing them differently does not change their nature.

The developmental hierarchy of incentives has thus far included material consequences, symbolic consequences, and social contracting arrangements. At the highest level of development, individuals regulate their own behavior by self-evaluative and other self-produced consequences. After signs of progress and merited attainment become a source of personal satisfaction, knowledge that one has done well can function as a reward. As we shall see, in order to derive satisfaction from activities through self-reinforcement a number of complex functions must be developed.

EXTRINSIC AND INTRINSIC INCENTIVES

There has been some reluctance, both within professional circles and among the public, to acknowledge the influential role of reinforcing consequences in the regulation of behavior. Some believe that behavior should be performed for its own sake. Others see behavior as being motivated by innate drives for exploration and competence, which they believe can be thwarted by social influences. They voice concern that incentive practices may impede development of self-direction and diminish inherent interest. Still others are reacting to the older conceptions of reinforcement as a mechanical controller of conduct rather than as an informative and motivating influence. In fact, the development of self-motivation and self-direction requires certain basic functions that are developed through the aid of external incentives.

Many of the activities that enhance competencies are initially tiresome and uninteresting. It is not until one acquires proficiency in them that they become rewarding. Without the aid of positive incentives during early phases of skill acquisition, potentialities remain undeveloped. Instead, more often than not, coercion and threats are brought to bear, which instill antipathies rather than competencies. The best way to ensure the prerequisite learning is to support children's efforts until their behavior is developed to the point that it produces natural sustaining consequences. Thus, for example, children may initially require some encouragement to learn to read, but after they become proficient they read on their own for the enjoyment and valuable information it provides. Once people have learned verbal, cognitive, and manual skills for dealing effectively with their environment, they no longer require extraneous inducements to use them.

Distinctions are frequently made between extrinsic and intrinsic sources of reinforcement as though they were anti-

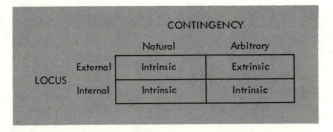

Figure 5 Social learning conceptions of the arrangements between behavior and its consequences that distinguish between extrinsic and intrinsic operations of reinforcement.

thetical. What is commonly referred to as intrinsic reinforcement includes several contingent arrangements. This is illustrated in Figure 5 by distinguishing between the locus and the contingency of reinforcement.

In extrinsic reinforcement, the consequences are externally produced and their relationship to the behavior is arbitrary. It is not in the natural course of things that work should produce paychecks, that good performances should evoke praise, or that reprehensible conduct should bring censure. Approval, money, privileges, penalties, and the like are socially arranged rather than natural consequences of behavior. When these outcomes are no longer forthcoming, the behavior declines unless it acquires other functional value.

Intrinsic reinforcement, as the concept is commonly used, comprises three types of arrangements between behavior and its consequences. In one form, the consequences originate externally, but are naturally related to the behavior. Stepping out of the rain reduces wetness, watching television provides audiovisual stimulation, and striking piano keys generates sound patterns. Under these conditions behavior is influenced by its sensory effects.

Many human activities are self-regulated by the sensory feedback they produce. Infants, for example, repeatedly perform responses in order to experience certain sounds and sights, and older children and adults spend long hours playing musical instruments that create pleasing sounds. Although the sensory effects are intrinsically related to the actions, the value of the feedback is learned in most instances. Grand opera or atonal music is not innately pleasing. Through repeated exposure, internal prototypes of patterns of stimulation are developed which serve as references for experiencing what is seen and heard as rewarding or unpleasant.

In the second intrinsic form, behavior produces naturally occurring consequences that are internal to the organism. Responses that generate physiological effects directly rather than through the action of external stimuli typify this contingency arrangement. Repetitive performance creates fatigue, relaxation exercises relieve muscular tension, and the like. Although cognitive activities can also produce physiological effects directly, this ability originates in exposure to arbitrary contingencies. After thoughts acquire emotion-activating potential through rewarding and punishing experiences, aversive arousal generated by perturbing thoughts can be reduced by engaging in serene thoughts.

Most of the things that people enjoy doing for their own sake originally had no reinforcing value. It is not the behavior itself or its feedback that is rewarding. Rather, it is people's self-reactions to their own performances that constitute the principal source of reward. To cite an example, there is nothing inherently rewarding about a tuba solo. To an aspiring tuba instrumentalist, however, an accomplished performance is a source of considerable self-satisfaction that can sustain much tuba blowing. Improvements in athletic and intellectual pursuits, similarly, activate self-evaluative reactions that serve as reinforcers of performance.

The self-reinforcement process described above represents the third form of intrinsic reinforcement. The evaluative consequences are internally generated, but the contingencies are arbitrary in that any activity can become invested with self-evaluative significance. What is a source of self-satisfaction for one person may be devalued or of no self-consequence for another.

The capability for evaluative self-reinforcement is established partly through the influence of extrinsic reinforcement. Internal evaluative regulation of behavior requires skill acquisition, adoption of performance standards, and self-generation of evaluative consequences. After some proficiency, judgmental standards, and self-reinforcing functions are acquired, qualitative variations in performance become sources of personal satisfaction or dissatisfaction.

The paramount role played by self-reinforcement in the regulation of human thought and conduct receives detailed consideration in a later section of this chapter. Behavior is least susceptible to the vagaries of situational inducements when the main consequences are either intrinsically related to the behavior or are self-produced.

Effects of Extrinsic Rewards on Intrinsic Motivation

According to attribution theory, people's perceptions of the causes of their behavior influence how they behave on future occasions (Bem, 1972; Nisbett & Valins, 1971). They presumably judge their motivation partly from the circumstances under which they behave. If they perform activities for external rewards they infer a lack of personal interest, whereas if they perform without external inducement, they judge themselves to be intrinsically interested in the activities. Extrinsic reinforcement for activities can therefore reduce intrinsic motivation to engage in them. How perception of causes changes intrinsic motivation remains to be explained. In Deci's (1975) view, rewards reduce intrinsic motivation by creating the impression that one's behavior is externally prompted and by weakening feelings of competence and self-determination.

A number of studies have been reported in which children who were promised rewards for doing things they like later engaged in them for a shorter time than those who were rewarded unexpectedly or received no rewards (Lepper & Greene, 1975; Lepper, Greene, & Nesbitt, 1973). Further experiments investigating the factors that might be operative in producing these effects have yielded variable results. Depending upon the activities involved and the way in which rewards are used, extrinsic incentives can increase interest in activities, reduce interest, or have no effect (Calder & Straw, 1975; Kruglanski, 1975; Reiss & Sushinsky, 1975; Ross, 1976). Despite these variable results, it is widely assumed that research has demonstrated that incentives weaken intrinsic motivation. In fact, questions exist about the derivations made from attribution theory, the limiting conditions under which extraneous incentives reduce performance, the conceptualization of intrinsic motivation, the experimental procedures used, the interpretation of conflicting findings, and even their relevance to reinforcement practices.

Let us first examine the deductions that are often drawn from attribution theory. If individuals are rewarded for engaging in interesting activities, they infer they must lack interest in them. Consider the main proposition and the inference: I like to perform certain activities that are inherently interesting; I am rewarded for engaging in them; therefore, I lack interest in them. The first two propositions jointly do not imply only a single consequence. Indeed, a number of attributional judgments are possible. Since people usually already know what they like, when needlessly rewarded, they are more apt to make inferences about the values, obtuseness, or manipulativeness of the rewarder than about their own interests. Although causal attribution is regarded as the intervening cause of performance, the types of attributions actually evoked by unnecessary rewards are seldom, if ever, measured. If extraneous rewards reduce performance by changing causal attributions, feelings of competence or self-determination, then these intervening causes should be measured rather than assumed to be operating just because behavior changes.

Intrinsic motivation is a highly appealing but elusive construct. Intrinsic motivation is usually defined as performance of activities for no apparent external reward. Identifying the existence of intrinsic motivation from persistence of behavior and absence of noticeable extrinsic incentives is no easy task, however. To begin with, one would be hard put to find any situations that lack external inducements for behavior. The physical and social structures of situations, the materials they contain, the expectations of others, and a host of other stimulus determinants all exert a substantial influence on behavior. How long one persists in a given activity will vary depending upon the alternatives available in the situation. People will appear intrinsically motivated to engage in a particular activity when they do not have anything better to do, but intrinsically unmotivated for the same activity when they have more attractive options. The activation and persistence of behavior is therefore best understood as a continuous interaction between personal and situational sources of influence.

Most human behavior is maintained by anticipated rather than by immediate consequences. Athletes, students, and entertainers put in long hard hours of preparatory work for the prospect of fame and fortune even though their endeavors bring little in the way of immediate tangible rewards. It is difficult to tell in a given instance whether an activity is pursued for inherent interest or for anticipated future benefits. To complicate matters further, the terms intrinsic interest and intrinsic motivation are often used interchangeably, and both are inferred from level of performance. Ascribing to activities the capacity to arouse interest and to motivate behavior is markedly different from invoking intrinsic motives. People spend many hours watching television without extraneous reward, for example, but one would hardly regard such viewing as springing from intrinsic motivation.

There are problems in building and testing a theory of motivation when the existence of that motivation is inferred from the very behavior it supposedly causes. This is because behavior is affected by many different factors. In the attribution research, decreases in performance are taken as evidence of reductions in intrinsic motivation. Applications of reinforcement can produce later reductions in performance without transforming the nature of motivation. This can result from several alternative processes. The first concerns reinforcement contrast effects. The motivating potential of incentives is determined relationally rather than by their absolute value. Therefore, one and the same outcome can be rewarding or punishing depending upon how the behavior has been previously reinforced. Abrupt withdrawal of rewards is not a neutral event. Not rewarding behavior after it has been consistently rewarded functions as a punisher that can reduce performance until people become accustomed to the change in reinforcement. Because reductions in usual incentives can temporarily affect the level of motivation by changing the value of incentives, preference for activities should be assessed over a period of time. This reduces the likelihood of misinterpreting temporary changes in motivational level as being a lasting transformation of intrinsic motivation by reinforcement. In a study specifically addressed to this issue, Feingold and Mahoney (1975) found that contingent rewards increased childrens' preference for an activity, but they reverted to their previous level of interest immediately after the rewards were withdrawn. However, when their preferences were again measured several weeks later, without any reward, the children showed twice as much spontaneous interest in the formerly reinforced activity as they had originally.

Another factor that can affect later involvement in an activity is satiation and tedium. When incentives are used to get people to perform the same activity over and over again, they eventually tire of it. In efforts to equate for amount of monotonous repetitiveness experienced by subjects in reward and nonreward conditions, researchers arrange things so that rewards do not increase performance. This solves the problem of differential satiation but reduces the relevance of the research because the reason for using incentives is to raise the level or scope of behavioral functioning. What is the point of using incentives if they do not affect behavior at the time they are applied? Research findings have limited applicability to reinforcement practices when the effects of incentives are studied under circumstances in which rewards serve no incentive function. From the social learning perspective, it would seem well worth exploring how positive incentives can aid development of skills and potentialities that serve as enduring sources of personal satisfaction and contribute to a sense of efficacy.

Decreases in performance may also reflect reactions to how incentives are presented rather than to the incentives themselves. Incentives can be used in a coercive manner ("You will not receive certain benefits unless you perform x"). Coercive contingencies tend to evoke oppositional behavior. Positive incentives can be presented as supportive aids ("This is to help you do x"), as expressions of appreciation ("This is in recognition of your achieving x"), or they can convey evaluative reactions ("This is what we think your performance is worth"). It is unlikely that concert pianists lose interest in the keyboard because they are offered high performance fees. Indeed, they would feel devalued and insulted by low fees. Bestowal of rewards is not only a social act that evokes positive or negative reactions in others. It can lower or raise the valuation of the activities themselves depending on whether the rewarders convey the impression that the reinforced activity is uninteresting, or that it eventually becomes enjoyable for its own sake after some proficiency is achieved. The same incentives can thus have differential effects on behavior depending upon the message conveyed.

Other differences in how incentives are used in attribution studies and in traditional reinforcement practices raise questions concerning the generality and relevance of research findings. In attribution studies, subjects gain the rewards regardless of how they perform, or if there is a contingency between performance and amount of reward it is loosely defined. Subjects are usually rewarded only once. By contrast, in the usual incentive applications, participants determine the amount of reward they secure by the level or quality of their performance, and they are reinforced on numerous occasions. Reiss and Sushinsky (1975) found that a reward dispensed in the attribution manner reduced interest, whereas when children were rewarded contingently, over a period of time, they showed twice as much spontaneous interest in the reinforced activity than in other nonreinforced activities after the rewards were discontinued. Similar results were obtained by Ross (1976) in tests of the hypothesis that extrinsic rewards foster intrinsic interest when they enhance mastery of an activity. Both children and adults increased their interest in activities when they were rewarded for performance attainments, whereas their interest declined when they were rewarded for undertaking activities irrespective of quality of performance.

A study conducted by Greene (1974) within the attribution framework corresponds more closely to appropriate incentive practices. The interest shown by children in four sets of mathematical play materials was measured during a baseline period. During the experimental phase, one group was rewarded for performing the two activities they preferred most during baseline; a second group was reinforced for performing the two activities they preferred least; while a third group chose which two activities they wanted to have reinforced. The rewards were credits earned toward certificates and trophies presented at assemblies. Later the rewards were discontinued. The amount of time children devoted to the formerly rewarded activities was compared with the time spent by control children on their two most and two least preferred activities.

When rewards were withdrawn, children who had been reinforced for low-interest activities performed them less than did the controls. But, contrary to attribution predictions, children who had been reinforced for the highly preferred activities maintained the same level of interest as did the nonreinforced controls.

The conflicting findings were explained in terms of salience of contingencies and phenomenology. According to the salience hypothesis, people are most likely to view their behavior as extrinsically motivated when contingent rewards are highly conspicuous. Ross (1975) investigated whether conspicuously administered rewards have different effects on behavior than if they are less noticeable. He found that expected rewards reduced subsequent performance only if they were physically present or imagined while the activity was first performed. Unfortunately, there was no measure of whether the contingencies were any less apparent to the children when the incentives were out of sight than when they were present. Children who were promised rewards for performing the activity later displayed the same level of interest as children who were neither promised nor given any rewards. This additional evidence is at variance with both the findings of other attributional studies and the salience hypothesis. In the study by Greene, it seems unlikely that children who earned a specific number of credits for each unit of work completed and were publicly rewarded with certificates and trophies at school assemblies for their progress would fail to notice why they were being rewarded. It would appear from other evidence that interest in reinforced activities increases as incentive contingencies are made more explicit (Reiss & Sushinsky, 1975), and that contingency salience does not adequately explain the variable results of attribution studies.

Phenomenological explanations—which state that the effects of reinforcement depend on how it is perceived—reduce the predictive value of attribution theory unless they specify what determines how people will view incentive arrangements. In such explanations, changes in motivation are attributed to subjective perceptions but it is the actual incentive practices that are questioned. If the issue is one of subjective appearances, then it is what people make of incentives rather than the incentives themselves that determines how extrinsic rewards will affect motivation.

The preceding discussion should not be interpreted as advocacy for wholesale use of extraneous incentives. One can point to instances in which material incentives are applied thoughtlessly and more for purposes of social regulation than for personal development. Incentives should be used, if necessary, primarily to promote competencies and enduring interests. To reinforce people materially for activities that already hold high interest for them, or that they would pursue for symbolic rewards, is not only inappropriate but contraindicated by reinforcement theory. To introduce excessive rewards invites unnecessary difficulties when the time comes to fade them out. Incentives encourage participation in activities that people would otherwise disregard, and thus never develop any interest in them. As involvement and skills in the activities increases, social, symbolic, and self-evaluative rewards assume the incentive functions (Bandura, 1969).

In attributional studies of incentives, people are typically rewarded for performing the same activities over and over again. It is important to distinguish between repetitive performance of the same behavior and acquisition of competencies when evaluating the enduring effects of incentive practices. When positive incentives facilitate the development of generalizable skills, the skills endure after the incentives have been withdrawn. Thus, for example, children who have learned to read with the aid of positive incentives will not lose their reading abilities simply because they are no longer extrinsically rewarded. Practices derived from social learning theory are well suited for cultivating personal competencies that serve as a genuine basis for exercise and perception of self-determination.

Generalization of behavior and its persistence are often discussed as though these features were unmitigated virtues.

They are not. It is difficult to achieve generalized enduring changes when the activities reinforced are primarily for the convenience or benefit of others. This is not an entirely lamentable state of affairs. If one could instill, through brief reinforcement, lasting behavioral changes that benefit the promoters but not the recipients, people would be amenable to wholesale arbitrary control. Because reinforcement practices serve as incentives for, rather than implanters of, behavior, people retain what is useful for them and discard what is not. In the case of activities that are personally inconvenient or uninteresting but important to the general welfare, sanctions and rewarding supports must be provided on a continuing basis. Every society adopts contingency structures for this purpose. The same is true of many service and production activities that are not socially prescribed. No methods exist for making menial labor intrinsically interesting so that laborers would perform the same routine day after day for little pay. Were it possible to do so, people could be easily exploited by those who possess the power to engineer whatever intrinsic interests served their purposes.

Multiform Incentives in Psychological Functioning

Although what people find to be reinforcing undergoes developmental changes, it should be noted that different aspects of human behavior are regulated by different combinations and levels of incentives. Many activities are governed by their physical effects. People go to great lengths to reduce or eliminate aversive conditions, and to gain physical comfort, sexual gratification, appetizing foods, and the like. Large segments of behavior are maintained by sensory reinforcement of the sights, sounds, and tactile sensations they produce.

People do a lot of things for money, or to gain access to enjoyable activities. Social commentators who voice objections to the use of extrinsic incentives would cease many of their own activities if they were no longer paid to do them. People will go to great lengths to secure the positive regard of others or to avoid social censure. It would be a rare, unfeeling person who could remain totally indifferent to the sentiments of others.

Many of the outcomes experienced in daily interchanges

are mediated through the actions of others. By resorting to persuasive or coercive behavior people can obtain valued goods and services, get others to perform onerous tasks for them, alter regulations to their own liking, eliminate conditions that adversely affect their well-being, and resist pressures for courses of action that do not serve their interests. In such instances, social behavior is reinforced by its success in influencing the conduct of others.

Much time and effort is expended in activities for the self-satisfaction derived from accomplished performances. And finally, one's self-regard often outweighs the inducements of money, social recognition, and physical comforts in determining how one behaves. Developmental experiences thus expand the range of effective incentives and alter their priority but do not replace those that may be considered lower in the hierarchy of reinforcements.

STRUCTURAL VARIATIONS IN CONTINGENCIES

The frequency and durability of a given behavior depends on how the prevailing contingencies of reinforcement are structured. Outcomes can be arranged according to time schedules or linked to performance. Most activities that become part of daily routines, such as daily meals, trips on public buses and planes and recreational pastimes are available only at appropriate times. Behavior is accordingly regulated in terms of time schedules under time-bound consequences, so that people need not do things when the things they seek are unavailable. Temporal scheduling of reinforcement is well suited to organizing activities, but not to sustaining them over any given period. For the latter purpose, behavior must be reinforced on the basis of quality or productivity rather than only at certain times. When outcomes depend upon one's own behavior, efforts are well maintained.

Another dimension on which response consequences vary is their predictability. Individuals whose behavior has been consistently reinforced expect quick results and are easily discouraged if their efforts fail. In contrast, those who have been reinforced irregularly tend to persist, despite repeated setbacks and only occasional success. Unpredictable outcomes produce behavior that is highly resistant to change because one's efforts are sustained by the belief that they will eventually prove successful. Behavior is most persistent when it is reinforced at a low, variable level and better means of securing reinforcement are lacking.

At a broader social level, some of the major rewards and privileges are linked to ranks rather than to specific performances. In these hierarchical structures, members are stratified into various positions on the basis of characteristics such as education, seniority, or competence. Higher status brings such benefits as higher social or monetary rewards, greater privileges, and better services. Rank-contingent reinforcement can have stronger impact on behavior than practices in which specific responses are individually reinforced (Martin, Burkholder, Rosenthal, Tharp & Thorne, 1968). To lose a specific reward for neglecting some task is of no great import. But when a few foolhardy or faulty actions can result in a demotion in rank with forfeiture of a vast array of benefits, the threat of loss of status creates general pressure for exemplary performances.

Societies, and the subgroups within them, differ in the extent to which reinforcements are structured on an individual or a collective basis. In the individualized system, people are rewarded or punished in terms of their own actions. Social arrangements in which one's outcomes are personally determined encourage self-reliance and self-interest. Collective contingency systems subordinate self-interest to group welfare. This is achieved by rewarding and punishing the entire group so that members are affected by each other's behavior. Individual benefits here are based on group accomplishments, and censurable behavior by individual members produces negative consequences for the entire group. When people share the consequences of their decisions and actions, their interests are best served by committing their efforts to common goals, by helping each other, and by assuming mutual responsibility. Group-oriented contingencies are most prevalent in societies espousing a collectivist ethic (Bronfenbrenner, 1970).

Reinforcement practices can be further differentiated in

terms of who sets and manages the prevailing contingencies. In self-governing systems of reinforcement, the group members themselves play an active role in deciding which values and behaviors will be encouraged or discouraged. In the more authoritarian systems, contingencies defining how people are expected to behave emanate from those who command power.

Because different social goals require different incentive practices, no single structure can be prescribed as the best. Individual oriented reinforcement, for example, is well suited for creating independent, self-seeking people. If, on the other hand, one wishes to promote a sense of shared responsibility and concern for others, then group-based consequences are more appropriate. The negative effects of excessive individualism or collectivism can be reduced by using both individual and group-oriented incentive systems. Under such arrangements, people's outcomes are determined both by the extent of their own contribution and by the overall accomplishments of the group.

Vicarious Reinforcement

People can profit from the successes and mistakes of others as well as from their own experiences. In everyday situations numerous opportunities exist to observe the actions of others and the occasions on which they are rewarded, ignored, or punished. There are several reasons why consideration of observed consequences is critical to the understanding of reinforcement influences. Observed outcomes can alter behavior in their own right in much the same way as directly experienced consequences. As a general rule, seeing behavior succeed for others increases the tendency to behave in similar ways, while seeing behavior punished decreases the tendency.

Of even greater importance is evidence that observed outcomes partly determine the strength and functional properties of external reinforcers. The value of a given incentive depends largely on its relation to other incentives rather than solely on its intrinsic qualities. Research on the relational nature of reinforcement has shown that the same outcomes can have either rewarding or punishing effects on behavior depending upon the type, frequency, and generosity with which behavior was previously reinforced. Thus, rewards function as punishers when contrasted with more attractive rewards, but as positive reinforcers when they occur in relation to nonreward or punishment (Buchwald, 1959, 1960).

Incentive contrast effects, resulting from disparity between observed and experienced consequences, operate in a similar manner. Observed consequences provide reference standards that determine whether particular extrinsic incentives will serve as rewards or punishments. The same compliment for a performance, for instance, is likely to be discouraging to persons who have seen similar performances by others more highly acclaimed, but rewarding when others have been less generously praised. Some of the conditions governing the effects of inequitable reinforcement will be discussed later.

Relational properties of reinforcement affect not only behavior, but also the level of personal satisfaction or discontent. Sensitivity to differential treatment is developed early in life when children are often treated unequally before they can fully understand the reasons for it. Children who see their older siblings staying up later, doing more interesting things, and enjoying greater freedom are not easily placated by explanations, even if they understand that certain rewards and privileges are linked to age and competence. Inequities become even more upsetting when they are based upon arbitrary favoritism. The displeasing aspects of unfair treatment continue to be reinforced in later years by inequities in services received, in social recognition, in wages, and in occupational advancement. Equitable reward tends to promote a sense of well-being, whereas inequitable reinforcement generates resentments and dissatisfactions. The subjective effects of perceived inequity are a further reason for emphasizing the social comparative aspects of reinforcement.

VICARIOUS REINFORCEMENT

Vicarious reinforcement is indicated when observers increase behavior for which they have seen others reinforced. Results of numerous studies generally show that rewarded modeling is more effective than modeling alone in fostering similar patterns of behavior. Observed positive consequences are especially likely to foster adoption of behaviors that have unpleasant aspects and hence, require incentives if they are to be performed. To cite but a few examples from laboratory studies, people will adopt high performance standards that reduce self-gratification, they will select nonpreferred foods, they will sacrifice material goods, they will divulge personal problems, and they will pursue formerly resisted courses of action more readily if they see models praised for exhibiting such conduct than if models receive no recognition for their actions. The amount of influence exerted by observed consequences, however, varies with how highly observers value the outcomes and the type of behavior being modeled.

When others engage in enjoyable activities that are ordinarily inhibited by social prohibition, seeing the behavior go unpunished increases similar conduct in observers to the same degree as witnessing the models rewarded (Bandura, 1965; Walters & Parke, 1964; Walters, Parke, & Cane, 1965). Because consequences derive their value relationally, the omission of anticipated negative outcomes is indeed a significant consequence. Individuals who expected punishment but got off free would hardly react as though they were nonrewarded. When anticipated consequences exist, observed nonreward is likely to operate as a positive reinforcer in the context of expected punishment, and as a punisher in the context of expected reward.

VICARIOUS PUNISHMENT

Behavior can be both enhanced and inhibited by observed consequences. In the process of vicarious punishment, observed negative consequences reduce the tendency to behave in similar or related ways. This phenomenon has been studied most extensively with respect to physically aggressive behavior. Witnessing aggression punished usually produces less imitative aggression than seeing it rewarded or unaccompanied by any evident consequences (Bandura, 1973).

Because of the variety and complexity of social influences, people are not always consistent in their response to aggressive behavior. Rosekrans and Hartup (1967) examined how observing discrepant consequences affected imitative aggression. Children who saw assaultive conduct consistently rewarded were most aggressive; those who saw it consistently punished displayed virtually no imitative behavior; while those who saw aggression sometimes rewarded and sometimes punished were moderately aggressive.

Vicarious punishment has been shown to have similar inhibitory effects on transgressive behavior. People who have seen models punished for violating prohibitions are less inclined to transgress themselves than if modeled violations were either rewarded or simply ignored (Walters and Parke, 1964; Walters, Parke, & Cane, 1965). Results of a comparative study by Benton (1967) indicate that, under some conditions, observed and directly experienced punishment may be equally effective in reducing transgressive behavior. Children who observed peers punished for engaging in prohibited activities later showed the same degree of response inhibition in temptation situations as did the punished transgressors.

In the preceding instances the models' behavior was punished either verbally or physically by someone else. On many occasions, models respond by punishing themselves for their own conduct, which can also have an inhibitory impact on observers. Seeing models criticize some of their own performances as undeserving of self-reward reduces observers' tendencies to treat themselves to freely available rewards for similar attainments (Bandura, 1971b). With regard to transgressive behavior, Porro (1968) found that when children saw a model praise herself for violating prohibitions, 80% subsequently engaged in forbidden activities, whereas the transgressive rate was only 20% for children who saw the same model respond self-critically toward her own transgressions.

It is generally easier to disinhibit than to inhibit behavior by either direct or vicarious means. This is because negative sanctions are usually applied to behavior that is rewarding for the user but is suppressed for the convenience or benefit of others. Therefore, it does not require much successful modeling of transgressive conduct to reduce vicariously restraints over activities people find personally rewarding. In contrast, inhibitions are more difficult to induce and sustain

by punishment when they involve relinquishing behaviors that are functional for the users.

EXEMPLARY PUNISHMENT AND LEGAL
DETERRENTS

The legal system of deterrence relies heavily on the inhibitory effects of exemplary punishment. The threat and
example of punishment are designed to serve a broad preven-
tive function by restraining others should they encounter circumstances that tempt them to transgressive conduct
(Packer, 1968; Zimring, 1973).

As we have already seen, observed punishment can
strengthen restraints over forbidden behavior. Modeling influences, however, can also reduce the deterrent efficacy of
threatened legal consequences. The chances of being caught
and punished for criminal conduct are relatively low. In lo-
cales in which transgressions are common, people have personal knowledge of many crimes being committed without
detection. Such exposure to unpunished transgressions tends
to increase prohibited behavior in observers.

Punishment that is observed to occur infrequently has an
especially weak restraining effect on people whose range of
options for securing valued rewards is limited largely to antisocial means. Observed punishment is informative as well as
inhibitory. When better options are lacking and the prohibited behavior holds some prospect of success, witnessing the
failures of others will more likely cause people to refine the
disallowed behavior to improve its chances of success than to
be deterred from performing it by the observed reprimands.

Systematic study of the restraining power of exemplary
punishment would probably show that it is most effective for
those who need it least. Included here are the people who
pursue rewarding lifestyles that make criminal alternatives
uninviting, who have too high a stake in their community to
risk the devastating consequences of criminal stigmatization,
and who are least frequently exposed to examples of unde-
tected offenses. For those who lack socially acceptable means
for getting what they seek, the best mode of prevention is to
combine deterrents with the cultivation of more functional

alternatives. Most law-abiding behavior relies more on deterrence through preferable prosocial options than on threats of legal sanctions.

COMPARATIVE EFFECTIVENESS OF EXPERIENCED AND VICARIOUS CONSEQUENCES

Learning Effects

The relative strength of observed and directly experienced consequences partly depends upon whether the effects are measured in terms of learning or of performance. By attending to the pattern of successes and failures of others, observers generally learn faster than do the performers themselves. This is especially true if the tasks depend more heavily on conceptual than on manual skills (Berger, 1961; Hillix & Marx, 1960; Rosenbaum & Hewitt, 1966). It is not difficult to find reasons for the relative superiority of vicarious reinforcement. Performers may have difficulty discovering the connections between actions and outcomes because they must devote at least some of their attention to creating, selecting, and enacting the responses and to their reactions to the consequences impinging upon them. Observers, on the other hand, can give their undivided attention to discovering the correct solutions.

Observed punishment generally serves as a performance inhibitor, but it can promote learning of the very acts being punished by heightening and focusing attention on those acts. Given originally low attentional involvement, both observed reward and punishment increase attentiveness to the modeled behaviors which, in turn, increases observational learning (Yussen, 1973). In addition, observed consequences are likely to prompt covert rehearsal of reinforceable responses to ensure that the information is retained for future use. Negative consequences, however, do not always enhance attention and rehearsal. Should they reach distressing levels, outcomes experienced by models are more likely to elicit avoidance than vigilance (Bandura & Rosenthal, 1966). Observers can often easily avoid what the performers cannot.

Motivational Effects

Direct incentives have greater motivational power than vicarious ones when it comes to maintaining behavior over time. For example, one would not advise employers to maintain the productivity of their employees by having them witness a small group of workers receiving paychecks at the end of each month. Seeing others rewarded may temporarily enhance responsiveness, but it is unlikely by itself to have much sustaining power. Observation of other people's outcomes, however, can exert a substantial influence on the effectiveness of directly experienced consequences. Since both direct and vicarious reinforcements inevitably occur together in everyday life, it is their interactive effects rather than their independent ones that are of primary interest.

INTERACTION OF OBSERVED AND EXPERIENCED OUTCOMES

Vicarious reinforcement introduces comparative judgmental processes into the operation of reinforcement influences. That is, the observed consequences accruing to others provide a standard for judging whether the reinforcements one customarily receives are equitable, beneficent, or unfair. The same outcome can thus function as a reward or a punishment depending on which sample of observed reinforcement is used for comparison.

The psychological effects of different patterns of direct and vicarious reinforcement have received surprisingly little attention considering the prevalence of their joint influence. People who have been reinforced both directly and vicariously persevere longer in the face of nonreward than do those who have experienced direct reinforcement alone. Unfavorable disparities between the levels of observed and experienced outcomes temporarily intensify performances (Bruning, 1965). The reactions to continuing inequitable conditions of reinforcement are more variable, however.

When grievance procedures exist and complaints carry low risk of reprisal, people take steps to remedy unfairness. Those who possess coercive power may resort to coercive measures to force preferred improvements by using such means as protest, strikes, and boycotts. Under conditions of limited power and threatening consequences for protest, the discontented eventually become resigned to inequitable treatment (Bandura, 1973). When the inequitably underrewarded find themselves trapped in dissatisfying situations for lack of better alternatives, they may respond to the perceived exploitation by lowering the productivity or quality of their work.

Inequitable conditions of reinforcement are often socially structured and justified in ways designed to reduce their negative impact. When people are graded by custom into social ranks and rewarded according to position rather than by performance, they tend to accept inequitable reinforcement. Arbitrary inequities are also likely to be tolerated if the underrewarded are led to believe that they are somehow less deserving of equal treatment. Persuasively justified inequities have more detrimental personal effects than acknowledged unfairness because they foster self-devaluation in the maltreated.

Negative reactions to inequitable reinforcement, even when it is acknowledged to be unwarranted, can likewise be diminished by temporizing: if people are led to believe that unfair treatment will be corrected within the foreseeable future, it becomes less aversive to them. Given the many factors that determine reactions to inequitable reinforcement, behavior is not fully predictable from a simple relational coefficient based on observed and experienced outcomes.

EXPLANATION OF VICARIOUS
REINFORCEMENT

Social learning theory sets forth several mechanisms by which observed rewards and punishments alter the thoughts, feelings, and actions of others (Bandura, 1971b). Events involving vicarious consequences may vary in a number of aspects, including the type of behavior being modeled, the characteristics of models and reinforcing agents, the type and intensity of consequences, their justifiability, the contexts in which they occur, and the reactions of models to the outcomes they experience. The number and type of mechanisms operating in any given instance will therefore depend upon the particular combination of circumstances.

Informative Function

Response consequences experienced by others convey information to observers about the types of actions that are likely to be rewarded or negatively sanctioned. Having gained knowledge observationally about probable response consequences, people are inclined to do the things they see well received and avoid those they see punished. Observed consequences are likely to be less influential when observers have reason to believe that, due to such factors as differences in age, sex, social rank, and legitimized roles, what is acceptable for models would be considered inappropriate for them.

The same behavior can have markedly different consequences depending upon the settings in which it is expressed, the persons toward whom it is directed, and when it is performed. What is permissible in one set of circumstances may be censurable in another. When others are rewarded for certain conduct in one context, but ignored or punished for the same type of behavior in a different situation, observers gain information about the aspects of the environment that signify how similar behavior is likely to be received (McDavid, 1964; Wilson, 1958). As a result, vicarious reinforcement later increases responsiveness in circumstances signifying favorable reception and decreases responsiveness in those forewarning punishment.

Motivational Function

Observed reinforcement not only informs, it also motivates. Seeing others reinforced can function as a motivator by arousing expectations in observers that they will receive similar benefits for comparable performances.

Variations in the amount, type, and frequency of observed outcomes provide equivalent information about the kinds of activities that produce certain outcomes. But such differences in incentives have differential motivational effects as reflected in the vigor and persistence with which the observers themselves behave. As a rule, observers are more persistent in the face of failure when they have seen the efforts of others rewarded only occasionally than when others have been continuously reinforced (Berger, 1971; Borden & White, 1973).

Emotional Learning Function

Models generally express emotional reactions while undergoing rewarding or punishing experiences. Observers are easily aroused by the emotional expressions of others. It was shown earlier how vicariously elicited arousal can become established either to the modeled behavior or to the environmental cues that are regularly associated with performers' distress reactions. After these contingencies are learned, the occurrence of the foreboding cues alone can frighten and inhibit observers.

Fears and inhibitions can be reduced as well as acquired through the observation of response consequences. Therapeutic applications of modeling provide the best example of this process. Observing models engage in threatening activities without adverse consequences initially evokes strong emotional arousal which decreases with repeated exposures. The more thoroughly the fear arousal is vicariously extinguished, the greater the reduction in defensive behavior and the more generalized the behavioral changes (Bandura & Barab, 1973; Blanchard, 1970b). These findings indicate that some of the changes resulting from observing affective consequences are partly due to vicarious learning and extinction of emotional arousal.

Valuation Function

Behavior is partly determined by value preferences. The personal values of observers can be developed, and preexisting ones altered, by the way in which modeled conduct is reinforced. Children are more apt to develop a liking for things they previously disfavored if they see modeled preferences rewarded than if they are not rewarded (Barnwell, 1966). Loathsome evaluations of long standing in adults can be changed to neutral or even favorable ones through modeling of positive reactions toward disliked objects (Bandura, Blanchard & Ritter, 1969; Blanchard, 1970a).

In the above studies, exemplified consequences altered

observers' valuation of objects used by models. Some of the behavioral changes accompanying observed outcomes may be mediated through modification of the model's status itself. Individuals who possess high status are generally emulated more than those of subordinate standing. Status can be conferred on people by the way in which their behavior is reinforced (Hastorf, 1965). Punishment tends to devalue models and their behavior, whereas the same models become sources of emulation when their actions are well received.

In some circumstances, observed punishment raises rather than lowers the model's social status. People who risk punishment by upholding beliefs and conduct cherished by a group or by challenging social practices that violate the professed values of society gain the admiration of others. It is for this reason that agents of authority are usually careful not to discipline challengers or transgressors in ways that might martyr them.

Observed consequences can change observers' valuation of the reinforcing agents as well as of the recipients. People who reward others lavishly may be considered insincere, ingratiating, or lacking in standards, which in turn detracts from their influence. Valuation is changed even more strongly by the exercise of punitive power. Restrained and principled use of coercive power commands respect. When societal officials misuse their power to reward and punish, they undermine the legitimacy of their own authority and arouse strong resentment. Seeing inequitable punishment is, therefore, more likely to generate opposition than compliance in observers.

Influenceability Function
People usually see not only the consequences experienced by models but also the manner in which they respond to their treatment. The exemplified responsiveness is an integral aspect of vicarious reinforcement that must also be considered in explaining the effects of observed outcomes. Observers' susceptibility to change by direct reinforcement is apt to be increased through prior exposure to modeled responsiveness, and reduced by modeled resistance. Ditrichs, Simon, and Greene (1967) provide evidence regarding this point. They

found that observers increased rewarded behavior when they had previously seen models respond positively to rewards, whereas they remained unresponsive to positive reinforcement after seeing models resist similar influence attempts.

Although the preceding discussion is concerned with possible mechanisms by which vicarious consequences affect observers, the alternative explanations apply also to how direct reinforcement influences the actions of performers. Reinforcement conveys information to performers about the types of responses that are appropriate; selective reinforcement directs performers' attention to environmental cues that signify the probable consequences of various behaviors; previously experienced outcomes create expectations that motivate actions designed to secure desired rewards and to avoid painful outcomes; punishing experiences can render persons, places, and things threatening and inhibit responsiveness; repeated successes and failures can alter people's self-evaluations in ways that affect their determination and willingness to engage in conduct that is discrepant with their self-attitudes; and finally, the treatment one receives can alter the effectiveness of those who exercise influence by creating attraction or antipathy toward them.

Self-Reinforcement

The discussion thus far has analyzed how behavior is regulated by external consequences that are either observed or experienced first-hand. If actions were determined solely by external rewards and punishments, people would behave like weathervanes, constantly shifting in different directions to conform to the momentary influences impinging upon them. They would act corruptly with unprincipled individuals and honorably with righteous ones, and liberally with libertarians and dogmatically with authoritarians.

Examination of social interactions however—aside from strong coercive pressures—would reveal that people hold firmly to ideological positions rather than undergo compliant behavior reversals. Anyone who attempted to change a pacifist into an aggressor or a devout religionist into an atheist would quickly come to appreciate the existence of personal sources of behavior control.

The notion that behavior is regulated by its consequences is usually misinterpreted to mean that actions are at the mercy of situational influences. Theories that explain human behavior as solely the product of external rewards and punishments present a truncated image of people because they possess self-reactive capacities that enable them to exercise some control over their own feelings, thoughts, and actions. Behavior is therefore regulated by the interplay of self-generated and external sources of influence.

Behavior is commonly performed in the absence of immediate external reinforcement. Some activities are maintained by anticipated consequences, but most are under self-reinforcement control. In this process, people set certain standards of behavior for themselves and respond to their own actions in self-rewarding or self-punishing ways.

The act of writing is a familiar example of a behavior that is continously self-regulated through evaluative self-reinforcement. Authors do not need someone sitting at their sides selectively reinforcing each written statement until a satisfactory manuscript is produced. Rather, they possess a standard of what constitutes an acceptable piece of work. Ideas are generated and phrased in thought several times before anything is committed to paper. Initial constructions are successively revised until authors are satisfied with what they have written. The more exacting the personal standards, the more extensive are the corrective improvements. Self-editing often exceeds external requirements of what would be acceptable to others. Indeed, some people are such critical self-editors that they essentially paralyze their own writing efforts. Others who lack suitable standards exercise little self-correction.

Because of their symbolizing and self-reactive capacities, humans are less dependent upon immediate external supports for their behavior. Including self-reinforcement processes in learning theory thus greatly increases the explanatory power of reinforcement principles as applied to human functioning.

COMPONENT PROCESSES IN
SELF-REGULATION

Self-reinforcement refers to a process in which individuals enhance and maintain their own behavior by rewarding themselves with rewards that they control whenever they attain self-prescribed standards. Because behavior can also be reduced by negative self-reactions, the broader term self-regulation will be used to encompass both the enhancing and reducing effects of self-reactive influences.

According to social learning theory (Bandura, 1976 b), self-regulated reinforcement increases performance mainly through its motivational function. By making self-reward conditional upon attaining a certain level of performance, individuals create self-inducements to persist in their efforts until their performances match self-prescribed standards. The level of self-motivation generated by this means will vary according to the type and value of the incentives and the nature of the performance standards. Figure 6 summarizes

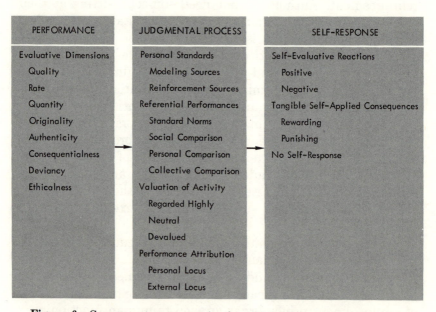

Figure 6   Component processes in the self-regulation of behavior by self-produced consequences.

the different component processes in the self-regulation of behavior through self-managed incentives.

Behavior may vary along a number of evaluative dimensions, some of which are listed in the figure. The importance of these dimensions will vary according to the activity. Track performances, for example, are gauged in terms of speed. Achievement-oriented activities are evaluated on the basis of quality, quantity, or originality. Social conduct is judged along such dimensions as authenticity, consequentialness, and deviancy, just to mention a few.

Behavior generates self-reactions through a judgmental function which includes several subsidiary processes. Whether a given performance will be regarded as rewardable or punishable depends upon the personal standards against which it is evaluated. Actions that measure up to internal standards give rise to positive appraisals, while those that fall short are judged negatively.

For most activities there are no absolute measures of adequacy. The time in which a mile is run, the scores obtained on tasks, or the size of charitable contributions, do not convey in themselves sufficient information for self-appraisal. When adequacy is defined relationally, performances are evaluated by comparing them with those of others. Thus, a student who scores 115 points on an examination and who wants to be in the upper 10% of the group would have no basis for making either a positive or a negative self-assessment without knowing the accomplishments of the other students. In performances gauged by social criteria, self-appraisals require relational comparisons of at least three sources of information to judge a given performance: absolute performance level, one's own personal standards, and a social referent.

The referential comparisons may take different forms for different tasks. For some regular activities, standard norms based on representative groups are used to determine one's relative standing. More often, however, people compare themselves to particular associates in similar situations. Performance judgments will therefore vary substantially depending upon the level of ability of those chosen for comparison: self-estimates are enhanced when comparison is made to others of lesser ability, and diminished when the accomplishments of the more talented are used to set the relative standard of adequacy.

One's previous behavior is continuously used as the reference against which ongoing performance is judged. In this process, it is self-comparison that supplies the measure of adequacy. Past performance determines self-appraisal mainly through its effect on standard setting. After a given level of performance is attained, it is no longer challenging, and new self-satisfactions are sought through progressive improvement. People tend to raise their performance standards after success and to lower them to more realistic levels after repeated failure.

The view is widely endorsed that social learning practices should be structured so that people come to judge themselves in reference to their own capabilities and standards, rather than by comparing themselves with others. In competitive, individualistic societies, however, where one person's success represents another person's failure, social comparison figures prominently in self-appraisal. The standards by which behavior is judged take other forms in societies organized around a collectivist ethic. Comparison processes still operate to some extent under such arrangements, but self-appraisal is primarily in terms of one's relative contribution to common goals and the level of group accomplishment.

Another factor in the judgmental component of self-regulation concerns the valuation of activities. People do not much care how they do on activities that have little or no significance for them. And little effort is expended on devalued activities. It is in areas affecting one's welfare and self-esteem that self-appraisals generate personal consequences.

Self-reactions will also vary depending upon how one perceives the determinants of one's behavior. People take pride in their accomplishments when they ascribe their successes to their own ability and effort. They do not derive much self-satisfaction, however, from behavior they attribute to external factors. The same is true for judgments of failure and blameworthy conduct. People respond self-critically to inadequate performances for which they hold themselves responsible but not to those which they perceive are due to irregular circumstances or to insufficient capabilities. Evidence will be presented later in this chapter on how people disengage self-evaluative consequences from their misconduct by restructuring the actions, distorting their effects, or obscuring responsibility for them.

Self-appraisals of performance set the occasion for self-produced consequences. Favorable judgments give rise to rewarding self-reactions, whereas unfavorable appraisals activate punishing self-responses. Performances that are regarded as having no personal significance do not generate any reactions one way or another. Much human behavior is regulated through self-evaluative consequences as expressed variously by self-satisfaction, self-pride, self-dissatisfaction, and self-criticism. People also get themselves to do things they would otherwise put off by making tangible outcomes conditional upon goal attainment.

Although both tangible and evaluative consequences can affect behavior separately, they are not entirely independent. Goal attainments for tangible benefits are likely to activate positive self-evaluations as well. And self-evaluative reactions acquire and retain their rewarding and punishing value through correlation with tangible consequences. That is, people usually engage in self-gratifications after achieving a sense of self-pride, whereas they treat themselves badly when they judge themselves self-critically.

ESTABLISHMENT OF SELF-REGULATIVE
FUNCTIONS

Behavioral standards for determining self-reinforcing responses can be established either by tuition or by modeling. People learn to evaluate their behavior partly on the basis of how others have reacted to it. Adults subscribe to certain standards of worthy behavior. They are generally pleased when children achieve or exceed valued standards and disappointed when their behavior falls short of the valued levels. As a result of such differential reactions, children eventually come to respond to their own behavior in self-approving and self-critical ways, depending on how it compares with the evaluative standards set by others. The effects of direct training on self-reinforcement practices are illustrated in a study conducted by Kanfer and Marston (1963). Adults who were treated indulgently later self-rewarded their own performances more generously than did those who had been stringently trained, even though the actual achievements of both groups were comparable.

People not only prescribe self-evaluative standards for others, they also exemplify them when responding to their own behavior. The influence of models in the transmission of differential standards that provide the basis for self-reinforcing reactions has received substantial attention. In the paradigm typically used to study this process, children observe models performing a task in which the models adopt either high or low performance standards for self-reward. When models attain or exceed the performance they find personally satisfying, they reward themselves tangibly and voice self-praise, but when they fall short of their self-prescribed requirements, they deny themselves freely available rewards and react self-critically. The observers later perform the task alone, and the performance levels for which they reward or punish themselves are recorded.

The findings show that children tend to adopt evaluative standards modeled by others, they judge their own performances relative to those standards, and reinforce themselves accordingly (Bandura & Kupers, 1964). When they are exposed to models who set high standards, children reward themselves only when they achieve superior performances; whereas other children exposed to models who regard low achievements as sufficient reinforce themselves for minimal performances. The behavioral standards of adults are similarly affected by modeling influences (Marston, 1965).

A number of selective factors operate in determining the types of self-evaluative standards that will be adopted from the profusion of modeling influences. Disparity in competence between models and observers is one such factor. Ordinarily, people favor reference models similar to their own ability over highly divergent ones whose behavior they can match only through great effort. In a study by Bandura and Whalen (1966), children readily adopted the standards displayed either by low-achieving models, who were satisfied with mediocre performances, or by moderately competent models who subscribed to self-reward standards within the children's reach. However, children rejected the lofty standards of highly skilled models and instead set their own requirements within the range of their achievements.

When self-satisfaction is made conditional upon high accomplishments, considerable time and effort must be expended to attain the rewardable levels of behavior. Reluctance to emulate exacting standards is therefore understandable. Nevertheless, it is not uncommon for people to subscribe to high standards. Indeed, many organizations, including universities and various professions, are heavily populated with members who are self-satisfied only with superior performances in the tasks they undertake.

High standards are widely emulated, despite some of their vexing effects, because they are actively cultivated through social rewards. People are praised, and honored for adhering to exemplary standards, and criticized for self-rewarding insignificant performances. Besides direct consequences, vicarious reinforcement serves as a source of social support for standard-setting behavior. Observing others publicly recognized for seeking excellence encourages emulative behavior.

Social environments contain numerous modeling influences which may be compatible or conflicting. As will be shown later, the social transmission of standards is facilitated by consistency in modeling. The effects that multiple modeling has on social learning are most often discussed in the context of conflicting influences of adults and peers. For reasons mentioned earlier, children might favor peer standards when conflicts arise. Because adult standards may be relatively high, children who adopted them would judge their lesser accomplishments as substandard and thus experience many self-disappointments.

Conditions favorable to emulating standards usually occur in combination with each other rather than alone. The way in which multiple influences affect adoption of exacting standards of self-reward is revealed in an experiment by Bandura, Grusec, and Menlove (1967). Children who observed only adult models adhering to a stringent performance standard were much less inclined to reward themselves for low attainments than if they were exposed to conflicting standards—high ones exemplified by adults and low ones by peers. Children were also more likely to impose high performance requirements for self-reward on themselves when they saw adult models praised for adherence to high standards. In addition, children who had experienced an indulgent relationship with the adult models were more lenient with themselves.

Analysis of various combinations of determinants in this study revealed that the expected tendency for peer modeling to reduce the impact of adult modeling was counteracted by observing social recognition of high standard-setting behavior. The most stringent standards of all were adopted by children for whom all three conditions prevailed: they observed social recognition bestowed upon adult models for maintaining high standards, they were not exposed to conflicting peer norms, and they were not treated indulgently by the adult models. Under these social conditions, children rarely considered performances below the adults' standards worthy of self-reward even though they seldom attained or surpassed that level. The adoption of, and continued adherence to, unrealistically high self-evaluative standards is especially striking considering that the children performed alone and were at liberty to reward themselves whenever they wished, without anyone around to judge their actions. By contrast, children disregarded stringent standards when they were modeled in the context of adult indulgence, peer self-leniency, and were not vicariously reinforced.

The process of learning standards is complicated by inconsistencies in the types of self-evaluative reactions exemplified by different people or by the same individual on different occasions. Observers must therefore process the conflicting information and eventually arrive at a personal standard against which to measure their own performances. Such inconsistencies are most likely to generate conflicts in modeling when people know what is expected but see others differing in the extent to which they adhere to the standards. Discrepancies in modeling influences reduce adoption of high standards (Allen & Liebert, 1969; Hildebrant, Feldman & Ditrichs, 1973), but the relative potency of the influences is determined by a number of interacting factors. Some of these include characteristics of the observers such as their achievement orientation and their predilection to perceive events as being either personally or externally determined (Soule & Firestone, 1975; Stouwie, Hetherington, & Parke, 1970).

Although standards can be conveyed by either example or by tuition alone, these two modes of influence usually operate jointly. People do not always practice what they preach. In familial situations, for instance, some parents lead austere lives but are lenient in what they ask of their children. Others are self-indulgent while expecting their children to adhere to exacting standards of achievement, requiring long hours of work and sacrifice. Contradictions between what is taught and what is modeled arise repeatedly in other settings as well.

Transmission of standards has been studied under conditions in which adults prescribe either high or low performance demands for children while requiring much or little of themselves for self-reward (McMains & Liebert, 1968; Rosenhan, Frederick & Burrowes, 1968). Findings show that children tend to adopt stringent performance requirements and to reward themselves sparingly when high standards are consistently prescribed and modeled. When adults both practice and teach leniency, children are self-satisfied with mediocre performance and reward themselves for such attainments. Discrepant practices, in which models impose exacting standards on others but lenient ones on themselves, or set higher standards for themselves than for others, reduce the likelihood that high standards of self-reward will be adopted. Of the two types of inconsistencies, the hypocritical form has the stronger negating effects. Practicing self-leniency while advocating stringencies for others lessens the models' attractiveness and increases rejection of the standards they propagate (Ormiston, 1972).

GENERALIZATION OF PERFORMANCE
STANDARDS OF SELF-REWARD

Development of performance standards and self-reinforcement practices would have limited value if they never generalized beyond the specific activity for which they were established. In fact, the principal goal of social development is to transmit general standards of conduct that could serve as guides for self-regulation of behavior in a variety of activities.

Generic standards are best transmitted by varying the nature of the activities that are performed but requiring a similar level of performance for self-reward (Bandura & Mahoney, 1974). The common standard is thus seperated from the specific activities in the same way as rules are extracted from events that may otherwise differ in certain ways. Standards will generalize to some extent even when acquired on a single task. Children who adopt, through modeling, high performance standards of self-reward tend to apply similar standards on later occasions, even with different activities and dissimilar situations (Lepper, Sagotsky, & Mailer, 1975).

The manner in which self-reward patterns may be passed on through a succession of models is demonstrated by Mischel and Liebert (1966). Children who had adopted high adult standards of self-reward later modeled and applied the same standards to peers. Marston (1965) has likewise shown in an experiment with adults that seeing models reinforce their performances, either generously or sparingly, affected not only how liberally observers rewarded their own behavior, but also how generously they reinforced others.

The laboratory findings corroborate field studies that include data on the cultural modeling of standards (Hughes, Tremblay, Rapoport & Leighton, 1960). In homogeneous communities in which the ethic of self-betterment predominates, people adhere to high self-demands and take pride and pleasure in their accomplishments. By contrast, in neighboring communities, in which more generous self-gratification patterns prevail, people reward themselves freely regardless of how they behave.

SELF-EVALUATION AND
PHENOMENOLOGY

Analyses of theories of behavior generally represent phenomenological approaches, in which self-conceptions receive emphasis, as incompatible with behavioral orientations that supposedly disregard self-evaluative experiences. Behavior theories differ among themselves, of course, in what they choose to study. As we have already seen, self-evaluative reactions figure prominently in social learning theory. In addition to serving as incentives for conduct, self-evaluations are of interest in their own right. Levels of both self-satisfaction and self-dissatisfaction are not determined only by one's accomplishments but also by the standards against which the accomplishments are judged. Performances that make one person happy can leave another highly dissatisfied because of differing standards. In traditional assessments of self-concepts, people are presented with evaluative statements in the form of adjective checklists, Q-sorts, or inventories and are asked to rate which statements apply to them. The individual responses are then summed to provide a global self-concept.

Social learning theory defines negative self-concepts in terms of proneness to devalue oneself and positive self-concepts as a tendency to judge oneself favorably. Because competencies and evaluative standards vary for different activities, performances in dissimilar areas (e.g., social, intellectual, vocational, and athletic) are likely to produce different self-evaluations. Individuals may, for example, regard themselves highly in their vocational specialty, moderately positive in social relationships, and negatively in athletic pursuits. A person's self-conceptions may vary even for different aspects of the same sphere of activities. For this reason, measures of self-evaluation in particular areas of functioning are more meaningful than is a conglomerate index.

Personality theories tend to attribute variations in behavior to differences in values, but they do not adequately explain how values regulate conduct. In the social learning analysis, one mode of operation is in terms of incentive preferences. People differ in the value they place on approval, money, material possessions, social status, exemption from restrictions, and the like. Values determine behavior in that prized incentives can motivate activities required to secure them, disvalued incentives do not. The higher the incentive value, the higher the level of performance.

Value can be invested in activities themselves as well as

in extrinsic incentives. As we have seen, the value does not inhere in the behavior itself but rather in the positive and negative self-reactions it generates. Evaluative self-reinforcement thus provides a second mechanism by which values influence conduct. The evaluative standards represent the values; the anticipatory self-pride and self-criticism for actions that correspond to, or fall short of, adopted standards serve as the regulatory influences.

DYSFUNCTIONAL SELF-EVALUATIVE
SYSTEMS

When analyses of self-regulation dwell mainly on performance standards, conditional self-evaluations, mobilization of effort, and the like, the process sounds like one of self-inflicting hardships. In fact, the development of self-reactive functions provides an important and continuing source of personal satisfaction, interest, and self-esteem. Performance accomplishments build a sense of personal efficacy, increase interest in the activities, and produce self-satisfactions. Without standards and evaluative involvement in activities, people are unmotivated, bored, and dependent upon momentary external stimulation for their satisfactions. Unfortunately, internalization of severe standards for self-evaluation can also serve as a continuing source of personal distress.

Dysfunctional self-evaluative systems figure prominently in some forms of psychopathology by activating excessive self-punishment or creating self-produced distress that motivates various defensive reactions. Many seekers of psychotherapy are talented and free of anxiety, but they experience considerable personal distress stemming from excessively high standards of self-evaluation and unfavorable comparisons with models noted for extraordinary achievements. As an unidentified sage once remarked, "If you compare yourself with others, you may become vain or bitter; for always there will be greater and lesser persons than oneself." Yet social comparison is inevitable, especially in societies that place a premium on competitiveness and individual achievement. Ironically, talented individuals who have high aspirations that are possible but difficult to realize are especially vulnerable to self-dissatisfaction despite their notable achievements. In the graphic portrayal of this phenomenon by Boyd (1969), "Each violinist in any second chair started out as a prodigy in velvet knickers who expected one day to solo exquisitely amid flowers flung by dazzled devotees. The 45-year old violinist with spectacles on his nose and a bald spot in the middle of his hair is the most disappointed man on earth." Linus, the security-blanketed member of the "Peanuts" clan, also alluded to this phenomenon when he observed, "There is no heavier burden than a great potential."

In its more extreme forms, harsh standards for self-evaluation give rise to depressive reactions, chronic discouragement, feelings of worthlessness, and lack of purposefulness. Excessive self-disparagement, in fact, is one of the defining characteristics of depression. As Loeb, Beck, Diggory, and Tuthill (1967) have shown, depressed adults evaluate their performances as poorer than do the nondepressed, even for identical accomplishments. Those who both overaspire and belittle their actual attainments are most vulnerable to depression. Treatments that promote accurate self-observation, realistic subgoals for positive self-evaluation, and self-reward for attainable accomplishments diminish depressive reactions (Fuchs & Rehm, 1975; Jackson, 1972). High aspirations do not produce self-discouragement as long as current attainments are measured against realistic subgoals rather than in terms of lofty ultimate goals.

People also suffer considerable self-devaluation when they experience a loss in ability due to age or physical injury but continue to adhere to their original standards of achievement. As a result, they self-criticize their performances so severely that they eventually become apathetic and abandon activities that previously brought them a great deal of personal satisfaction.

When a person's behavior is a source of self-criticism, defensive reactions that avert or lessen discomfort are thereby reinforced. Self-produced distress thus creates the conditions for the development of various forms of deviant behavior. Some people whose accomplishments bring them a sense of failure resort to alcoholic self-anesthetization; others escape into grandiose ideation where they achieve in fantasy what is unattainable in reality; many renounce pursuits having self-evaluative implications and gravitate to groups embracing antiachievement norms; others protect themselves from self-condemnation for their self-alleged faults by imputing persecutory schemes; and tragically still others are driven by relentless self-disparagement to suicide. Ernest Hemingway, who died by suicide, suffered from this type of self-generated tyranny (Yalom & Yalom, 1971). Throughout his life he imposed upon himself demands that were unattainable, pushed himself to extraordinary feats, and constantly demeaned his own accomplishments.

The preceding discussion portrays the personal misery that can result from stringent standards for self-appraisal. Deficient or deviant standards also create problems, although the resultant adverse effects are more likely to be social than personal. Unprincipled individuals who pursue an ethic of expediency and those who pride themselves on excelling at antisocial activities readily engage in injurious conduct unless deterred by external sanctions.

REGULATION OF BEHAVIOR THROUGH
SELF-PRODUCED CONSEQUENCES

After individuals learn to set standards for themselves and to generate conditional self-reactions, they can influence their behavior by self-produced consequences. The development of self-reactive functions thus gives humans a capacity for self-direction.

The motivating effects of contingent self-reward have been studied under both laboratory and natural conditions. Bandura and Perloff (1967) compared the relative effectiveness of self-administered and externally applied reinforcement in an experiment that proceeded as follows: Children worked at a manual task in which the more responses they performed the higher the scores they could achieve. In the self-reinforcement condition, children selected their own performance standards and rewarded themselves with tokens redeemable for prizes whenever they attained their self-prescribed goals. Children in the externally-reinforced group were matched with members of the self-reward group so that the same standards were set for them, and they were rewarded by others when they reached the predetermined levels. Other groups of children performed the same task, but either received the rewards without any strings attached or worked without any rewards at all.

One of the two major properties of reinforcement is its capacity to maintain effortful behavior. Children in all groups therefore performed the task alone until they no longer wished to continue the activity. Children whose attainments were reinforced either by themselves or by others were more than twice as productive as children who received the rewards noncontingently or who were never rewarded.

The higher the performance goals the children set for themselves, the harder they had to work for the same amount of self-reward. Of special interest is the prevalence with which children in the self-directed group imposed upon themselves difficult performance requirements. Although they worked alone and were at liberty to select any goal, not a single child chose the lowest standard, which required the least effort. Many selected the highest level of achievement as the minimal performance meriting self-reward. Still others raised their initial standard to a higher level without a corresponding increase in amount of self-reward, thereby demanding of themselves more work for the same recompense.

Why do people demand of themselves high levels of performance when no one requires them to do so? Once achievement standards are adopted through example and precept, self-regard becomes conditional upon valued attainments. Conflicts are likely to arise when material gains can be increased by resorting to behavior that has low self-regard value. In this case, individuals are tempted to maximize rewards for minimum effort by lowering their standards. However, rewarding mediocre performances incurs self-esteem costs. In the study just cited, children apparently were willing to deny themselves rewards over which they had full control rather than risk self-disapproval for unmerited self-reward. Many of the children, in fact, set themselves goals that necessitated much effort at minimum material recompense. These findings are at variance with utility theories that explain behavior in terms of optimal reward-cost balances, un-

less such formulations include the self-esteem costs of rewarding oneself for devalued behavior. When people engage in
activities of such little personal value that self-evaluative
consequences are not activated, they behave more in accordance with external reward-cost values—expending the
least amount of effort for each material self-reward (Felixbrod
& O'Leary, 1974).

There have been numerous applications of self-
reinforcement practices aimed at teaching children and adults
how to regulate their own behavior by arranging incentives for
themselves. Results of these studies show that people can
improve and maintain behavior on their own over long periods just as well as when others apply incentives for change
(Bolstad & Johnson, 1972; Drabman, Spitalnik, & O'Leary,
1973; Glynn, 1970; McLaughlin & Malaby, 1974). Those who
influence their own behavior by contingent self-reward attain
higher levels of performance than those who perform the same
activities but receive no reinforcement, are rewarded noncontingently, or observe their own behavior and set goals but do
not self-reward their successful efforts (Bandura, 1976c).
Self-administered negative consequences have been used with
some degree of success to reduce stuttering, obsessional ruminations, and injurious habits of long standing (Thoresen &
Mahoney, 1974).

Although both external and self-directed procedures alter
behavior, the practice of self-reward can have the added advantage of developing a generalizable skill in self-regulation
that can be used continually. It is perhaps for this reason
that self-rewarded behavior tends to be maintained more effectively than if it has been externally reinforced. Moreover,
personal changes achieved mainly through one's own efforts
increase a sense of personal causality (Jeffrey, 1974).

Evidence that people can exercise some control over their
own behavior has provided the impetus for the development
of self-regulatory techniques (Goldfried & Merbaum, 1973;
Mahoney & Thoresen, 1974). In these approaches people
change their own refractory behavior by creating environmental inducements, cognitive aids, and suitable consequences for
desired activities. Self-reinforcement plays a prominent role
in successful self-directed change.

Personal change is often difficult to achieve because it tends to be associated, at least initially, with unfavorable conditions of reinforcement. Activities such as excessive smoking and overeating are powerfully maintained by their immediate reinforcing effects, whereas their detrimental consequences accumulate slowly and are not experienced for some time. Efforts to control such behaviors produce immediate discomfort, while benefits are considerably delayed. Contingent self-rewards are therefore used to provide the motivational inducements for self-controlling behavior until the benefits that are eventually gained assume the reinforcing function.

Methods for achieving self-directed change have relied heavily upon self-administration of tangible reinforcers. Of considerable interest is evidence that symbolized consequences can also serve as incentives in regulating overt behavior. Weiner (1965) reports an experiment in which inappropriate responses by adults were penalized by having others fine them, they penalized themselves by imagining the same fines, or their behavior had no effect. Both the covert self-punishment and the actual punishment reduced inappropriate responding, although the covert form was somewhat weaker.

Much current theorizing and research is addressed to the role of covert self-influences in the regulation of behavior and the extension of self-control techniques to cognitive events (Bandura, 1969; Mahoney, 1974; Mischel, 1973). Findings of several lines of research on self-regulatory processes indicate that social learning approaches hold considerable promise for increasing people's capacity to regulate their own feelings, thoughts, and actions.

CONDITIONS MAINTAINING
SELF-REINFORCEMENT SYSTEMS

In analyzing regulation of behavior through self-reinforcement, it is important to distinguish between two sources of incentives that operate in the process. First, there is the arrangement of self-reward contingent upon designated performances to create incentives for oneself to engage in the activities. Second, there are the incentives for adhering to the performance contingency. The interesting but insufficiently explored questions requiring explanation are why people deny themselves rewards over which they have full control, why they adhere to exacting standards requiring difficult performances, and why they punish themselves.

Negative Sanctions

Adherence to performance requirements for self-reward is partly sustained by periodic environmental influences which take a variety of forms. When standards for self-reinforcing reactions are being acquired or when they are later applied inconsistently, unmerited self-reward often results in negative consequences. Rewarding oneself for inadequate or undeserving performances is more likely than not to evoke critical reactions from others. And lowering one's performance standards is rarely considered praiseworthy.

The role of negative sanctions in the maintenance of contingent self-reward is revealed in studies of self-reinforcement in infrahumans. Such research provides a paradigm for analyzing some of the basic processes in self-reinforcement that cannot be definitively elucidated with humans who have undergone years of social learning (Mahoney & Bandura, 1972). Through selective reinforcement, animals adopt performance standards and maintain effortful behavior by treating themselves to rewards they control only after they attain the preselected levels of performance. When all environmental supports are removed, they continue to maintain their behavior by self-reward for some time but eventually discard self-imposed contingencies, especially if they entail much work. However, periodic punishment for unmerited self-reward helps to sustain contingent self-reinforcement. The higher the certainty of negative sanctions for noncontingent self-reward, the greater is their sustaining capacity (Bandura & Mahoney, 1974).

Predictive Situational Determinants

Situational factors which predict probable consequences for unmerited self-reward influence the likelihood that people will withhold rewards from themselves until performance

standards are met. Environmental settings in which performance was previously required for self-reward foster adherence to self-imposed contingencies, even though negative
sanctions for rewarding oneself noncontingently no longer exist (Bandura, Mahoney, & Dirks, 1976). Thus, contextual
influences, which signify past environmental prescripts that
self-reward should be made dependent upon performance,
provide additional supports.

Threat of negative sanctions is not the most reliable
basis upon which to rest a system of self-regulation. Fortunately, there are more advantageous reasons for exercising
some influence over one's own behavior through self-arranged
incentives. Some of the benefits are extrinsic to the behavior;
others derive from the behavior itself.

Personal Benefits

People are motivated to impose upon themselves requirements for self-reward when the behavior they seek to change
is aversive. To overweight persons, for example, the discom-
forts, maladies, and social costs of obesity create inducements
to control overeating. Heavy smokers are motivated to reduce
their consumption of cigarettes by physical maladies and fear
of cancer. Students are prompted to alter avoidant study
habits when failures in completing assignments make academic life sufficiently distressing.

By making self-reward conditional upon performance attainments, individuals can reduce aversive behavior, thereby
creating a natural source of reinforcement for their efforts:
they lose weight, they curtail or stop smoking, and they raise
their course grades by improving study habits. When people
procrastinate on required tasks, thoughts about what they put
off continuously intrude on, and detract from enjoyment of
their ongoing activities. By setting themselves a given accomplishment for self-reward, they mobilize their efforts to complete what needs to be done and are thus spared intrusive
self-reminders.

The benefits of self-regulated change may provide natural incentives for continued self-imposition of contingencies
in the case of valued activities as well as aversive ones.
People commonly motivate themselves, through contingent

self-reward, to improve their skil s in activities they aspire to master and to enhance their competencies in dealing with the demands of everyday life. Here the personal gains derived from improved proficiency can strengthen self-prescription of contingencies. Similar self-inducements are used to ensure continual progress in creative endeavors. In commenting on the writing habits and self-discipline of novelists, Irving Wallace (1976) illustrates how famous novelists regulate their writing output by making self-reward contingent upon completion of a certain amount of writing each day.

As indicated in the foregoing discussion, because self-regulated reinforcement involves brief self-denial it does not necessarily create an adverse state of affairs. Singling out self-privation from the total effects accompanying self-directed change overemphasizes the negative aspects of the process. Let us compare the overall rather than only the momentary consequences of behavior with and without the aid of conditional self-reward. Under noncontingent arrangements, rewards are available for the taking, but the likelihood of engaging in potentially advantageous behavior is reduced for lack of self-motivation. In addition to the lost benefits there are the punishment costs for failure to fulfill obligations. In contrast, self-directed change provides both the rewards that were temporarily withheld as well as the benefits accruing from increased proficiency. For activities that have some potential value, self-reinforcement can provide the more favorable total consequences. Thus, on closer analysis, the exercise of momentary self-denial becomes less perplexing than it might originally appear. However, there are no particular advantages for self-regulation of behavior that is devoid of any value. It is in the latter instances that continued extraneous supports for adherence to self-reward contingencies assume special importance.

Upholding high standards is actively promoted by a vast system of rewards including praise, social recognition, and awards, whereas few accolades are bestowed on people for self-rewarding mediocre performances. Praise fosters adherence to high performance standards. Moreover, seeing others publicly recognized for upholding excellence aids emulation of high standards. Vicarious reinforcement can therefore supplement periodic direct consequences as another source of support for abiding by self-prescribed contingencies.

Because people choose reference groups whose members share similar behavioral norms for self-reinforcement, individuals' self-evaluations are influenced by actual or anticipated reactions of members whose judgment they value. When the immediate reference group is small, the individuals appear to be "inner-directed" (Riesman, 1950) because their self-evaluations are not much influenced by the views of most people. In fact, the members of such a group are highly responsive to the few whose good opinion they prize. Individuals who regard their behavior so highly that the reactions of their associates have no effect on their self-evaluation are rare indeed.

Modeling Supports

Modeling has been shown to be a powerful means for establishing behavior, but it has rarely been studied as a maintenance factor. In view of evidence that human behavior is extensively under modeling stimulus control, there is every reason to expect that seeing others successfully regulate their own behavior by holding to contingent self-reward would increase the likelihood of adherence to self-prescribed contingencies in observers.

In social learning theory, self-managed reinforcement is conceptualized not as an autonomous regulator of behavior but as a personal source of influence that operates in conjunction with environmental factors. Although self-reinforcing functions are created and occasionally supported by external influences, this does not negate the fact that exercise of that function partly determines how people behave. In the case of refractory habits, environmental inducements alone often fail to produce change, while the same inducements with contingent self-reinforcement prove successful. In other instances, the behavior developed through the aid of self-reward activates environmental influences that would otherwise not come into play. Here the potential benefit cannot occur until self-reinforced improvements in performance produce them. In still other instances, the behavior fashioned through contingent self-reward transforms the environment. Formerly passive individuals who facilitate development of assertive behavior through conditional self-reward will alter their social environment by their firm actions.

Because personal and environmental determinants affect each other in a reciprocal fashion, attempts to assign causal priority to these two sources of influence reduce to the "chicken-or-egg" debate. Situational influences prompt self-generated influences which in turn alter the situational determinants. For example, overweight individuals who refrain, through the aid of self-reward, from buying an assortment of chocolates on a shopping tour create a different environment for themselves than those who head home with a generous supply of the high-caloric delicacies. A full explanation of self-regulatory processes must include the self-control determinants of environments as well as the environmental determinants of self-control. Searching for the ultimate environmental contingency for activities regulated by self-reward is a regressive exercise that in no way resolves the issue under discussion because, for every ultimate environmental contingency that is invoked, one can find prior actions that created it. Promotion systems for occupational pursuits, grading schemes for academic activities, and reverence of slimness are human creations, not decrees of an autonomous, impersonal environment.

Operant theorists have always argued against attributing behavior to causes that extend far into the future. However, in explaining increases in self-reinforced behavior, some adherents of this view appeal to ultimate benefits of prospective behavior but neglect self-reactive determinants of behavior in the here and now (Rachlin, 1974). Although anticipated benefits of future accomplishment undoubtedly provide some incentive for pursuing self-directed change, it is self-regulated incentives that serve as continual immediate inducements for change.

Determinants of Self-Punishment

The question of why people punish themselves is even more perplexing than why they temporarily impose self-privations. In the explanation proposed by Aronfreed (1964), people punish themselves because such behavior has become endowed with anxiety relief value through prior conditioning. This *conditioned relief* interpretation assumes that when parents discipline their children, they often voice their criticism as they cease punishing them. If verbal criticism is repeatedly associated with the termination of punishment, criticism becomes a relief signal indicating the end of punishment, thus allaying anxiety. Thereafter, when transgressive behavior arouses anticipatory fear, people criticize themselves for its conditioned tranquilizing effects. Self-criticism persists, according to this explanation, because it is automatically reinforced by anxiety reduction.

In a test of this view, Aronfreed found that when a word intended as a reprimand was uttered as punishment ceased, children were more inclined to say the word when they transgressed than were children who heard the critical word uttered at onset of punishment. These findings are consistent with the classical conditioning view, but other aspects of the data cast doubt on this interpretation. After transgressing, the children rarely uttered the critical word on their own; they did so only after the punisher prompted them by questioning them about their behavior. Given anxiety arousal, one would expect an anxiety reducer to be used quickly and spontaneously. Why endure discomfort if one can relieve it by a soothing self-critical word?

The children's initially reluctant but later differential use of the critical word is better explained by its assumed functional value than by its conditioned tranquilizing effects. Children for whom the critical word brought punishment would have little reason to use it, while those who had observed that the critical verbalization ended punishment would be inclined to try it as a way of placating the probing punisher. Having seen that uttering the critical word apparently eliminated at least the punisher's verbal reprimand, children would tend to repeat it for its presumed instrumental value.

Children will adopt self-punitive behavior through exposure to self-critical models (Bandura & Kupers, 1964; Herbert, Gelfand, & Hartmann, 1969). The conditioned relief theory would require several complicated assumptions to explain how self-punitive behavior is acquired observationally because the observers actually do not receive any painful treatment.

In the social learning view, self-punishment is maintained by its acquired capacity to *alleviate thought-produced distress* and to *attenuate external punishment.* When people perform inadequately or violate their own standards of conduct, they tend to engage in self-critical and other distressing thoughts. During the course of socialization the sequence of transgression—internal distress—punishment—relief is repeatedly experienced. In this process, wrongdoing arouses anticipatory fears and self-devaluative reactions that often persist in varying intensity until reprimanded. Punishment not only terminates worries over discovery of wrongdoing and the resultant consequences, but tends to restore the favor of others.

Punishment can thus provide relief from thought-produced anguish that is enduring and is often more painful than the reprimand itself. This process is vividly illustrated by cases in which individuals torment themselves for years over minor transgressions and do not achieve relief until they make some type of restitution. Self-punishment can serve a similar distress-relief function. Having criticized or punished themselves for reprehensible conduct, individuals are likely to discontinue further upsetting ruminations about their past behavior.

In psychotic disorders, self-punishment is often powerfully maintained by delusional contingencies that have little relationship to reality. In a case to be cited later, a psychotic who regarded trivial acts as heinous sins could relieve his self-contempt and his visions of hellish torture only by performing self-torturous behaviors for long hours.

The analysis of the role of self-punishment in reducing distressing thoughts can be applied to self-disappointing performances as well as to moral conduct. Like transgressive conduct, faulty performances can cause disconcerting thoughts that are reducible by self-criticism.

Self-punishment often serves as an effective means of lessening negative reactions from others. When certain behavior is almost certain to evoke disciplinary actions, self-punishment may be the lesser of two evils. Stone and Hokanson (1969) show how self-punitive behavior can indeed be maintained by its self-protective and stress reducing value. When adults could avoid painful shocks by administering shocks of lesser intensity to themselves, they increased self-punitive responses and became less emotionally distressed.

Self-punishment that is successful in averting anticipated threats can prevent reality testing so that it persists long after the threats have ceased to exist. Sandler and Quagliano (1964) document the durability of anticipatory self-punishment in studies with animals. After monkeys learned to press a lever to avoid shock, conditions for learning self-punishment were introduced. The animals could prevent shock by pressing the lever, but by doing so, they administered a weaker shock to themselves. As the experiment progressed, the strength of the self-administered shock was gradually increased until it equaled the one being avoided. However, the animals did not reduce their self-punishment even though it no longer was the lesser of two evils. After the avoided shock was permanently abolished, the animals continued to punish themselves needlessly with the shock intensities that they previously worked hard to avoid. These findings show how self-punishment can become dissociated from current conditions of reinforcement through its capacity to forestall anticipated threats that in fact no longer exist.

In addition, self-punishment can be used to extract compliments from others. By criticizing and belittling themselves, people can get others to enumerate the criticizers' praiseworthy qualities and achievements and to reassure them of future successes. Self-punishing behavior is thus intermittently reinforced by both subjectively created contingencies and various external sources.

INTERACTION BETWEEN PERSONAL
AND EXTERNAL SOURCES OF
REINFORCEMENT

After a self-reinforcement system has been developed, a given act typically produces two sets of consequences: self-evaluative reactions and external outcomes. Personal and external sources of reinforcement may operate as complementary or as opposing influences on behavior.

People commonly experience conflict when they are rewarded socially or materially for behavior they themselves devalue. The anticipation of self-reproach for conduct that violates one's standards provides a source of motivation to keep behavior in line with standards in the face of opposing inducements. There is no more devastating punishment than self-contempt. When self-devaluative consequences outweigh the force of external rewards for accommodating behavior, the external influences are relatively ineffective. On the one hand, if certain courses of action produce greater rewards than self-censure, the result can be cheerless compliance. People, however, possess cognitive skills for reconciling upsetting discrepancies between standards and conduct. The processes by which losses of self-respect for devalued conduct are reduced will be considered later.

Another type of conflict between external and self-produced consequences arises when individuals are punished for behavior they value highly. Principled dissenters and non-conformists often find themselves in this predicament. Here the relative strengths of self-approval and external censure determine whether the behavior will be restrained or expressed. Should threatened consequences be severe, self-praiseworthy acts are inhibited under high risk of penalty but readily performed when the chances of escaping punishment are good. There are individuals, however, whose sense of self-worth is so strongly invested in certain convictions that they will submit to prolonged maltreatment rather than accede to what they regard as unjust or immoral. Thomas More, who was beheaded for refusing to compromise his resolute convictions, is a notable example from history. One can cite many other historical and contemporary figures who have endured considerable punishment for unyielding adherence to ideological and moral principles.

Another common situation is one in which the external reinforcement for given activities is minimal or lacking, and individuals sustain their efforts largely through self-encouragement. This is illustrated by innovators who persist, despite repeated failures, in endeavors that provide neither rewards nor recognition for long periods, if at all. In order to persist, they must be sufficiently convinced of the worth of their activities to self-reward their efforts, and not be much concerned with the opinions of others.

External consequences exert greatest influence on behavior when they are compatible with those that are self-produced. These conditions exist when externally rewardable acts provide self-satisfaction and externally punishable ones are self-censured. To enhance compatibility between personal and social influences, people select associates who share similar standards of conduct, thereby ensuring social support for their own system of self-reinforcement.

SELECTIVE ACTIVATION AND
DISENGAGEMENT OF
SELF-EVALUATIVE CONSEQUENCES

Development of self-reactive capabilities does not create an invariant control mechanism within a person, as is implied by theories of internalization that portray incorporated entities (e.g., the conscience or superego) as continuous internal overseers of conduct. Self-evaluative influences do not operate unless activated, and there are many factors that exercise selective control over their activation. Therefore, the same behavior is not uniformly self-rewarded or self-punished regardless of the circumstances under which it is performed.

The processes by which self-sanctions are acquired have been examined in some detail. However, the selective activation and disengagement of internal control, which have considerable theoretical and social import, have only recently received systematic study. After ethical and moral standards of conduct are adopted, anticipatory self-condemning reactions for violating personal standards ordinarily serve as self-deterrents against reprehensible acts. Individuals normally refrain from conduct that produces self-devaluative consequences, and they pursue activities that serve as sources of self-satisfaction.

Self-deterring consequences are likely to be activated most strongly when the causal connection between reprehensible conduct and its injurious effects is unambiguous. There are various means, however, by which self-evaluative consequences can be dissociated from censurable behavior. Figure 7 shows the several points in the process at which the disengagement can occur.

To begin with, what is culpable can be made to seem

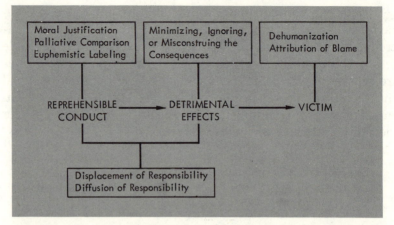

Figure 7 Mechanisms through which behavior is disengaged from self-evaluative consequences at different points in the behavioral process.

honorable through cognitive restructuring. One method is to make reprehensible conduct personally and socially acceptable by portraying it in the service of moral ends. Over the years, much cruelty has been perpetrated by decent, moral people in the name of religious principles, righteous ideologies, and social order. Self-deplored acts can also be made righteous by contrasting them with more flagrant inhumanities. The more outrageous the comparison practices, the more likely are one's own reprehensible acts to appear trifling. Euphemistic language provides an additional convenient device for masking reprehensible activities or even according them a respectable status. Through convoluted verbiage pernicious conduct is made benign and those who engage in it are relieved of a sense of personal agency.

Moral justifications and palliative characterizations are especially effective disinhibitors because they not only eliminate self-generated deterrents, but engage self-reward in the service of inhumane conduct. What was morally unacceptable becomes a source of self-pride.

A further set of dissociative practices operates by obscuring or distorting the relationship between actions and the effects they cause. People will behave in ways they normally repudiate if a legitimate authority sanctions their conduct and acknowledges responsibility for its consequences (Kelman, 1973; Milgram, 1974). By displacing responsibility people do not see themselves as personally accountable for their actions and are thus spared self-prohibiting reactions. Nor is there much reason for engaging in self-censure when the link between conduct and its social consequences is obscured by diffusing the responsibility for culpable behavior. Through division of labor, diffusion of decision making, and collective action, people can behave injuriously without any one person feeling personally responsible. They therefore act more harshly when responsibility is obscured by a collective instrumentality (Bandura, Underwood, & Fromson, 1975).

Additional ways of weakening self-deterring reactions operate by misrepresenting the consequences of actions. When people choose to pursue a self-disapproved course of action for personal gain, or because of other inducements, they tend to minimize the harm they cause. As long as they disregard the detrimental effects of their conduct, there is little likelihood that self-censuring reactions will be activated.

The strength of self-evaluative reactions partly depends upon how the people toward whom actions are directed are viewed. Maltreatment of individuals who are regarded as subhuman or debased is less apt to arouse self-reproof than if they are seen as human beings with dignifying qualities. People who are perceived as base creatures are considered insensitive and responsive only to crass treatment. The dehumanization of victims thus serves as a further means of reducing self-punishment for cruel actions (Zimbardo, 1969). Analysis of the cognitive concomitants of punitive behavior reveals that dehumanization fosters a variety of self-exonerating maneuvers (Bandura, Underwood & Fromson, 1975). People strongly disapprove of punitive behavior and rarely excuse its use when they interact with humanized individuals. By contrast, people seldom condemn punitive conduct and generate self-disinhibiting justifications for it when they direct their behavior toward individuals divested of humanness.

Many conditions of contemporary life are conducive to dehumanizing behavior. Bureaucratization, automation, urbanization, and high social mobility lead people to relate to each other in anonymous, impersonal ways. In addition, social practices that divide people into in-group and out-group members produce human estrangement that fosters dehumanization. Strangers can be more easily cast as unfeeling beings than can personal acquaintances.

Psychological research tends to focus on the disinhibiting effects of practices that divest people of human qualities. This emphasis is understandable considering the prevalence and the serious consequences of people's inhumanities toward each other. Of equal theoretical and social significance is the power of humanization to counteract injurious conduct. Studies examining this process reveal that, even under conditions that ordinarily weaken self-deterrents, it is difficult for individuals to behave cruelly toward people when they are characterized in ways that personalize and humanize them (Bandura, Underwood, & Fromson, 1975).

Attributing the blame to one's victims is still another expedient that can serve self-exonerative purposes. Detrimental interactions usually involve a series of reciprocally escalative actions in which the victims are rarely faultless. One can always select from the chain of causes an instance of defensive behavior by the adversary and view it as the original instigation. Victims then get blamed for bringing suffering on themselves, or extraordinary circumstances are invoked to vindicate irresponsible conduct. By blaming others, one's own actions become excusable.

Because internalized controls are subject to dissociative operations, marked changes in people's moral conduct can be achieved without altering their personality structures, moral principles, or self-evaluative systems. It is self-exonerative processes rather than character flaws that account for most inhumanities.

5

Cognitive Control

IF HUMAN BEHAVIOR COULD BE FULLY EXPLAINED in terms of antecedent inducements and response consequences, there would be no need to postulate any additional regulatory mechanisms. However, most external influences affect behavior through intermediary cognitive processes. Cognitive factors partly determine which external events will be observed, how they will be perceived, whether they leave any lasting effects, what valence and efficacy they have, and how the information they convey will be organized for future use. By manipulating symbolically the information that is derived from experience, one can comprehend events and generate new knowledge about them. In the present discussion, cognitive events refer to imagery, to representation of experiences in symbolic form, and to thought processes. Some attention has already been given to the various ways in which cognitive functioning enters into the regulation of human behavior. These and other issues receive further consideration in this chapter.

Cognitively Based Motivation

Motivation is primarily concerned with how behavior is activated and maintained. Some instigators arise from the stimulation of environmental events and bodily conditions—people are moved to action by thirst, hunger, sexual arousal, pain, and various types of aversive external stimuli.

A great deal of human behavior, however, is initiated and sustained over long periods in the absence of compelling immediate external stimulation. In these instances, the inducements to action are rooted in cognitive activities.

The capacity to represent future consequences in thought provides one cognitively based source of motivation. Cognitive representations of future outcomes function as current motivators of behavior. Many of the things we do are designed to gain anticipated benefits and to avert future difficulties. It will be recalled from earlier discussions that reinforcement operations affect behavior largely by creating expectations that conditional behavior will produce desired outcomes.

A second cognitively based source of motivation operates through the intervening influences of goal setting and self-regulated reinforcement. Self-motivation requires standards against which performance is evaluated. When individuals commit themselves to explicit goals, perceived negative discrepancies between what they do and what they seek to achieve create dissatisfactions that serve as motivational inducements for change.

The motivational effects do not derive from the goals themselves, but rather from the fact that people respond evaluatively to their own behavior. Goals specify the conditional requirements for positive self-evaluation. Once individuals have made self-satisfaction contingent upon goal attainment, they tend to persist in their efforts until their performances match what they are seeking to achieve. Both the anticipated satisfactions of desired accomplishments and the negative appraisals of insufficient performances provide incentives for action. Most successes do not bring lasting satisfaction; having accomplished a given level of performance, individuals ordinarily are no longer satisfied with it and make further positive self-evaluation contingent upon higher attainments.

Goals do not automatically activate the evaluative processes that affect performance. Certain properties of goals determine the likelihood that self-evaluations will be elicited by any given activity. The degree to which goals create incentives for action is partly determined by *goal specificity*. Explicitly defined goals regulate performance by designating the type and the amount of effort required, and they foster self-satisfaction by furnishing clear signs of personal accomplishments. General intentions, on the other hand, provide little basis for regulating one's efforts or for evaluating how one is doing.

The amount of effort and satisfaction that accompany variations in goals depends upon the *level* at which they are set. When self-satisfaction is made contingent upon attainment of difficult goals, more effort is expended then if easy ones are adopted as adequate. For activities that are readily amenable to voluntary control, the higher the goals, the higher the performance level (Locke, 1968). On difficult tasks, however, one would not expect a linear relationship between intentions and performance. When goals are set unrealistically high, most performances prove disappointing. Strong effort that produces repeated failure weakens efficacy expectations, thereby reducing motivation to perform the activity. Subgoals of moderate difficulty are therefore likely to be most motivating and satisfying.

Goal proximity is another relevant factor. The effectiveness of intentions in regulating behavior is partially determined by how far into the future they are projected. Immediate goals mobilize effort and direct what one does in the here and now. Remote intentions are too far removed in time to serve as effective incentives for action, especially when there are many competing influences at hand, as is usually the case. By focusing on the distant future, it is easy to put off matters in the present—one can always begin in earnest tomorrow. Self-motivation is best maintained by explicit proximate subgoals that are instrumental in achieving larger future ones. Subgoals help to create present inducements for action, while subgoal attainments provide the self-satisfactions that reinforce and sustain one's efforts along the way.

Self-motivation through self-reactive influences, wherein individuals observe their own behavior, set goals, and reinforce their performances, is a major factor in a variety of motivational phenomena. Achievement motivation is one such instance. The higher the performance standards people set for themselves, the greater their attainments are likely to be. High achievers tend to make self-satisfaction contingent upon attainment of difficult goals; low achievers adopt easy goals as sufficient.

Self-reactive influences mediate the effects of many forms of extrinsic feedback that are assumed to possess reinforcing properties. Knowledge that one is performing correctly or wrongly can improve and sustain behavior over an extended time. Some of the benefits of such feedback derive from the information it provides on the types of errors one is making and how they might be corrected. Knowledge of results, however, enhances performance even when feedback information specifies the level of attainment but does not furnish a basis for correcting errors. In these instances, informative feedback serves as a motivator rather than as a response corrective.

Informative feedback is not by itself inherently rewarding. Rather, knowledge of performance assumes significance in relation to the performers' standards and provides the basis for self-evaluative reinforcement. Hence, correctness feedback on tasks that are personally devalued or regarded as trifling will, if anything, reduce the amount of effort expended on them. In contrast, informative feedback indicating that one's performances match personal standards will sustain efforts by creating self-satisfaction about subgoal achievements and by raising goals for subsequent performance.

There is some evidence to suggest that self-reactive influences may partly account even for changes produced by extrinsic consequences. In the course of being reinforced by others for their performances, people set goals for themselves and respond evaluatively toward their accomplishments. When changes in goal setting accompanying reinforcement are controlled or partialled out, the effects on performance attributable to extrinsic incentives are substantially reduced (Locke, Cartledge & Knerr, 1970). Incentives thus motivate partly through their effects on personal goals and intentions.

Self-motivation has been explained by some theorists in terms of an inborn motivating mechanism. According to Piaget (1960), people are inherently motivated to advance in cognitive development by moderate discrepancies between new experiences and established cognitive structures. The resulting disequilibrium motivates exploration of the source of the discrepancy until internal structures are brought in line with incongruent experiences. There are several reasons why a motivational system of this type might be viewed with some reservation. An automatic self-motivator explains more than has ever been observed. If disparities between events and mental structure were in fact automatically motivating, learning should be much more indiscriminate than it really is. As a rule, people do not pursue most activities that differ moderately from what they know or can do. A teacher may be motivated by instructional failures to gain better understanding of how children learn, but show little curiosity about the workings of the internal combustion engine because of mechanical difficulties with a car. When faced with contradictions between facts and their conceptions, people often discount or reinterpret the "facts" rather than change their way of thinking. If they were motivated by an innate drive to know, they should all be highly knowledgeable about the world around them and progressing continually toward higher levels of reasoning. The evidence does not seem to bear this out. Similar problems of making fact fit theory arise when self-motivated behavior, which varies considerably between individuals and for the same individual in different areas of functioning, is attributed to a universal motive for competency (White, 1959) or self-determination (Deci, 1975).

Until criteria are specified for determining optimal disequilibrium, the Piagetian theory of self-motivation does not lend itself readily to empirical verification. If mismatches between conceptions and evidence fail to arouse and sustain efforts to change, it can always be argued that the discrepancy was not within the optimal range. When highly novel activities are pursued until mastered, the resultant learning tends to be discounted as "superficial." Simply demonstrating that children are bored by what they already know and discouraged by things beyond their capabilities can be explained without requiring an automatic self-moving mechanism. Arousal of interest is by no means confined only to what is partially known. Nor does moderate discrepancy in experience alone guarantee learning. As for the instructional implications of motivation through disequilibrium, they are much the same as those of any other theory: children will most readily learn what is only slightly beyond what they already know or can do.

According to social learning theory, people function as active agents in their own self-motivation. Their standard setting determines which discrepancies are motivating and which activities they strive to master. Strength of self-inducement varies curvilinearly with level of discrepancy between standards and demonstrated competence: relatively easy goals are insufficiently challenging to arouse much interest, moderately difficult ones maintain high effort and produce satisfactions through subgoal achievements, while goals set well beyond one's reach are discouraging. Self-regulated motivation, although of considerable importance, is only one of several sources of incentives for developing competencies. Skills that enable people to manage their environment are rapidly perfected because of their generalized functional value.

Cognitive Representation of Contingencies

It was previously shown that changes in behavior resulting from the association of environmental events or response consequences rely heavily upon cognitive representations of contingencies. People do not learn much from repeated paired experiences unless they recognize that events are correlated. Nor are they much affected by response consequences if they are unaware of what is being reinforced. Sudden increases in appropriate behavior upon discovery of the reinforcement contingency is indicative of the acquisition of insight.

Another way of analyzing the process of cognitive control is to pit the power of belief against experienced consequences in the regulation of behavior. Several researchers have examined how cognitive influences weaken, distort, or nullify the effects of response consequences. Kaufman, Baron, and Kopp (1966) conducted a study in which all participants were rewarded approximately once a minute (variable-interval schedule) for performing manual responses, but were given different information about the reward schedule. One group was correctly informed about how often their performances would be rewarded, whereas other groups were misled into believing that their behavior would be reinforced either every minute (fixed-interval schedule), or after they had performed 150 responses on the average (variable-ratio schedule). Beliefs about the prevailing conditions of reinforcement outweighed the influence of experienced consequences. Although everyone was actually rewarded on the same schedule, those who thought they were being reinforced once every minute produced very low rates of response (mean = 6); those who thought they were reinforced on the variable-ratio schedule maintained an exceedingly high output (mean = 259) during the same period; while those who were correctly informed that their behavior would be rewarded on the average every minute displayed an intermediate level of responsiveness (mean = 65). Participants regulated their level and distribution of effort in accordance with their reinforcement expectations, producing markedly different performances under the same actual reinforcement contingencies.

The preceding study varied beliefs about how often behavior is likely to be reinforced. Identical environmental consequences can have different behavioral effects depending on beliefs about why they occur. Physically aversive consequences increase responses when people believe these unpleasant outcomes signify correctness but reduce responses when they believe that these same outcomes indicate errors (Dulany, 1968). Behavior is similarly enhanced or reduced by physically pleasing consequences depending on whether they are believed to signify appropriate or inappropriate responses.

The widely accepted dictum that behavior is governed by its consequences fares better for anticipated than for actual consequences. As people are exposed to variations in the frequency and predictability of reinforcement, they behave on the basis of the outcomes they expect to prevail in the future. In most instances, customary outcomes are good predictors of behavior because what people anticipate is accurately derived from, and therefore corresponds closely to, prevailing conditions of reinforcement. Belief and actuality, however, do not always coincide, because anticipated consequences are also partly inferred from the observed outcomes of others, from what one reads or is told, and from other indicators of likely consequences.

Individuals may accurately assess existing conditions of reinforcement but fail to act in accordance with them because of false hopes that their actions may eventually bring favorable results. In one study, some children persisted in modeling behavior that was never reinforced in the mistaken belief that their continued imitativeness might change the adults' reinforcement practices (Bandura and Barab, 1971). People often lead themselves astray by erroneous expectations when they wrongly assume that persistence or certain changes in their behavior will alter future consequences.

When belief differs from actuality, which is not uncommon, behavior is weakly controlled by its actual consequences until repeated experience instills realistic expectations. It is not always one's expectations that change in the direction of the social reality. Acting on erroneous expectations can alter how others behave, thus shaping the social reality in the direction of the expectations.

In some of the more severe behavior disorders, psychotic acts are so powerfully controlled by bizarre subjective contingencies that the behavior remains unaffected even by intense external consequences. This process is graphically illustrated in the passages quoted below (Bateson, 1961), taken from a patient's account of his psychotic experiences in an insane asylum during the early nineteenth century. The patient, who had received a scrupulously moralistic upbringing, considered innocuous conduct sinful enough to provoke the wrath of God; hence, many of his innocent acts aroused dreadful apprehensions, leading him to perform, for hours on end, torturous atonement rituals designed to forestall the imagined disastrous consequences.

> In the night I awoke under the most dreadful impressions; I heard a voice addressing me, and I was made to imagine that my disobedience to the faith, in taking the medicine overnight, had not only offended the Lord, but had rendered the work of my salvation extremely difficult, by its effect upon my spirits

and humours. I heard that I could only be saved now by being changed into a spiritual body. . . . A spirit came upon me and prepared to guide me in my actions. I was lying on my back, and the spirit seemed to light on my pillow by my right ear, and to command my body. I was placed in a fatiguing attitude, resting on my feet, my knees drawn up and on my head, and made to swing my body from side to side without ceasing. In the meantime, I heard voices without and within me, and sounds as of the clanking of iron, and the breathing of great forge bellows, and the force of flames. . . . I was told, however, that my salvation depended on my maintaining that position as well as I could until the morning; and oh! great was my joy when I perceived the first brightness of the dawn, which I could scarcely believe had arrived so early [pp. 28—29]

Both the inducements for the self-torturing rituals and their reinforcing consequences are internally created. The patient's acceptance of medicine, an act he later considered as rebellious distrust of the Almighty, aroused dreadful hallucinations of hellish torture, which could be banished only by enacting the arduous, bizarre rituals.

Reduction of acute distress through the nonoccurrence of subjectively feared, but objectively nonexistent, threats provides a source of reinforcement for other types of psychotic behavior. Given powerful contingencies created and confirmed in thought, behavior is likely to remain under poor environmental control even in the face of severe penalties and blatant disconfirming experiences. The punishments administered to the patient by the attendants were pale compared with his imagined Hadean torture. When the prophecies of divine inner voices failed to materialize, the patient discounted these otherwise disconfirming experiences as tests by the Almighty of the strength of his religious convictions.

When I opened the door, I found a stout man servant on the landing, who told me that he was placed there to forbid my going out, by the orders of Dr. P. and my friend; on my remonstrating, he followed me into my room and stood before the door. I insisted on going out; he, on preventing me. I warned him of the danger he incurred in opposing the will of the Holy Spirit, I prayed him to let me pass, or otherwise an evil would befall him, for that I was a prophet of the Lord. He was not a whit shaken by my address, so, after again and again adjuring him, by the desire of the Spirit whose word I heard, I seized one of his arms, desiring it to wither; my words were idle, no effect followed, and I was ashamed and astonished.

Then, thought I, I have been made a fool of! But I did not on that account mistrust the doctrines by which I had been exposed to this error. The doctrines, thought I, are true; but I am mocked at by the Almighty for my disobedience to them, and at the same time, I have the guilt and the grief, of bringing discredit upon the truth, by my obedience to a spirit of mockery, or, by my disobedience to the Holy Spirit; for there were not wanting voices to suggest to me, that the reason why the miracle had failed, was, that I had not waited for the Spirit to guide my action when the word was spoken, and that I had seized the man's arm with the wrong hand [p. 33]. . .

The voices informed me, that my conduct was owing to a spirit of mockery and blasphemy having possession of me . . . that I must, in the power of the Holy Spirit, *redeem myself*, and rid myself of the spirits of blasphemy and mockery that had taken possession of me.
The way in which I was tempted to do this was by throwing myself on the top of my head backwards, and so resting on the top of my head and on my feet alone, to turn from one side to the other until I had broken my neck. I suppose by this time I was already in a state of feverish delirium, but my good sense and prudence still refused to undertake this strange action. I was then accused for faithlessness and cowardice, of fearing man more than God. . .

I attempted the command, the servant prevented me. I lay down contented to have proved myself willing to obey in spite of his presence, but now I was accused of not daring to wrestle with him unto blows. I again attempted what I was enjoined. The man seized me, I tore myself from him, telling him it was necessary for my salvation; he left me and went down stairs. I then tried to perform what I had begun; but now I found, either that I could not so jerk myself round on my head, or that my fear of breaking my neck was really too strong for my faith. In that case I then certainly mocked, for my efforts were not sincere. . .

Failing in my attempts, I was directed to expectorate vio-
lently, in order to get rid of my two formidable enemies; and
then again I was told to drink water, and that the Almighty
was satisfied; but that if I was not satisfied (neither could I be
sincerely, for I knew I had not fulfilled his commands), I was
to take up my position again; I did so; my attendant came up
with an assistant and they forced me into a straight waistcoat.
Even then I again tried to resume the position to which I was
again challenged. They then tied my legs to the bed-posts, and
so secured me. [pp. 34-35].

Grotesque homicidal actions provide further illustrations
of how behavior can come under bizarre cognitive control.
Every so often tragic episodes occur in which individuals are
led by delusional beliefs to commit acts of violence. Some
follow divine inner voices commanding them to murder.
Others are instigated by paranoid suspicions to protect themselves from people who are supposedly conspiring to harm
them. And still others are motivated by grandiose convictions
that it is their heroic responsibility to eliminate evil persons
in positions of power.

A study of the assassins of American presidents (Weisz &
Taylor, 1970) shows that, with one exception, the murderous
assaults were partly under delusional control. The assassins
acted by divine mandate, through alarm that the president
was in conspiracy with treacherous foreign agents to over-
throw the government, or on the conviction that their own
adversities resulted from presidential persecution. Being unusually seclusive in their behavior, the assassins effectively
shielded their erroneous beliefs from corrective influences.

Representational Guidance of Behavior

Cognitive processes play a prominent role in the acquisition and retention of behavior as well as in its expression.
Transitory experiences leave lasting effects by being coded
and stored in symbolic form for memory representation. Internal representations of behavior, constructed from observed

examples and from informative response consequences, serve as guides to overt action on later occasions. Representational guides are especially influential in early and intermediate phases of learning. After response patterns become routinized through repeated execution, they are performed in recurring situations without requiring prior visualization or thought. When learning to drive a car, thought is used to guide actions. After driving becomes a well-integrated routine, people think of other matters while navigating the streets and highways. Attending to the mechanics of what one is doing after proficiency is achieved tends, if anything, to disrupt skilled performance. Moreover, if one had to think before carrying out every routine function, it would consume most of one's attention and create a monotonously dull inner life. There are obviously considerable benefits to be being able to think about and do different things at the same time.

Although it is difficult to learn without awareness and the aid of thought, once patterns of behavior are well established they are typically executed without much conscious deliberation. Therefore, evidence that people perform common routines without being fully conscious of what they are doing, has no bearing on the role of thought and awareness in the original mastery of the behavior.

Thought Control of Action by Covert Problem Solving

Coping with the demands of everyday life would be exceedingly trying if one could arrive at solutions to problems only by actually performing possible options and suffering the consequences. Fortunately, higher cognitive capacities enable people to conduct most problem solving in thought rather than in action. They design sturdy dwellings and bridges, for example, without having to continue building them until they happen to hit upon a structure that does not collapse. Rather, they consider relevant information, apply cognitive operations to it, and generate possible solutions. The alternatives are typically tested by symbolic exploration and are either dis-

carded or retained on the basis of the calculated consequences. Favored symbolic solutions are then actually
executed.

THOUGHT AS SYMBOLIC
CONSTRUCTIONS

Symbols that represent events, cognitive operations, and
relationships serve as the vehicles of thought. Thinking depends to a large extent upon language symbols. Thinking also
occurs in terms of numerical and musical notations, and other
symbols. By manipulating symbols that convey relevant information, one can gain understanding of causal relationships, create new forms of knowledge, solve problems, and
deduce consequences without actually performing any activities. The functional value of thought rests on the close corre-
spondence between the symbolic system and external events,
so the former can be substituted for the latter. Thus, subtracting the number two from ten yields the same outcome as
physically performing the operation of removing two objects
from a group of ten.

Symbols, being infinitely easier to manipulate than their
physical counterparts, greatly increase the flexibility and
power of cognitive problem solving. Symbols provide the instruments of thought; internal representations of experiences
serve as important sources for the symbolic constructions
which constitute the thoughts.

The process by which people learn to solve problems
symbolically has received comparatively little attention despite its central role in human functioning. Because thought
is a private activity, it is not readily accessible to empirical
study. Requisite cognitive skills are usually developed by initially performing operations on actual objects and then
translating the external functions into covert symbolic ones of
increasing complexity and abstraction. In the teaching of a-
rithmetic principles, for example, children first learn the formal operations of addition and subtraction by physically
combining and withdrawing actual objects and receiving corrective feedback on their performances. Pictorial representations are also used in early phases as concrete referents in the
acquisition of arithmetic principles. After children have

learned to solve problems through physical manipulation, the objects are symbolized by numbers. Correct solutions are now achieved by manipulating numerical symbols on paper, where each step in the cognitive operations can be checked and corrected. The activity at this stage is still partially overt, but the solutions are worked out internally. Eventually solutions are generated entirely symbolically by having children think out the problem without any external aids.

In this way thought processes gradually become independent of immediate concrete referents. Symbols can then be manipulated to produce thoughts that are not necessarily limited to those directly translatable to external events. Many fantasies and unusual ideas in fact involve novel symbolic constructions that transcend the bounds of reality. One can easily think of cows jumping over the moon and elephants riding on flies even though these events are impossible to enact. The remarkable flexibility of symbolization and its independence from reality constraints, expands the scope of thought.

After people acquire cognitive skills and operations for processing information, they can formulate alternative solutions and evaluate the probable immediate and long range consequences of different courses of action. The result of weighing the effort required, the relative risks and benefits, and the subjective probabilities of gaining the desired outcomes influences which actions, from among the various alternatives, are chosen. This is not to say that the decisions are necessarily good ones or that reason always prevails. Decisions may be based on inadequate assessment of information and misjudgment of anticipated consequences. Moreover, people often know what they ought to do but are swayed by immediately compelling circumstances to behave otherwise.

LANGUAGE DEVELOPMENT

Because a great deal of human thought is linguistically based, the process by which language develops is of major interest. Until recently, it was commonly assumed that learning had only a secondary influence on language development. This conclusion was largely based on a limited view of learning processes. Grammatical speech is not produced by differential reinforcement; however, results of laboratory and field studies reveal that corrective feedback substantially aids grammatical learning. With regard to modeling processes, psycholinguistic theorizing and research have been essentially confined to verbal mimicry. By restricting analyses to children's repetition of what they hear, researchers have concluded that by modeling one can learn only specific utterances, not the grammatical rules of speech. Rather than simply copying individual utterances, children learn sets of rules which enable them to generate an almost infinite variety of new sentences that they have never heard. It is abstract modeling, with its perceptual, cognitive, and reproductive component processes, rather than simple verbal mimicry, that is most germane to the development of generative grammar.

The contribution of learning influences to language development has also been downplayed on the basis of certain observations. During initial language learning, children usually convert adult speech to simpler grammars. They can acquire linguistic rules without engaging in any motor speech. In addition, it has been claimed that children's imitations are no more advanced linguistically than are their nonimitative spontaneous utterances. Imitation, it is therefore argued, cannot produce new grammatical forms. Nor is reinforcement believed to play a significant role in grammatical learning, since adults are more inclined to approve the factual accuracy than the grammatical correctness of children's utterances. And finally, language is acquired too rapidly to occur by tuition.

Many of the above criticisms are valid when applied to theories of imitation that emphasize verbatim repetition of modeled responses and that assume that learning requires reinforced performance. It is evident from the material already discussed at length that the social learning interpretation of modeling is compatible with rule-learning theories proposed by psycholinguists. Both conceptualizations assign special importance to the process of abstracting productive grammatical rules from diverse utterances. The differentiation made by psycholinguists between language competence and performance corresponds to the distinction made between learning and performance in social learning theory. Since observational learning does not require performance, it provides a medium for rapid acquisition of new competencies.

Some of the limitations attributed to learning theory have resulted from the failure to distinguish between response mimicry and abstract modeling. Consider the widely cited argument that imitation cannot serve as a vehicle of language learning, because spontaneous imitations diminish during the second year of life when language is developing at a rapidly accelerating rate. Parents are initially amused over mimicking of vocalizations and simple acts by young children but consider it inappropriate as they grow older. As children's discriminative capacities increase, they are disinclined to mimic everything they see or hear. However, humans do not cease observational learning at age two. On the contrary, as children's attentional, cognitive, and ideomotor functions develop with age, their capabilities for observational learning are greatly enhanced.

The role of example in grammatical learning has also been questioned on the grounds that children often display ungrammatical speech unlikely to have been modeled by adults (e.g., "I runned"). Many of these errors represent children's overgeneralizing learned rules from regular to irregular grammatical constructions. Such novel utterances arise because the children model too well. The inappropriate transfer is easily eliminated by corrective feedback on the exceptions to the rules (Sherman, 1971). Other reservations concerning learning determinants stem from limited evidence or gross measurement of children's speech. The notion that children cannot imitate linguistic features extending beyond their current grammar is questioned by more recent findings that young children can adopt new linguistic forms by means of modeling (Bloom, Hood, & Lightbown, 1974; Kemp & Dale, 1973).

Given the evidence of widespread regularities in language acquisition and the supposed deficiencies of learning mechanisms, innate grammatical predispositions were postulated as the source of linguistic categories. Common grammatical features, however, do not necessarily arise from innate programming. Behaviors that are universally functional will be found in all cultures. An innate propensity for tools, for example, is rarely proposed to explain why all people use tools (Rosenthal & Zimmerman, 1977). There are basic uniformities in environmental events, involving agents, actions, and objects, that are related analogously in every society. Utterances used to represent these events will therefore contain similar syntactic features (e.g., nouns and verbs) in diverse cultural contexts. Regularities in order in which different grammatical features are mastered may reflect the differential ease of learning various concepts arising more from cognitive complexity than from linguistic features.

Psycholinguists disagree on the nature of the innate component in language acquisition. Some believe that the basic grammatical categories are biologically preprogrammed and require only minimal environmental input to be activated. It would follow from this theory that exposure to speech alone is sufficient to produce grammatical competence without requiring any corrective feedback. Others, who believe in a lesser degree of preprogramming, assume that people are innately equipped with information-processing capacities that enable them to discover the structural properties of languages. In this view, the cognitive capacity is given, but the development of linguistic proficiency requires instructive examples and some corrective feedback. Whatever the innate potentiality may be, few would question that social learning experiences influence the rate of language development. Rules about grammatical relations between words cannot be developed unless they are exemplified by the utterances of models.

Researchers have begun to examine systematically how children learn to comprehend and use language through social learning processes. In learning to communicate symbolically, children must acquire appropriate verbal symbols for objects and events and the syntactic rules for representing relationships among them. The process of acquiring language involves not only learning grammatical relations between words, but also correlating the linguistic forms with the events to which they apply. Language learning therefore depends upon semantic aids and nonlinguistic understanding of the events to which the utterances refer. For this reason, it is difficult to transmit linguistic forms that children do not already know by verbal modeling alone. Adults, of course, do not converse abstractly with young children who have a poor grasp of speech. Verbal expressions that convey grammatical relations are usually matched to meaningful ongoing activities about which children already have some knowledge. Grammatical features of speech are more informative and distinguishable when the semantic referents for the utterances are present than when they are absent. Young children, for example, are aided in comprehending plural forms if they hear singular and plural labels applied to single and multiple objects, respectively.

That acquisition of language rules is greatly facilitated by pairing linguistic modeling with perceptual referents was confirmed by Brown (1976) in an experimental study. Young children, who had little or no understanding of passive constructions, heard a model narrate in passive form a series of events while she enacted the corresponding activities, or showed pictures portraying the same activities, or used no referential aids. Modeling with enacted referents substantially increased children's comprehension of passive constructions. Linguistic modeling without referential correlates improved comprehension in children who already had partial understanding of passive constructions, whereas modeling with enacted referents facilitated learning of the grammatical form even in children who did not previously know it. The results attained by Brown and those of Moeser and Bregman (1973), using an artificial language, indicate that initial language learning requires referential aids but that after some verbal competence is achieved further learning becomes less dependent upon immediate perceptual referents.

Parents usually adapt their speech to their children's verbal skills in an effort to facilitate language learning. Rules for organizing words into sentences are discovered more easily in short simple utterances than when they are obscured in ponderous verbiage. When addressing young children, parents use utterances that are shorter, more redundant, and grammatically simpler than when they speak to older children (Baldwin & Baldwin, 1973; Moerk, 1974; Snow, 1972). Misunderstanding of what people say can result in inappropriate actions, which, in turn, create informative feedback for improving comprehension of speech. Acquisition of language rules is therefore accelerated by the consequences of acting on verbal prompts as well as by linguistic modeling and referential inputs.

Contingent analysis of verbal interchanges between parents and their young children reveals that parents are active language teachers, frequently providing phonetic, semantic, and grammatical corrections after incomplete or incorrect utterances by their children (Moerk, 1976; Mann & Van Wagenen, 1975). The instructional and corrective methods include didactic modeling, prompting, questioning, informing, answering, labeling, pictorial structuring, and accenting grammatically significant speech elements. Parents diminish their instructional activity as their children's linguistic competence increases.

Corrective feedback contains both linguistic modeling and social reactions which could well affect the level and accuracy of children's speech. The current trend in psycholinguistic theory has been away from a predominantly structural orientation toward an analysis of psychological processes underlying syntactic encoding of semantic relationships. The change has increased interest in experiential determinants of linguistic development. Because of the early antagonism between researchers favoring structural and functional approaches to language, however, the contribution of reinforcement influences to linguistic behavior remains largely unexplored. In the concern over the form of speech, its social function was neglected.

Adults do not make arbitrary rewards contingent upon correct grammar, but this does not mean that grammatical accuracy has no differential effects. Children's language will be influenced more strongly by its natural consequences than by arbitrary extrinsic ones. The most effective natural consequences are the benefits derived from influencing people and events. Thus, for example, young children with limited language skills do not adopt modeled linguistic features for verbal approval alone. However, they readily pick up these more advanced speech forms when they can obtain desired play materials only by asking for them in the advanced grammatical way (Hart & Risley, 1968). Success in influencing the behavior of others, which has strong reinforcing effects, is better achieved by grammatical articulation than by utterances that are poorly understood. The demands for communicative accuracy, although minimal initially, increase as children grow older.

Some theorists have speculated about whether immediate imitation, comprehension, and production form a developmentally causal sequence in language acquisition. There is currently some debate over whether imitation produces comprehension or comprehension produces imitation (Bloom, Hood, & Lightbown, 1974; Whitehurst & Vasta, 1975). In the social learning analysis, both comprehension and imitative performance are viewed as products of observational learning, rather than as being causally related. Through observation of referential modeling, children can gain understanding of grammatical relations which aids later imitative reconstructions. Instant mimicry need not require either learning or comprehension. It reflects more the capacity for short-term memory. Because grammatical features that are initially imitative are later used spontaneously does not prove that linguistic competence results from mimicry.

Although productive speech depends upon knowledge of linguistic rules, such knowledge does not automatically transfer to speech performance. As shown earlier, learning and performance are governed by different component processes. To perfect a productive skill, one must develop the ability to convert knowledge into appropriate performance. Hence, language proficiency is best developed by modeling combined with language production and corrective feedback.

Modeling, either alone or coupled with corrective feedback, has proved highly successful in encouraging children to use grammatical forms they comprehend but do not often use in everyday speech (Zimmerman & Rosenthal, 1974; Whitehurst and Vasta, 1975). These methods are equally effective in establishing generalized usage of grammatical forms in speech-deficient children (Sherman, 1971). Through these social learning influences, children identify the rules governing models' utterances and generate speech incorporating the same structures.

Verification Processes and Thought

People form conceptions about themselves and the world around them by observing and extracting the regularities of events in their environment. By representing symbolically the information derived from such experiences, they gain knowledge about the properties of objects, about relationships, and how to predict what is likely to happen under given conditions. Effective cognitive functioning requires some means of distinguishing accurate from inaccurate thinking. Thoughts about thoughts are developed through a verification process. As we have noted, knowledge concerning oneself and the environment is represented in symbolic constructions. Judgments concerning their validity and value are formed by comparing the thought representations with experiential evidence. Good matches confirm the provisional thoughts, mismatches refute them.

Evidence for verification of thoughts can come from several different sources. People derive much of their knowledge from direct experience of the effects produced by their actions. It does not require many encounters with flames set by matches, for example, to come to know the properties of matches and that striking them will cause things to burn. Based on experiences of when things will or will not burn, people develop conceptions about fire and the conditions under which it is likely to occur. Other concepts, such as those of time, quality, causality, and so on, are developed through a similar process.

Most theories of cognitive development focus almost exclusively on cognitive change through feedback from direct experimentation. According to Piagetian theory, children's experience of manipulating the environment is the chief source of their information for cognitive development. Interestingly, although behavioristic and Piagetian conceptions of behavior are often presented as antithetical, they share the assumption that development proceeds mainly through the actual effects of one's own behavior. In the social learning view, results of one's own actions are not the sole source of knowledge. As extensively documented in preceding chapters, information about the nature of things is frequently extracted from vicarious experience. In this mode of verification, observation of the effects produced by somebody else's actions provides the check on one's own thoughts. Symbolic modeling by verbal or pictorial means greatly expands the range of verification experiences that cannot otherwise be secured by personal action because of social prohibitions or the limitations of time, resources, and ability. For this reason, theories of human development formulated before the recent revolutionary advances in communications technology may present a less than adequate account of the determinants of cognitive development under contemporary conditions of life.

A third mode of verification relies upon comparison with the judgments of others. Often there is no easy way to check the validity of one's thoughts. Some of these situations involve matters that, because of their complexity or limited accessibility, restrict how much any one person can get to know about them. Consequently, views will differ from individual to individual depending upon their own particular experiences. Other thoughts involve metaphysical ideas that cannot be confirmed by objective means, as, for example, beliefs about supernatural forces. When experiential verification is either difficult or impossible, people evaluate the soundness of their views by comparing them against the judgments of others. Social verification can foster conventional, unorthodox, or even bizarre ways of thinking depending upon the beliefs of the reference groups one selects.

In the course of development, people acquire some rules of inference. They then can detect certain errors in thought by logical verification. Thoughts convey information about events. If the information contained in these propositions is accepted as valid, they create logical implications that can be used to gauge the correctness of derivative propositions. In this mode of verification, it is the logic of thought that provides a means of checking the validity of one's reasoning. Knowledge can be generated as well as evaluated by using rules of inference. By deducing consequences from generalizations they have found to be true, people can derive knowledge about things that extend beyond their experiences. Thus, if one knows that a persimmon is a deciduous tree and that deciduous trees shed their leaves in the autumn, then one can arrive at the knowledge that a persimmon tree will remain bare during the winter without having to observe the foliage of such a plant throughout the different seasons.

The discussion thus far has been concerned with the development of veridical thought through enactive, vicarious, social, and logical verification. Under certain conditions each of these ways of checking thought against reality can lead to faulty thinking. To begin with, appearances can be misleading, especially to young children who lack the experiences necessary to interpret accurately what they see. The study of developmental changes in children's conceptions of environmental events has been a major focus of research within the Piagetian tradition. Many of these studies are concerned with the principle of conservation, which reflects a child's ability to recognize that a given property remains the same despite external changes that make it look different. In the study of conservation of quantity, for example, the same amount of liquid is poured into containers of different shapes (e.g., a tall narrow beaker and a short wide beaker), and children are asked whether the two beakers contain equal amounts of water. Young children tend to evaluate things on the basis of appearance—believing that the tall narrow beaker contains more water—whereas older children judge things to be alike although altered in appearance.

Young children who have not yet learned to conserve acquire this capacity through corrective learning experiences. These experiences are provided by modeling appropriate conservation judgments alone or with supporting explanations, by correcting children's misconceptions, or by explaining the rules for arriving at accurate solutions (Brainerd, 1976; Zimmerman & Rosenthal, 1974). Conservation judgments developed by children through modeling do not differ from conservation concepts acquired by children in the course of everyday experiences (Sullivan, 1967). This is not surprising considering that modeled judgments undoubtedly play an influential role in conceptual learning under natural conditions.

Developmental theorists who subscribe to fixed stage theories assume that thinking occurs in terms of unvarying sequences of cognitive stages, and that these uniform mental structures restrict what one can learn from informative experiences. Development of reasoning by instructive experiences therefore tends to be discounted by stage theorists as reflecting only alterations in verbalizations rather than in how one thinks about matters. Changes in thinking presumably result from maturation and from one's own cumulative spontaneous experiences.

Portraying development as a spontaneous self-discovery process has considerable appeal. However, the negative features of stage theories are rarely given much thought. Such theories tend to cast people into prefixed types, thus lending themselves readily to sterotyping people by stage classification. After they have been categorized, people tend to be viewed in terms of the category rather than by the individuality of their thought and conduct. As a consequence, classification practices often do more harm than good. Stage theories can also provide convenient excuses for weak programs that are supposed to foster intellectual development. When failures occur in cognitive learning they are readily attributable to lack of "cognitive readiness." Rather than creating environments conducive to learning, some adherents of stage views are inclined to wait for children to become ready for learning. For many it turns out to be a long wait.

As in the case of moral judgments, the theoretical foundation for stage notions becomes more shaky as evidence from improved methods accumulates. For example, children's conservation judgments vary with different items in the same conservation task (Baker, 1967; Uzgiris, 1964). Thus, they may be misled by changes in appearance when judging some materials but not others. Such variations in judgments are not easily explainable in terms of uniform thought structures. Studies cited earlier demonstrated that children who allegedly lack the stage readiness can learn abstract concepts, generalize them to new situations, and retain them over time. Such findings are sufficiently promising to warrant detailed analysis of the social learning determinants of cognitive functioning. These studies further show why researchers should not be too quick to attribute performance deficiencies to limitations in children's cognitive capabilities. When the process has been explored further, changes in learning procedures have often produced improvements in cognitive functioning. This is not to imply that children of any age can be taught anything. All learning requires certain prior capabilities. The issue in question is whether the requisites for change, which all theories acknowledge, are cognitive skills or uniform mental structures. It might also be noted that cognitive learning is studied experimentally not for the pragmatic purpose of rushing children through "stages", but to advance understanding of the determinants and processes of thought.

So much for errors in thought arising out of misleading appearances. Inaccuracies in thinking occur, even though events are correctly perceived, when information is derived from insufficient evidence. The proverbial blind-folded persons feeling different parts of the same elephant developed diverse views corresponding to their particular realities, but they were all misled by their limited experiences. The same is true of knowledge gained vicariously. Biased conceptions are often developed observationally by overgeneralizing from exposure to a restricted range of the activities and experiences of others. Learning from the images conveyed by the mass media is a good case in point. People partly form impressions of the social realities with which they have little or no contact from televised representations of society. Because the world of television is heavily populated with villainous and unscrupulous characters it can distort knowledge about the real world. Gerbner, who has been studying how television cultivates certain views about people and life, reports evidence which bears on this process (Gerbner & Gross, 1976). He found that heavy viewers of television are less trustful of others and over-estimate their chances of being victimized than do light viewers. Heavy viewers tend to see the world as more dangerous regardless of their educational level, sex, age, and amount of newspaper reading. Many of the misconceptions that people develop about occupations, ethnic groups, social roles, and other aspects of life are similarly cultivated through symbolic modeling of sterotypes (McArthur & Eisen, 1976; Siegel, 1958).

Information, whether generated by direct or vicarious

forms of experience, is not absorbed automatically. Preconceptions partly determine which aspects of experience are extracted and how they are perceived. Because of the selective bias to see what one is looking for, erroneous preconceptions can easily become self-perpetuating. A misguiding verification process, of course, involves more than selective processing and transforming of information. By acting in accordance with false beliefs, people create for themselves realities supporting their thoughts and avoid situations that would provide corrective reality testing. Once the reciprocal contingencies have become well established, misconceptions can be altered only by disconfirming experiences that are too compelling to be ignored or misconstrued (Bandura, 1977).

There are certain conditions under which social verification tends to promote styles of thought that may have little basis in reality. This typically occurs when individuals become exclusively dependent, by attraction or lack of better options, on a tight-knit group that espouses the idiosyncratic beliefs of a charismatic leader. By isolating themselves from other groups and outside sources of information, the members shield their faulty notions from beliefs contrary to those they hold. The various cults and messianic groups that emerge from time to time typify this process.

Fallacies in thinking can arise from faulty logical processing of information. Reasoning about events involves acquiring knowledge by tuition or induction from observed uniformities, and by deducing new information from the knowledge one already possesses. We have already examined how many fallacies in thinking result from incorrect inductive inferences. People distort what they see and hear through their personal biases. They form strong beliefs about things on the basis of insufficient or inadequate evidence. They frequently overgeneralize from their limited experiences. Inaccurate suppositions, which are due largely to nonlogical factors, will produce inferences that are deductively valid but factually erroneous. As an example, a person who has come to believe that all athletes lack intellectual interests will logically conclude that baseball players are disinterested in intellectual matters. People also make mistakes in what logically follows from valid information they possess. In these instances the errors in thought reflect faulty deductive reasoning. However, people are probably misled more by their beliefs concerning what they are reasoning about than by their logical intuitions.

Interaction of Regulatory Systems

The regulatory systems by which behavior is organized and controlled do not operate independently. Most actions are controlled simultaneously by two or more sources of influence. Moreover, the various regulatory systems are closely interdependent in acquiring and retaining their power to affect behavior. In order to establish and maintain the effectiveness of predictive stimuli, the same actions must produce different consequences in different circumstances. If crossing the street on red or green signals made one equally vulnerable to being hit by a car, pedestrians would quickly disregard traffic lights and rely on other informative cues to guide them safely through busy intersections, as in the case of New York City. Earlier we noted how the effectiveness of verbal and other social influences is negated by faulty reinforcement practices and reinstated by ensuring that predictable consequences ensue for actions appropriate to the circumstances.

The preceding examples illustrate how antecedent determinants of behavior depend upon their correlation with response consequences. Stimulus and cognitive influences, in turn, can alter the impact of prevailing conditions of reinforcement. Threatening cues sometimes acquire such powerful control over defensive behavior that people avoid renewed encounters with feared persons, places, or things. When the original threats no longer exist, self-protective behavior remains insulated, by continued avoidance, from existing conditions of reinforcement. Through procedures fostering reality testing, behavioral contact with the environment can be eventually restored (Bandura, 1976a).

Even when the object of one's antipathy or fear is not completely avoided, highly evocative cues activate defensive behavior that creates adverse contingencies where they may not ordinarily exist. We might draw again on a newspaper advice column to illustrate how anticipatory reactions can result in a reality of one's own making:

Dear Abby:

I have trouble with blondes. Every time I go for a girl and she is a blonde she turns out to be a gold-digger. I notice on TV whenever they have a gold-digger she is blonde. The last blonde I went with asked me to buy a record every time I took her out. She kept me busted buying her records. Should I pass up all blondes from now on?

Blonde Trouble

Dear Blonde Trouble:

Plenty of golden heads have golden hearts.

Abby

To the extent that the correspondent's distrust of blonde women leads him to behave in ways that provoke their unfriendly counterreactions, the predictive significance of blonde hair is repeatedly confirmed, which, in turn, prompts anticipatory rejections with reciprocal negative consequences. Both the processes of antecedent and consequent control, thus support each other. Sequential analyses of the interactions of people who repeatedly become involved in interpersonal difficulties show that anticipations shape reality in a self-confirming fashion (Toch, 1969).

The way in which beliefs can enhance, distort, or negate the influence of reinforcing consequences has already been reviewed and needs no further illustration. Cognitive events, however, do not occur spontaneously, nor do they function as autonomous causes of behavior. Their nature, their valence, and their occurrence are governed by stimulus and reinforcement influences. Therefore, no analysis of cognitive control of behavior is complete without specifying what regulates the influential cognitions.

Cognitively based emotional learning, for instance, cannot occur unless the thoughts serving as sources of arousal have activating potential. Studies by Miller (1951) and Grose (1952) demonstrated that thoughts can become arousing by generalization from experiences associated with overt responses. Thoughts corresponding to verbalizations that had been punished generated physiological arousal, whereas thoughts representing nonpunished verbalizations elicited no emotional reactions. If the painful experiences are sufficiently intense, however, they can become so aversive that the disturbing thoughts themselves are inhibited (Ericksen & Kuethe, 1956; Marks & Gelder, 1967).

Thoughts are partly governed by external stimuli. Thus, the cognitions elicited in a hospital differ markedly from those aroused in a night club. A simple cue from a past experience can set one daydreaming of bygone events. And disturbing trains of thought can be turned off by directing one's attention to absorbing matters that elicit superseding cognitive activities. This form of self-control, in which thought-produced arousal is diminished by engrossment in absorbing books, television programs, vocational and avocational activities, and other engaging enterprises, is widely used to restore a sense of well-being.

The rules and principles that people use to guide their actions do not arise in a vacuum. When rules defining appropriate behavior are not explicitly designated, they are derived from information conveyed by observed or experienced response consequences. Provisional hypotheses that produce responses resulting in favorable outcomes are retained, partially correct hypotheses are successively refined on the basis of differential response feedback until the right one is hit upon, and erroneous hypotheses that give rise to faulty performances are discarded. While it is true that implicit rules govern behavior, the rules themselves are partly fashioned from feedback experiences.

One difficulty in influencing thoughts through consequences is that cognitions are not publicly observable. In the process described above, thoughts are modified indirectly by their correlated response effects. This works well when actions stemming from thoughts produce natural consequences. Ideas about how to get to a place will be retained if they get one there, but will be rapidly discarded if they lead one astray. When consequences are socially mediated rather than natural to the behavior, it can have different effects depending on the preferences of others. As a result, people will often say and do things publicly they do not believe privately. The susceptibility of beliefs to change through the consequences stemming from them, therefore, varies depending on whether the beliefs are naturally or socially functional.

Regulation of cognitions is not restricted solely to indirect response effects. Thoughts are observable by the person doing the thinking, and can be directly influenced by self-reinforcement. The growing recognition of human self-reactive capacities has increased studies of how thought processes are changed through contingently self-administered consequences (Mahoney, 1974). In this process, constructive lines of thought are enhanced by making self-reward conditional on their occurrence; trains of thought that are subjectively distressing or behaviorally disruptive, such as self-derogations, infuriating or vexatious ruminations, obsessions, and hallucinations, are reduced by contingent self-punishment or supplanted by rewarding alternative cognitive activities.

Thought processes are modifiable by modeling influences as well as by the self-produced or behavioral consequences of thought. Cognitive activities are not readily amenable to change by behavioral modeling when the covert components of thought processes cannot be adequately conveyed by behavioral cues alone. This problem can be easily overcome by having models verbalize aloud their thought processes as they engage in problem-solving activities. The covert thought component is thus given overt representation. Debus (1976) has successfully produced generalized, durable improvements in cognitive skills by modeling thought processes in conjunction with the action strategies.

Other approaches to the modification of cognitive control have been developed in programs designed to alter psychological dysfunctions arising from faulty styles of thinking. Many human difficulties and distresses stem from problems of thought. People repeatedly generate aversive arousal by anxiety-provoking ruminations; they debilitate their own performances by self-doubting, self-depricating, and other self-defeating thoughts; they act without thinking or on misconceptions that get them into trouble.

Meichenbaum (1974) devised self-instructional procedures as a means of modifying cognitive determinants. The rationale for focusing on self-instruction was based on Ellis's (1962) rational-emotive therapy and Luria's (1961) analysis of the internalization of verbal self-control. According to Ellis, psychological disorders arise from irrational thoughts which are expressed in negative internal dialogues. Treatment consists of challenging the irrational beliefs and prescribing behaviors that negate them. It is assumed that insight into the irrationality of one's beliefs eliminates negative self-statements, thereby reducing internal distress and troublesome patterns of behavior. Findings of controlled studies suggest that attempts to modify faulty ideation solely by rational analysis and cognitive restructuring achieve, at best, weak, inconsistent changes in behavior (Mahoney, 1974). If clinical applications of this approach produce better results, they probably derive more from the corrective assignments to behave differently than from exhortations to think better. Improvements in behavioral functioning produce cognitive changes (Bandura, 1977).

The second source for the self-instructional approach, which receives greater empirical support, is the developmental sequence of verbal self-control proposed by Luria. In this view, children's behavior is initially controlled by verbal instructions from others; later children regulate their actions by overt self-instructions and eventually by covert self-instructions.

The procedures developed by Meichenbaum follow the above sequence. Models demonstrate appropriate forms of behavior while thinking aloud the action strategies. The modeled verbalizations include analysis of task requirements, symbolic rehearsal of a plan of action, self-instructional guides for performance, coping self-statements to counteract self-debilitating thoughts, and verbal self-rewards for attainments. After exposure to the behavioral and self-instructional modeling, participants are instructed on how to perform the appropriate activities. They later perform the tasks while instructing themselves at first aloud, then quietly, and finally covertly. Results of numerous experiments reveal that self-guidance modeling combined with overt-to-covert symbolic rehearsal improves cognitive and behavioral functioning.

Because of the complex interdependence of antecedent, consequent, and cognitive regulatory systems, the sharp distinctions commonly drawn between behavioral and cognitive processes are more polemical than real. It has been customary in psychological theorizing to construct entire explanatory schemes around a single regulatory system, to the relative neglect of other influential determinants and processes. Some theorists have tended to concentrate upon antecedent control created principally through the association of environmental events; others have focused primarily upon regulation of behavior by external reinforcement; still others favor cognitive determinants and confine their studies largely to cognitive operations. Strong allegiances to part processes encourage intensive investigations of subfunctions, but considered independently they do not provide a complete understanding of human behavior.

6

Reciprocal
Determinism

FROM THE SOCIAL LEARNING PERSPECTIVE, psychological functioning is a continuous reciprocal interaction between personal, behavioral, and environmental determinants. The term reciprocal is used in the sense of mutual action between events rather than in the narrower meaning of similar or opposite counterreactions. As mentioned briefly before, theories that have attempted to incorporate both personal and environmental determinants usually depict behavior as resulting from the joint influence of these two factors. In studying the determinants of behavior within this paradigm, the responses of individuals are measured under varying situational conditions. The data are then analyzed to determine how much of the variation in behavior is due to personal characteristics, how much to situational conditions, and how much to their joint effects. The efforts to gauge the relative importance of these factors, have not been especially informative because one can obtain almost any pattern of results depending upon the types of persons, behavior, and situations selected. For example, in deciding which movie to attend from many alternatives in a large city there are few constraints on the individual so that personal preferences emerge as the predominant determinants. In contrast, if people are immersed in a deep pool of water their behavior will be remarkably similar however uniquely varied they might be in their cognitive and behavioral make-up.

Interdependence of Personal and Environmental Influences

As a short-hand convenience for the present discussion, the influence exerted by the individual and by his or her behavior will be designated together as the personal determinant. As we know, internal personal factors and behavior also operate as reciprocal determinants of each other. To take one example, people's expectations influence how they behave, and the outcomes of their behavior change their expectations. The major weakness of the traditional formulations is that they treat behavioral dispositions and the environment as separate entities when in fact, each determines the operation of the other. For the most part, the environment is only a potentiality until actualized by appropriate actions; it is not a fixed property that inevitably impinges upon individuals. Lecturers do not influence students unless they attend their classes, books do not affect people unless they select and read them, fires do not burn people unless they touch them, and rewarding and punishing influences remain in abeyance until activated by conditional performances. Similarly, personal determinants are only potentialities that do not operate as influences unless they are activated. People who can converse knowledgeably about certain issues can affect others if they speak but not if they remain silent, even though they possess the means to do so. Thus, behavior partly determines which of the many potential environmental influences will come into play and what forms they will take; environmental influences, in turn, partly determine which behavioral repertoires are developed and activated. In this two-way influence process, the environment is influenceable, as is the behavior it regulates.

SELECTIVE ACTIVATION OF POTENTIAL
INFLUENCES

The way in which behavioral and environmental influences affect each other is evident even in simple experimental situations in which fixed environments are imposed on animals. Consider a standard experiment in defensive learning in which shocks are scheduled to occur every minute, but each bar press forestalls the shock for 30 seconds, thus enabling the animals to determine the punitiveness of their environment by their actions. Those who quickly learn the controlling behavior can create an environment for themselves that is essentially free of punishment. Others who, for one reason or another, are slow in acquiring the requisite coping skill experience a highly unpleasant milieu.

Though the *potential environment* is identical for all animals, the *actual environment* depends upon their behavior. Is the animal controlling the environment or is the environment controlling the animal? What we have here is a two-way regulatory system in which the organism appears either as an object or an agent of control, depending upon which side of the reciprocal process one chooses to examine. When the rate of self-protective responses is measured, the environmental contingencies appear to be the controllers of behavior. If, instead, one measures the amount of punishment brought about by each animal, then it is the environment that is controlled and modified by behavior. The punitiveness of the environment can, therefore, vary considerably for different animals and at different times for the same animal. In examining how behavior determines the environment, one might test drunk and sober animals in the same programmed situation and compare the aversiveness of the environments animals create for themselves under intoxicated and under sober conditions.

The rewards of an environment are also only potentialities until actualized by appropriate behavior. A researcher once studied schizophrenic and normal children in a setting containing an extraordinary variety of attractive devices, including television sets, phonographs, pinball machines, electric trains, picture viewers, and electric organs. To activate these playthings, children had simply to deposit available coins, but only when a light on the device was turned on; coins deposited when the light was off increased the period that the device would remain inoperative. Normal children rapidly learned how to take advantage of what the environment had to offer and created unusually rewarding conditions for themselves. By contrast, schizophrenic children, who failed to master the simple controlling skill, experienced the same potentially rewarding environment as a depriving, unpleasant place.

In the preceding examples, the potential environment is fixed so that behavior determines only the extent to which it impinges on the organism. Behavior can create environmental conditions, as well as regulate their impact. Social environments provide an especially wide latitude for creating contingencies that reciprocally affect one's own behavior. People can converse on many topics, they can engage in a variety of activities, and their potential responsiveness is exceedingly diverse in other ways. In social interactions the behavior of each participant governs which aspects of their potential repertoires are actualized and which remain unexpressed. We are all acquainted with problem-prone individuals who, through their obnoxious conduct, predictably breed negative social climates wherever they go. Others are equally skilled at bringing out the best in those with whom they interact.

At the organizational level, people play an influential role through their collective action in creating social conditions that affect the course and quality of their lives. Labor unions, for example, negotiate the working conditions and pay schedules they favor. Other groups similarly use the power of collective pressure to change social practices in ways that improve their life situation.

Because personal and environmental sources of influence function as interdependent rather than separate determinants, research aimed at estimating what percentage of behavioral variation is due to persons and which to situations does not throw much light on the interactive aspects of regulatory processes. Nor is evidence that much of the variation is usually due to the joint effects of personal characteristics and situational conditions especially instructive. Rather, to elucidate the process of reciprocal interaction between personal and environmental influences, one must analyze how each is conditional on that of the other. The methodology best suited for this purpose specifies the conditional probabilities that the interacting factors will affect the likelihood of the occurrence of each other in an on-going sequence.

Analysis of sequential interchanges in social relationships provides one example of reciprocal influence processes. Studies of dyadic exchanges document how the behavior of one member activates particular responses from the repertoire of the other member which, in turn, prompt reciprocal counteractions that mutually shape the social milieu in a predictable direction (Bandura, Lipsher, & Miller, 1960). Raush and his associates have similarly shown that the antecedent acts of one person strongly influence how others respond, thus determining the course of the interaction (Raush, 1965; Raush, Barry, Hertel, & Swain, 1974). Hostile acts generally draw aggressive counterresponses from others, whereas cordial antecedent acts seldom do. Aggressive children thus create through their actions a hostile environment, while children who favor friendly modes of response generate an amicable social milieu.

Reciprocal processes are not governed solely by momentary behavioral contingencies. Counterresponses to antecedent actions are also influenced by judgments of later consequences of responding in a particular manner. Children who are well trained in coercive behavior will maintain, or even escalate, aversive conduct in the face of immediate punishment when persistence is expected to eventually get them what they want. The same momentary punishment will serve as an inhibitor rather than as an enhancer when continuance of aversive conduct is known to be ineffective. Aggression in interactions between adults may similarly elicit counteraggression, or conciliation, or some other response depending on the later effects anticipated for these alternative courses of action. The predictive power of momentary reciprocal effects therefore derives partly from changes in the consequences anticipated over the course of sequential interchanges.

When the predictors of likely consequences are personal characteristics, individuals can set in motion certain reciprocal sequences of interaction through their stimulus value alone. The research cited earlier showing that the mere appearance of adults elicits different amounts of cooperativeness depending on whether they had previously reinforced such behavior is a good example of this process. In addition, role prescriptions, specifying how people are supposed to behave in carrying out their assigned roles, serve as structuring influences on the nature of reciprocal exchanges. For instance, expected behaviors toward the same person in the same setting will differ for the roles of work supervisor and confidante. Therefore in analyzing how the behavior of one person affects the counterreactions of another, one must consider, in addition to immediate effects of each action, the anticipated changes in mutual consequences over time, predictive cues, and the socially structured constraints on behavior of roles and circumstances.

The preceding discussion is not meant to imply that all research should use reciprocal influence paradigms. On the contrary. It is important to understand how certain determinants produce change in the first place regardless of how the resultant changes, in turn, affect the subsequent operation of the determinants. To continue with the aggression example, the question of how environmental influences induce and initiate aggression requires a separate analysis apart from how the resultant aggression changes the environment. The study of initial and of reciprocal effects are separable and require different experimental procedures. Both approaches are needed for a full understanding of behavior. It should also be noted that not all reciprocal processes operate at the level of direct interpersonal exchanges. Many influences impinge on people and produce cognitive changes which, in turn, affect selection and symbolic processing of subsequent influences.

It might be argued that if individuals partly create their own environments, then there is no one remaining to be influenced. One's behavior, of course, is not the sole determinant of subsequent events. As we have seen, situational constraints, the roles people occupy, and many other factors partly determine what one can or cannot do in response to the actions of others. Moreover, it is precisely because influences are altered by their reciprocal effects that unidirectional control rarely exists. Rather, counterinfluences undergo reciprocal adjustments in ongoing sequences of interaction.

The operation of reciprocal reinforcement processes in the inadvertent production of coercive conduct in children is a familiar illustration of how the interdependent influences change through successive feedback. Children's mild requests often go unheeded because the parent is disinterested or preoccupied with other matters. If further bids for attention go unrewarded, children generally intensify their behavior until it becomes aversive to the parent. At this stage in the interaction sequence the child is exercising coercive control over the parent. Eventually the parent is forced to terminate the aversive behavior by attending to the child, thereby reinforcing such behavior. The parent's reactions thus selectively train the child to use coercive techniques. Since the child gains parental attention and the parent gains temporary peace, the behavior of both participants is reinforced, although the long-term effects benefit neither.

Detrimental reciprocal systems are readily created and mutually sustained when unfavorable social practices evoke coercive behavior, which, due to its aversive properties, creates the reinforcement conditions likely to perpetuate it. Analyses of the sequential probabilities of behavior in family interactions by Patterson and his colleagues (Patterson & Cobb, 1971) reveal how family members become, through interlocking contingencies, both developers and victims of coercive relationships. This pattern is most evident in families in which the members have trained each other to use painful control techniques. Antagonistic behavior rapidly accelerates aggressive counteractions in an escaling power struggle. By escalating reciprocal aggression each member provides aversive instigation for each other, and each member is periodically reinforced for behaving coercively by overpowering the other through more painful counteractions. Harmful reciprocal systems of this sort can be converted to wholesome ones by reducing the reinforcement supporting coercive conduct and developing more constructive means of securing desired responsiveness from others (Patterson, 1975).

Reciprocal Influence and the Exercise of Self-Direction

Discussion of causal processes raises the fundamental issue of determinism and personal freedom. In examining these questions it is essential to distinguish between the metaphysical and the social aspects of freedom. Many of the disputes on this topic arise as much, if not more, from ambiguities about the dimensions of freedom being discussed as from disagreements over the doctrine of determinism.

Let us first consider freedom in the social sense. Whether freedom is an illusion, as some writers maintain, or a social reality of considerable importance depends upon the meaning given to it. Within the social learning framework, freedom is defined in terms of the number of options available to people and the right to exercise them. The more behavioral alternatives and prerogatives people have, the greater is their freedom of action.

CONSTRAINTS ON PERSONAL
FREEDOM.

Personal freedom can be limited in many different ways. Behavioral deficencies restrict one's possible choices and otherwise curtail opportunities to realize one's preferences. Freedom can therefore be fostered by cultivating competencies. In addition, self-restraints resulting from unwarranted fears and excessive self-censure restrict the range of activities that individuals can engage in or even contemplate. Here freedom is enhanced by eliminating dysfunctional self-restraints.

In maximizing freedom a society must place some limits on conduct because complete license for any individual will encroach on the freedom of others. Societal prohibitions against behavior that is socially injurious create additional curbs on conduct. There are few disagreements about placing limits on behavior that directly injures or seriously infringes on the rights of others. Conflicts often arise, however, over behavioral restrictions when many members of society question conventional customs and when legal sanctions are used more to enforce a particular brand of morality than to prohibit socially detrimental conduct.

The issue of whether individuals should be allowed to engage in activities that are self-injurious but are not detrimental to society has been debated vigorously over the years. Prohibitionists argue that it is difficult for anyone, other than a recluse, to impair him or herself without inflicting secondary harm on others. Should self-injury produce incapacities, society usually ends up bearing the costs of treatment and subsistence. Libertarians do not find such arguments sufficiently convincing to justify a specific prohibition, for some of the self-injurious activities that society approves may be as bad or worse than those it outlaws. Normative changes over time regarding private conduct tend to favor an individualistic ethic. Consequently, many of the activities that were formerly prohibited by law have now been exempted from legal sanctions.

The freedom of some groups of people is curtailed by socially condoned discrimination. Here, the alternatives available to a person are limited by skin color, sex, religion, ethnic background, or social class, regardless of capabilities. When self-determination is restricted by prejudice, those who are affected attempt to remove inequities by altering practices that compromise or temporize the professed equality values of society.

The exercise of freedom involves rights as well as options and behavioral restraints. Struggles for freedom are principally aimed at structuring societal contingencies so that certain forms of behavior are exempted from aversive control. After protective laws are built into the system, there are certain things that a society may not do to individuals who challenge conventional values or vested interests, however much it might like to. Legal prohibitions against unauthorized societal control create freedoms that are realities, not simply feelings or states of mind. Societies differ in their institutions of freedom and in the number and types of behaviors that are officially exempted from punitive control. Social systems that protect journalists from criminal sanctions for criticizing government officials, for example, are freer than those that allow authoritative power to be used to silence critics or their vehicles of expression. Societies that possess a judiciary independent of other government institutions ensure greater social freedom than those that do not.

FREEDOM AND DETERMINISM.

In philosophical discourses, freedom is often considered antithetical to determinism. When freedom is defined in terms of options and rights, there is no incompatibility between freedom and determinism. From this perspective, freedom is not conceived negatively as the absence of influences or simply the lack of external constraints. Rather, it is defined positively in terms of the skills at one's command and the exercise of self-influence which choice of action requires. Given the same environmental constraints, individuals who have many behavioral options and are adept at regulating their own behavior will experience greater freedom than will individuals whose personal resources are limited.

Psychological analyses of freedom eventually lead to discourses on the metaphysics of determinism. Are people partial determiners of their own behavior, or are they ruled exclusively by forces beyond their control? The long-standing debate over this issue has been enlivened by Skinner's (1971) contention that, apart from genetic contributions, human behavior is controlled solely by environmental contingencies (e.g., "A person does not act upon the world, the world acts upon him," p. 211). A major problem with this type of analysis is that it depicts the environment as an autonomous force that automatically shapes and controls behavior.

Environments have causes, as do behaviors. It is true that behavior is regulated by its contingencies, but the contingencies are partly of a person's own making. By their actions, people play an active role in producing the reinforcing contingencies that impinge upon them. As was previously shown, behavior partly creates the environment, and the environment influences the behavior in a reciprocal fashion. To the oft-repeated dictum, "change contingencies and you change behavior," should be added the reciprocal side, "change behavior and you change the contingencies." In the regress of prior causes, for every chicken discovered by a unidirectional environmentalist, a social learning theorist can identify a prior egg.

The image of people's efficacy that emerges from psychological research depends upon which aspect of the reciprocal influence system is selected for analysis. In the paradigm favoring *environmental determinism*, investigators analyze how environmental influences change behavior [$B = f(E)$]. The paradigm that lends itself to the study of *personal determinism* examines how behavior determines the environment

$[E = f(B)]$. Behavior is the effect in the former case, and the cause in the latter.

Social learning theory conceives of regulatory processes in terms of *reciprocal determinism* $[B \underset{\longleftarrow}{\overset{P}{\longrightarrow}} E]$. Although the reciprocal sources of influence are separable for experimental purposes, in everyday life two-way control operates concurrently. In ongoing interchanges, one and the same event can thus be a stimulus, a response, or an environmental reinforcer depending upon the place in the sequence at which the analysis arbitrarily begins. Figure 8, which represents a sequence of reactions of two persons (A and B), shows how the same actions change their status from stimuli to responses to reinforcers at varying entry points in the flow of the interaction.

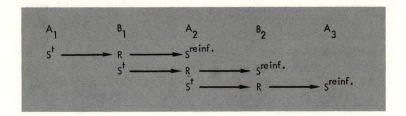

Figure 8 Illustration of how the same social behavior can be a stimulus, a response, or a reinforcer depending on where one begins the analysis in the continous flow of a social interaction. The A's are successive responses by one person, and the B's are successive responses by the second person in the dual interaction; S^t represents stimulus; R represents response; and S^{reinf} represents reinforcer.

A survey of the scope of research on causal processes confirms the heavy reliance upon a one-sided paradigm to map a bidirectional process. Environmental control is minutely analyzed, whereas personal control has been relatively neglected. To cite one example, there exist countless demonstrations of how behavior varies under different schedules of reinforcement, but one looks in vain for studies of how people succeed, either individually or by collective action, in negotiating the reinforcement schedules to their own liking. The scarcity of research on personal control is not because people exert no influence on their environment or because such efforts are without effect. Quite the contrary; behavior is one of the more influential determinants of future contingencies.

It should be noted that some theories that assign preeminent control to the environment are ultimately qualified by acknowledging that individuals exercise some measure of countercontrol (Skinner, 1971). The notion of reciprocal determinism, however, goes considerably beyond the concept of countercontrol. Countercontrol portrays the environment as an instigating force to which individuals react. As we have already seen, people activate and create environments as well as rebut them.

People may be considered partially free insofar as they can influence future conditions by managing their own behavior. Granted that selection of particular courses of action from available alternatives is itself determined, individuals can nevertheless exert some control over the factors that govern their choices. In philosophical analyses, all events can be submitted to an infinite regression of causes. Such discussions usually emphasize how people's actions are determined by prior conditions but neglect the reciprocal part of the process showing that the conditions themselves are partly determined by people's actions. Applications of self-control practices demonstrate that people are able to direct their courses of action toward valued goals by arranging the environmental conditions most likely to elicit appropriate behavior and by creating cognitive aids and self-reinforcing consequences to sustain it. Individuals may be told how to go about this process and be given some initial external support for their efforts, but that does not argue against the fact that self-produced influences contribute significantly to future goal attainment. Any account of the determinants of human behavior must therefore include self-generated influences as a contributing factor.

To contend, as environmental determinists often do, that people are controlled by external forces and then to advocate that they redesign society by applying psychotechnology undermines the basic premise of the argument. If humans were, in fact, incapable of influencing their own actions, they might describe and predict environmental events but they could hardly exercise any intentional control over them. When it comes to advocacy of social change, however, thoroughgoing environmental determinists become ardent advocates of people's power to transform environments in pursuit of a better life.

In backward causal analyses, environmental conditions are usually portrayed as ruling people, whereas forward deterministic analyses of the goals people set for themselves and their later attainments reveal how people can shape conditions for their own purposes. Some are better at it than others. The greater their foresight, proficiency, and self-influence, all of which are acquirable skills, the greater the progress toward their goals. Because of the capacity for reciprocal influence, people are at least partial architects of their own destinies. It is not determinism that is in dispute, but whether determinism should be treated as a one-way or a two-way control process. Due to the interdependence of behavior and environmental conditions, determinism does not imply the fatalistic view that individuals are only pawns of external influences.

Psychological perspectives on determinism, like other aspects of theorizing, influence the nature and scope of social practice. Environmental determinists are apt to use their methods primarily in the service of institutionally prescribed patterns of behavior. Personal determinists are more inclined to cultivate self-directing potentialities. The latter behavioral approach and humanism have much in common. Behavior theorists, however, recognize that "self-actualization" is by no means confined to human virtues. People have numerous potentialities that can be actualized for good or ill. Over the years, many have suffered considerably, and will continue to do so, at the hands of self-actualized tyrants. A self-centered ethic of self-realization must therefore be tempered by concern for the social consequences of one's conduct. Behaviorists generally emphasize environmental sources of control, whereas humanists tend to restrict their interest to personal control. Social learning encompasses both aspects of the bidirectional influence process.

When the environment is regarded as an autonomous

rather than as an influenceable determinant of behavior, valuation of dignifying human qualities and accomplishments is diminished. If inventiveness stems from external circumstances, it is environments that should be credited for people's achievements and blamed for their failings or inhumanities. Contrary to the unidirectional view, human accomplishments result from reciprocal interaction of external circumstances with a host of personal determinants, including endowed potentialities, acquired competencies, reflective thought, and a high level of self-initiative.

Composers, for example, help to shape tastes by their creative efforts, and the public in turn supports their performances until advocates of new musical styles generate new public preferences. Each succeeding form of artistry results from a similar two-way influence process for which neither artisans nor circumstances deserve sole credit.

Superior accomplishments, whatever the field, require considerable self-disciplined application. After individuals adopt evaluative standards, they spend large amounts of time, on their own, improving their performances to the point of self-satisfaction. At this level of functioning, persistence in an endeavor is extensively under self-reinforcement control. Skills are perfected as much, or more, to please oneself as to please the public.

Without self-generated influences, most innovative efforts would be difficult to sustain. This is because the unconventional is initially resisted and is accepted gradually only as it proves functionally valuable or wins prestigious advocates. As a result, the early efforts of innovators generally bring rebuffs rather than rewards or recognition. In the history of creative endeavors, it is not uncommon for artists and composers to be scorned when they depart markedly from conventional forms and styles. Some gain recognition later in their careers. Others are sufficiently convinced of the worth of their work that they labor tirelessly even though their productions are negatively received throughout their lifetimes. Ideological and, to a lesser extent, technological changes follow similar courses. While innovative endeavors may receive occasional social support in early phases, environmental conditions alone are not especially conducive to unconventional endeavors.

Reciprocal Influence and the Limits of Social Control

The operation of reciprocal influence also has bearing on the public's concern that advances in psychological knowledge will produce an increase in the calculated manipulation and control of people. A common response to such fears is that all behavior is inevitably controlled. Social influence, therefore, does not entail imposing controls where none existed before. This type of argument is valid in the sense that every act has a cause. But it is not the principle of causality that worries people. At the societal level, their misgivings center on the distribution of controlling power, the means and purposes for which it is used, and the availability of mechanisms for exercising reciprocal control over institutional practices. At the individual level, they are uneasy about the implications of psychotechnology for programming human relations.

INDIVIDUAL SAFEGUARDS

Possible remedies for exploitative use of psychological techniques are usually discussed in terms of individual safeguards. Increasing people's knowledge about modes of influence is prescribed as the best defense against such manipulation. When people are informed about how behavior can be controlled, they tend to resist evident attempts at influence, thus making manipulation more difficult. Awareness alone, however, is a weak countervalence. Most people are quite aware that advertisers attempt to influence their behavior by exaggerated claims, modeled testimonials, pseudo-experiments demonstrating the superiority of their products, paired association of events, and portrayal of benefits accruing to product users. Such knowledge does not make people immune to advertising influences. The same is true of persuasion through response consequences. Coercion can extract compliance and rewards can induce accommodating behavior, even though people recognize that the incentives are prompting their actions.

Exploitation was successfully thwarted long before the discipline of psychology existed to formulate principles and practices of behavior change. The most reliable source of opposition to manipulative control resides in the reciprocal consequences of human interactions. People resist being taken advantage of, and will continue to do so in the future, because compliant behavior produces unfavorable consequences for them. Sophisticated efforts at influence in no way reduce the aversiveness of yielding that is personally disadvantageous. Because of reciprocal consequences, no one is able to manipulate others at will, and everyone experiences some feeling of powerlessness in getting what they want. This is true at all levels of functioning, both individual and collective. Parents cannot get their children to follow all their wishes, while children feel constrained by their parents in doing what they desire. At universities, the administrators, faculty, students, and alumni each feel that the other constituencies are unduly influential in promoting their self-interests but that they themselves have insufficient power to alter the institutional practices. In the political arena, Congress feels that the executive branch possesses excessive power, and conversely the executive branch feels thwarted in implementing its policies by congressional counteraction.

SOCIAL SAFEGUARDS.

If protection against exploitation relied solely upon individual safeguards, people would be continually subjected to the most unscrupulous and coercive pressures. Accordingly, they create institutional sanctions which set limits on the control of human behavior. The integrity of individuals is largely secured by societal safeguards that place constraints on improper means and foster reciprocity through balancing of interests. This is achieved by establishing formal mechanisms for exercising reciprocal influence over organizational practices through legal systems, regulatory agencies, and due process and elective procedures. Institutional reciprocal

mechanisms not only safeguard against arbitrary or unwarranted control, they provide the means for changing institutions and the conditions of life. The limits set by law and
social rules on the degree and form of control people can
exercise over each other tends to be overlooked in discussions
of the implications of psychological knowledge.

Because individuals are conversant with psychological
techniques does not grant them license to impose them on
others. Industrialists, for example, know full well that productivity is higher when payment is made for amount of work
completed rather than for length of time at work. Nevertheless, they cannot use the reinforcement system most advantageous to them. When industrialists commanded exclusive
power, they paid workers at a piece-rate basis and hired and
fired them at will. Reductions in the disparity of power between employers and employees resulted in a gradual change
in the nature of the contingency contracts. As workers gained
coercive economic strength through collective action, they
were able to negotiate guaranteed wages on a daily, weekly,
monthly, and eventually on an annual basis. At periodic
intervals new contractual contingencies are adopted that are
mutually acceptable. In the course of time, as better means of
collective action are developed, other constituents will use
their influence to modify arrangements that benefit certain
segments of labor and industry but may adversely affect the
quality of life for other sectors of society.

As the previous example illustrates, improved knowledge
of how to influence behavior does not necessarily raise the
level of social control. If anything, recent years have wit-
nessed the diffusion of power, creating increased opportunities
for reciprocal influence. This has enabled people to challenge
social inequities, to effect changes in institutional practices,
to counteract infringements on their rights, and to extend
grievance procedures and due process of law to activities in
social contexts that hitherto operated under unilateral control. The fact that more people wield power does not in and of
itself ensure a humane society. In the final analysis, the
important consideration is the purposes that power serves,
however it might be distributed. Nor does knowledge about
means of psychological influence necessarily produce me-

chanical responsiveness in personal relations. Whatever their orientations, people model, expound, and reinforce what they value. Behavior arising out of purpose and commitment is no less genuine than improvised action.

Novels depicting authoritarian systems and utopian societies based on behavioral principles generate public fears that a particular mode of life may be imposed on everyone. Advocates of utopian societies prescribe the lifestyles they like. Since personal preferences differ widely, most people question the values reflected either in specific prescriptions of a particular utopia or in the value orientation of the whole design. Even those who regard the guiding values as acceptable, nevertheless express concern over the homogenization of life within a single social arrangement. Others fear that should the instruments of influence fall into the wrong hands, they could be used to engineer public consent for authoritarian rule or benevolent despotism. What is intended as a visionary process for an experimenting society, thus becomes a frightening prospect.

When only a single form of utopian social living is presented as founded on behavioral principles, as in *Walden Two* (Skinner, 1948), the general techniques for developing better social systems get confounded with the particular brand of lifestyle that is promulgated. As a result, procedures for achieving human ideals are repudiated because the advocated mode of life may be uninviting. Principles can be separated from social practices by providing alternative types of social living founded on the same behavioral principles. Under pluralistic arrangements, people have options as to the lifestyles they wish to pursue. Those who do not find a particular form of life to their liking can try other forms. Wholesale manipulation is difficult to achieve because the value preferences and networks of influences differ across groups. Given the appropriate value commitments, social learning principles can be used effectively to cultivate diversity.

The cliché of the futuristic nightmare of Orwell's *1984* and its more recent kin diverts public attention from less sensational regulative influences that pose continual threats to human welfare. Most societies have instituted reciprocal systems that are protected by rules of law or social regulations to prohibit such imperious control of human behavior. Although abuses of institutional power arise from time to time, it is not totalitarian rule that constitutes the impending peril. The hazards lie more in the intentional pursuit of personal gain, whether material or otherwise, than in control by coercion. Detrimental social practices occur and resist change, even within an open society, when many people benefit from them. To take a prevalent example, inequitable treatment of disadvantaged groups for private gain can enjoy public support without requiring despotic rule.

People, of course, have more to contend with than inhumane treatment at the hands of others. When the aversive consequences of otherwise rewarding lifestyles are delayed and accumulate imperceptibly, people can become willful agents of their own self-destruction. Thus, if enough people benefit from activities that progressively degrade their environment, then, barring contravening influences, they will eventually destroy their environment.

With growing populations and the spread of lifestyles emphasizing material consumption, both of which tax finite resources, people will have to learn to cope with new realities of existence. Widespread pursuit of activities that maximize personal rewards can produce harmful consequences that must be borne by all. These new realities will require a greater consideration of, and a heightened sense of responsibility for, the social consequences of one's behavior. Pressures will mount to subordinate individual choices to collective interests. The challenge ahead is the development of social practices which promote the common good in ways that still preserve the greatest possible individual freedom.

Modification of common practices that are immediately rewarding but detrimental in the long run does not necessarily require curtailing freedom of choice. Behavior is modified far more effectively by providing better alternatives than by imposing prohibitions. Birth rates, for example, have been substantially reduced through economic development, public enlightenment about the perils of overpopulation, family planning and the development of birth control devices—without resorting to the restriction of sexual activities or the imposition of breeding quotas. In this case, broader societal interests coincide with individual ones. In other instances, detrimental practices would also be rapidly discarded in favor of beneficial ones if their development were not resisted by vested interests. Heavy reliance on polluting automobiles, which also consume large quantities of materials, could be diminished faster by providing convenient and economical rapid-transit systems than by continuing to produce millions of automobiles yearly, constructing more freeways, and then increasing the costs and aversiveness of driving cars. Because large numbers of people benefit financially, either directly or indirectly, from the profusion of automobiles, the restriction of choice to alternatives that produce detrimental effects secures wide public support.

These are but a few examples of how collective survival practices are best promoted by expanding rather than curtailing individual choice. Change is achieved most rapidly both by providing advantageous options and by raising the costs of traditional practices that produce adverse delayed consequences. When alternative means of obtaining benefits are lacking, people are slow to abandon behavior that operates against their long-term welfare, even in the face of mounting negative consequences.

Psychology cannot tell people how they ought to live their lives. It can, however, provide them with the means for effecting personal and social change. And it can aid them in making value choices by assessing the consequences of alternative lifestyles and institutional arrangements. As a science concerned with the social consequences of its applications, psychology must promote public understanding of psychological issues that bear on social policies to ensure that its findings are used in the service of human betterment.

References

Allen, M. K., & Liebert, R. M. "Effects of Live and Symbolic Deviant Modeling Cues on Adoption of a Previously Learned Standard." *Journal of Personality and Social Psychology*, 1969, 11:253-260.

Aronfreed, J. "The Origin of Self-Criticism." *Psychological Review*, 1964, 71:193-218.

Ayllon, T., & Haughton, E. "Control of the Behavior of Schizophrenic Patients by Food." *Journal of the Experimental Analysis of Behavior*, 1962, 5:343-352.

Baer, D. M., & Sherman, J. A. "Reinforcement Control of Generalized Imitation in Young Children." *Journal of Experimental Child Psychology*, 1964, 1:37-49.

Baer, D. M., & Wolf, M. M. "The Entry into Natural Communities of Reinforcement." Paper presented at the American Psychological Association Meeting, Washington, D.C., September 1967.

Baker, N. "The Influence of Some Task and Organismic Variables on the Manifestation of Conservation of Number." Unpublished master's thesis, University of Toronto, 1967.

Baldwin, A. L., & Baldwin, C. P. "The Study of Mother-Child Interaction." *American Scientist*, 1973, 61:714-721.

Bandura, A. "Influence of Models' Reinforcement Contingencies on the Acquisition of Imitative Responses." *Journal of Personality and Social Psychology*, 1965, 1:589-595.

Bandura, A. *Principles of Behavior Modification.* New York: Holt, Rinehart & Winston, 1969.

Bandura A. (Ed.), *Psychological Modeling: Conflicting Theories.* Chicago: Aldine-Atherton, 1971a.

Bandura, A. "Vicarious and Self-Reinforcement Processes." In R. Glaser (Ed.), *The Nature of Reinforcement.* New York: Academic Press, 1971b.

Bandura, A. *Aggression: A Social Learning Analysis.* Englewood Cliffs, N.J.: Prentice-Hall, 1973.

Bandura, A. "Effecting Change Through Participant Modeling." In J. D. Krumboltz & C. E. Thoresen (Eds.), *Counseling Methods.* New York: Holt, Rinehart & Winston, 1976a.

Bandura, A. "Self-Efficiency: Toward a Unifying Theory of Behavioral Change." *Psychological Review,* 1977, 84:191-215.

Bandura, A. "Self-Reinforcement: Theoretical and Methodological Considerations." *Behaviorism,* 1976b, 4:135-155.

Bandura, A., Adams, N. E., & Beyer, J. "Cognitive Processes Mediating Behavioral Change." *Journal of Personality and Social Psychology,* 1977, 35:125-139.

Bandura, A., & Barab, P. G. "Conditions Governing Nonreinforced Imitation." *Developmental Psychology,* 1971, 5:244-255.

Bandura, A., & Barab, P. G. "Processes Governing Disinhibitory Effects Through Symbolic Modeling." *Journal of Abnormal Psychology,* 1973, 82:1-9.

Bandura, A., Blanchard, E. B., & Ritter, B. "The Relative Efficacy of Desensitization and Modeling Approaches for Inducing Behavioral, Affective, and Attitudinal Changes." *Journal of Personality and Social Psychology,* 1969, 13:173-199.

Bandura, A., Grusec, J. E., & Menlove, F. L. "Observational Learning as a Function of Symbolization and Incentive Set." *Child Development,* 1966, 37:499-506.

Bandura, A., Grusec, J. E., & Menlove, F. L. "Some Social Determinants of Self-Monitoring Reinforcement Systems." *Journal of Personality and Social Psychology,* 1967, 5:449-455.

Bandura, A., & Jeffery, R. W. "Role of Symbolic Coding and Rehearsal Processes in Observational Learning." *Journal of Personality and Social Psychology,* 1973, 26:122-130.

Bandura, A., Jeffery, R., & Bachicha, D. L. "Analysis of Memory Codes and Cumulative Rehearsal in Observational Learning." *Journal of Research in Personality,* 1974, 7:295-305.

Bandura, A., & Kupers, C. J. "The Transmission of Patterns of Self-Reinforcement through Modeling." *Journal of Abnormal and Social Psychology,* 1964, 69:1-9.

Bandura, A., Lipsher, D. H., & Miller, P. E. "Psychotherapists' Approach-Avoidance Reactions to Patient's Expressions of Hostility." *Journal of Consulting Psychology*, 1960, 24:1-8.

Bandura, A., & Mahoney, M. J. "Maintenance and Transfer of Self-Reinforcement Functions." *Behaviour Research and Therapy*, 1974, 12:89-97.

Bandura, A., Mahoney, M. J., & Dirks, S. J. "Discriminative Activation and Maintenance of Contingent Self-Reinforcement." *Behaviour Research and Therapy*, 1976, 14:1-6.

Bandura, A., & McDonald, F. J. "The Influence of Social Reinforcement and the Behavior of Models in Shaping Children's Moral Judgments." *Journal of Abnormal and Social Psychology*, 1963, 67:274-281.

Bandura, A., & Menlove, F. L. "Factors Determining Vicarious Extinction of Avoidance Behavior through Symbolic Modeling." *Journal of Personality and Social Psychology*, 1968, 8:99-108.

Bandura, A., & Perloff, B. "Relative Efficacy of Self-Monitored and Externally-Imposed Reinforcement Systems." *Journal of Personality and Social Psychology*, 1967, 7:111-116.

Bandura, A., & Rosenthal, T. L. "Vicarious Classical Conditioning as a Function of Arousal Level." *Journal of Personality and Social Psychology*, 1966, 3:54-62.

Bandura, A., Ross, D., & Ross, S. A. "A Comparative Test of the Status Envy, Social Power, and Secondary Reinforcement Theories of Identificatory Learning." *Journal of Abnormal and Social Psychology*, 1963, 67:527-534.

Bandura, A., Underwood, B., & Fromson, M. E. "Disinhibition of Aggression through Diffusion of Responsibility and Dehumanization of Victims." *Journal of Research in Personality*, 1975, 9: 253-269.

Bandura, A., & Walters, R. H. *Adolescent Aggression*. New York: Ronald Press, 1959.

Bandura, A., & Whalen, C. K. "The Influence of Antecedent Reinforcement and Divergent Modeling Cues on Patterns of Self-Reward." *Journal of Personality and Social Psychology*, 1966, 3:373-382.

Barber, T. X., & Hahn, K. W., Jr. "Experimental Studies in 'Hypnotic' Behavior: Physiological and Subjective Effects of Imagined Pain." *Journal of Nervous and Mental Disease*, 1964, 139:416-425.

Barnwell, A. K. "Potency of Modeling Cues in Imitation and Vicarious Reinforcement Activities." *Dissertation Abstracts*, 1966, 26: 7444.

Baron, A., Kaufman, A., & Stauber, K. A. "Effects of Instructions and Reinforcement-Feedback on Human Operant Behavior Maintained by Fixed-interval Reinforcement." *Journal of the Experimental Analysis of Behavior*, 1969, 12:701-712.

Bateson, G. (Ed.), *Perceval's Narrative: A Patient's Account of His Psychosis, 1830-1832*. Stanford, Calif.: Stanford University Press, 1961.

Baum, W. M. "The Correlation-based Law of Effect." *Journal of the Experimental Analysis of Behavior*, 1973, 20:137-153.

Bem, D. J. "Self-Perception Theory." In L. Berkowitz (Ed.), *Advances in Experimental Social Psychology*. Vol. 6. New York: Academic Press, 1972.

Bem, D. J., & Allen, A. "On Predicting Some of the People Some of the Time: The Search for Cross-situational Consistencies in Behavior." *Psychological Review*, 1974, 81:506-520.

Benton, A. A. "Effects of the Timing of Negative Response Consequences on the Observational Learning of Resistance to Temptation in Children." *Dissertation Abstracts*, 1967, 27:2153-2154.

Berger, S. M. "Incidental Learning Through Vicarious Reinforcement." *Psychological Reports*, 1961, 9:477-491.

Berger, S. M. "Conditioning through Vicarious Instigation." *Psychological Review*, 1962, 69:450-466.

Berger, S. M. "Observer Perseverance as Related to a Model's Success." *Journal of Personality and Social Psychology*, 1971, 19:341-350.

Berkowitz, L. "Words and Symbols as Stimuli to Aggressive Responses." In J. F. Knutson (Ed.), *The Control of Aggression: Implications from Basic Research*. Chicago: Aldine, 1973.

Blanchard, E. B. "The Relative Contributions of Modeling, Informational Influences, and Physical Contact in the Extinction of Phobic Behavior." *Journal of Abnormal Psychology*, 1970a, 76: 55-61.

Blanchard, E. B. "The Generalization of Vicarious Extinction Effects." *Behavior Research and Therapy*, 1970b, 8:323-330.

Blanchard, E. B., & Young, L. B. "Self-Control of Cardiac Functioning: A Promise as Yet Unfulfilled." *Psychological Bulletin*, 1973, 79:145-163.

Bloom, L., Hood, L., & Lightbown, P. "Imitation in Language Development: If, When, and Why." *Cognitive Psychology*, 1974, 6:380-420.

Bolles, R. C. "The Avoidance Learning Problem." In G. H. Bower

(Ed.), *The Psychology of Learning and Motivation* (Vol. 6). New York: Academic Press, 1972.

Bolles, R. C. *Theory of Motivation* (2nd ed.). New York: Harper & Row, 1975.

Bolstad, O. D., & Johnson, S. M. "Self-regulation in the Modification of Disruptive Behavior." *Journal of Applied Behavior Analysis*, 1972, 5:443-454.

Borden, B. L., & White, G. M. "Some Effects of Observing a Model's Reinforcement Schedule and Rate of Responding on Extinction and Response Rate." *Journal of Experimental Psychology*, 1973, 97:41-45.

Borkovec, T. D. "The Role of Expectancy and Physiological Feedback in Fear Research: A Review with Special Reference to Subject Characteristics." *Behavior Therapy*, 1973, 4:491-505.

Bowers, K. S. "Situationism in Psychology: An Analysis and a Critique." *Psychological Review*, 1973, 80:307-336.

Boyd, L. M. "Most Disappointed Men in the World." *San Francisco Chronicle*, March 15, 1969.

Brainerd, C. J. "Learning Research and Piagetian Theory." In L. S. Siegel & C. J. Brainerd (Eds.), *Alternatives to Piaget—Critical Essays on the Theory*. Hillsdale, N.J.: Erlbaum, 1976, in press.

Bridger, W. H., & Mandel, I. J. "A Comparison of GSR Fear Responses Produced by Threat and Electric Shock." *Journal of Psychiatric Research*, 1964, 2:31-40.

Bronfenbrenner, U. *Two Worlds of Childhood: U.S. and U.S.S.R.* New York: Russell Sage Foundation, 1970.

Brown, I. "Modeling Processes and Language Acquisition: The Role of Referents." *Journal of Experimental Child Psychology*, 1976, 22:185-199.

Bruning, J. L. "Direct and Vicarious Effects of a Shift in Magnitude of Reward on Performance." *Journal of Personality and Social Psychology*, 1965, 2:278-282.

Bryan, J. H., & Walbek, N. H. "Preaching and Practicing Generosity: Some Determinants of Sharing in Children." *Child Development*, 1970, 41:329-354.

Buchwald, A. M. "Experimental Alterations in the Effectiveness of Verbal Reinforcement Combinations." *Journal of Experimental Psychology*, 1959, 57:351-361.

Buchwald, A. M. "Effects of 'Right' and 'Wrong' on Subsequent Behavior: A New Interpretation." *Psychological Review*, 1969, 76: 132-145.

Budzynski, T., Stoyva, J., & Adler, C. "Feedback-induced Muscle

Relaxation: Application to Tension Headache." *Journal of Behavior Therapy and Experimental Psychiatry*, 1970, 1:205-211.

Calder, B. J., & Straw, B. M. "Self-Perception of Intrinsic and Extrinsic Motivation." *Journal of Personality and Social Psychology*, 1975, 31:599-605.

Chandler, M. J., Greenspan, S., & Barenboim, C. "Judgments of Intentionality in Response to Videotaped and Verbally Presented Moral Dilemmas: The Medium is the Message." *Child Development*, 1973, 44:315-320.

Chatterjee, B. B., & Eriksen, C. W. "Cognitive Factors in Heart Rate Conditioning." *Journal of Experimental Psychology*, 1962, 64: 272-279.

Church, R. M. "Emotional Reactions of Rats to the Pain of Others." *Journal of Comparative and Physiological Psychology*, 1959, 52: 132-134.

Coates, B., & Hartup, W. W. "Age and Verbalization in Observational Learning." *Developmental Psychology*, 1969, 1:556-562.

Craig, K. D., & Weinstein, M. S. "Conditioning Vicarious Affective Arousal," *Psychological Reports*, 1965, 17:955-963.

Crooks, J. L. "Observational Learning of Fear in Monkeys." Unpublished manuscript, University of Pennsylvania, 1967.

Dawson, M. E. "Comparison of Classical Conditioning and Relational Learning." Unpublished master's thesis, University of Southern California, 1966.

Dawson, M. E., & Furedy, J. J. "The Role of Awareness in Human Differential Autonomic Classical Conditioning: The Necessary-gate Hypothesis." *Psychophysiology*, 1976, 13:50-53.

Debus, R. L. "Observational Learning of Reflective Strategies by Impulsive Children." Unpublished manuscript, University of Sydney, 1976.

Deci, E. L. *Intrinsic Motivation.* New York: Plenum, 1975.

Dekker, E., & Groen, J. "Reproducible Psychogenic Attacks of Asthma: A Laboratory Study." *Journal of Psychosomatic Research*, 1956, 1:58-67.

Dekker, E., Pelser, H. E., & Groen, J. "Conditioning as a Cause of Asthmatic Attacks." *Journal of Psychosomatic Research*, 1957, 2:97-108.

Ditrichs, R., Simon, S., & Greene, B. "Effect of Vicarious Scheduling on the Verbal Conditioning of Hostility in Children." *Journal of Personality and Social Psychology*, 1967, 6:71-78.

Drabman, R. S., Spitalnik, R., & O'Leary, K. D. "Teaching Self-

Control to Disruptive Children." *Journal of Abnormal Psychology*, 1973, 82:10-16.

Dulany, D. E. "Awareness, Rules, and Propositional Control: A Confrontation with S-R Behavior Theory." In T. R. Dixon & D. L. Horton (Eds.), *Verbal Behavior and General Behavior Theory*, Englewood Cliffs, N.J.: Prentice-Hall, 1968.

Dulany, D. E., & O'Connell, D. C. "Does Partial Reinforcement Dissociate Verbal Rules and the Behavior They Might Be Presumed to Control?" *Journal of Verbal Learning and Verbal Behavior*, 1963, 2:361-372.

Ellis, A. *Reason and Emotion in Psychotherapy*. New York: Stuart, 1962.

Endler, N. S., & Magnusson, D. (Eds.) *Interactional Psychology and Personality*. Washington, D.C.: Hemisphere, 1975.

Eriksen, C. W., & Kuethe, J. L. "Avoidance Conditioning of Verbal Behavior Without Awareness: A Paradigm of Repression." *Journal of Abnormal and Social Psychology*, 1956, 53:203-209.

Estes, W. K. "Reinforcement in Human Behavior." *American Scientist*, 1972, 60:723-729.

Feingold, B. D., & Mahoney, M. J. "Reinforcing Effects on Intrinsic Interest: Undermining the Overjustification Hypothesis." *Behavior Therapy*, 1975, 6:367-377.

Felixbrod, J. J., & O'Leary, K. D. "Self-Determination of Academic Standards by Children." *Journal of Educational Psychology*, 1974, 66:845-850.

Flanders, J. P. "A Review of Research on Imitative Behavior." *Psychological Bulletin*, 1968, 69:316-337.

Fuchs, C., & Rehm, L. P. "The Treatment of Depression through the Modification of Self-control Behaviors." Unpublished manuscript, University of Pittsburgh, 1975.

Gale, E. N., & Jacobson, M. B. "The Relationship between Social Comments as Unconditioned Stimuli and Fear Responding." *Behaviour Research and Therapy*, 1970, 8:301-307.

Gardner, R. A., & Gardner, B. T. "Teaching Sign Language to a Chimpanzee." *Science*, 1969, 165:664-672.

Geer, J. H. "A Test of the Classical Conditioning Model of Emotion: The Use of Nonpainful Aversive Stimuli as Unconditioned Stimuli in a Conditioning Procedure." *Journal of Personality and Social Psychology*, 1968, 10:148-156.

Gerbner, G., & Gross, L. "Living with Television: The Violence Profile." *Journal of Communication*, 1976, 26:173-199.

Gerst, M. S. "Symbolic Coding Processes in Observational

Learning." *Journal of Personality and Social Psychology*, 1971, 19:7-17.

Gewirtz, J. L., & Stingle, K. G. "Learning of Generalized Imitation as the Basis for Identification." *Psychological Review*, 1968, 75: 374-397.

Glynn, E. L. "Classroom Applications of Self-Determined Reinforcement." *Journal of Applied Behavior Analysis*, 1970, 3:123-132.

Goldfried, M. R., & Merbaum, M. (Eds.), *Behavior Change through Self-Control*. New York: Holt, Rinehart & Winston, 1973.

Gray, V. "Innovation in the States: A Diffusion Study." *American Political Science Review*, 1973, 4:1174-1185.

Greene, D. Immediate and Subsequent Effects of Differential Reward Systems on Intrinsic Motivation in Public School Classrooms. Unpublished doctoral dissertation, Stanford University, 1974.

Grings, W. W. "The Role of Consciousness and Cognition in Autonomic Behavior Change." In F. J. McGuigan and R. Schoonover (Eds.), *The Psychophysiology of Thinking*. New York: Academic Press, 1973.

Grose, R. F. "A Comparison of Vocal and Subvocal Conditioning of the Galvanic Skin Response." Unpublished doctoral dissertation, Yale University, 1952.

Gutkin, D. C. "The Effect of Systematic Story Changes on Intentionality in Children's Moral Judgments," *Child Development*, 1972, 43:187-195.

Harris, F. R., Wolfe, M. M., & Baer, D. M. "Effects of Adult Social Reinforcement on Child Behavior." *Young Children*, 1964, 20:8-17.

Harris, M. B., & Evans, R. C. "Models and Creativity." *Psychological Reports*, 1973, 33:763-769.

Hart, B. M., & Risley, T. R. "Establishing Use of Descriptive Adjectives in the Spontaneous Speech of Disadvantaged Preschool Children." *Journal of Applied Behavior Analysis*, 1968, 1:109-120.

Hastorf, A. H. "The 'Reinforcement' of Individual Actions in a Group Situation." In L. Krasner & L. P. Ullmann (Eds.), *Research in Behavior Modification*. New York: Holt, Rinehart & Winston, 1965.

Hatano, G. "Subjective and Objective Cues in Moral Judgment." *Japanese Psychological Research*, 1970, 12:96-106.

Hayes, K. J., & Hayes, C. "Imitation in a Home-raised Chimpanzee." *Journal of Comparative and Physiological Psychology*, 1952, 45:450-459.

Hefferline, R. F., Bruno, L. J. J., & Davidowitz, J. E. "Feedback

Control of Covert Behaviour." In K. Connolly (Ed.), *Mechanisms of Motor Skill Development*. New York: Academic Press, 1970.

Herbert, E. W., Gelfand, D. M., & Hartmann, D. P. "Imitation and Self-Esteem as Determinants of Self-Critical Behavior." *Child Development*, 1969, 40:421-430.

Hernandez-Peon, R., Scherrer, H., & Jouvet, M. "Modification of Electric Activity in Cochlear Nucleus during 'Attention' in Unanesthetized Cats." *Science*, 1956, 23:331-332.

Herrnstein, R. J. "Method and Theory in the Study of Avoidance." *Psychological Review*, 1969, 76:49-69.

Hicks, D. J. "Girls' Attitudes toward Modeled Behaviors and the Content of Imitative Private Play." *Child Development*, 1971, 42:139-147.

Hildebrant, D. E., Feldman, S. E., & Ditrichs, R. A. "Rules, Models, and Self-reinforcement in Children." *Journal of Personality and Social Psychology*, 1973, 25:1-5.

Hillix, W. A., & Marx, M. H. "Response Strengthening by Information and Effect on Human Learning." *Journal of Experimental Psychology*, 1960, 60:97-102.

Hinde, R. A., & Hinde-Stevenson, J. *Constraints on Learning*. New York: Academic Press, 1973.

Horn, G. "Electrical Activity of the Cerebral Cortex of the Unanesthetized Cat during Attentive Behavior." *Brain*, 1960, 83:57-76.

Hughes, C., Tremblay, M., Rapoport, R. N., & Leighton, A. H. *People of Cove and Woodlot: Communities from the Viewpoint of Social Psychiatry*. New York: Basic Books, 1960.

Jackson, B. "Treatment of Depression by Self-Reinforcement." *Behavior Therapy*, 1972, 3:298-307.

Jeffery, R. W. "The Influence of Symbolic and Motor Rehearsal on Observational Learning." *Journal of Research In Personality*, 1976, 10:116-127.

Jeffrey, D. B. "A Comparison of the Effects of External Control and Self-Control on the Modification and Maintenance of Weight." *Journal of Abnormal Psychology*, 1974, 83:404-410.

Kanfer, K. H., & Marston, A. R. "Determinants of Self-Reinforcement in Human Learning." *Journal of Experimental Psychology*, 1963, 66:245-254.

Kaufman, A., Baron, A., & Kopp, R. E. "Some Effects of Instructions on Human Operant Behavior." *Psychonomic Monograph Supplements*, 1966, 1:243-250.

Kaye, K. "Learning by Imitation in Infants and Young Children."

Paper presented at the meeting of the Society for Research in Child Development, Minneapolis, 1971.

Kazdin, A. E. "Covert Modeling, Model Similarity, and Reduction of Avoidance Behavior." *Behavior Therapy*, 1974a, 5:325-340.

Kazdin, A. E. "Comparative Effects of Some Variations of Covert Modeling." *Journal of Behavior Therapy and Experimental Psychiatry*, 1974b, 5:225-232.

Kazdin, A. E. "Effects of Covert Modeling and Reinforcement on Assertive Behavior." *Journal of Abnormal Psychology*, 1974c, 83:240-252.

Kazdin, A. E. "Covert Modeling, Imagery Assessment, and Assertive Behavior." *Journal of Consulting and Clinical Psychology*, 1975, 43:716-724.

Kelman, H. C. "Violence Without Moral Restraint: Reflections on the Dehumanization of Victims and Victimizers." *Journal of Social Issues*, 1973, 29:25-61.

Kemp, J. C., & Dale, P. S. "Spontaneous Imitations and Free Speech: A Grammatical Comparison." Unpublished manuscript, Florida State University, 1973.

Kennedy, T. D. "Verbal Conditioning Without Awareness: The Use of Programmed Reinforcement and Recurring Assessment of Awareness." *Journal of Experimental Psychology*, 1970, 84:484-494.

Kennedy, T. D. "Reinforcement Frequency, Task Characteristics, and Interval of Awareness Assessment as Factors in Verbal Conditioning Without Awareness." *Journal of Experimental Psychology*, 1971, 88:103-112.

Kohlberg, L. "Stage and Sequence: The Cognitive-Developmental Approach to Socialization." In D. A. Goslin (Ed.), *Handbook of Socialization Theory and Research*. Chicago: Rand McNally, 1969.

Krane, R. V., & Wagner, A. R. "Taste Aversion Learning with a Delayed Shock US: Implications for the 'Generality of the Laws of Learning.'" *Journal of Comparative and Physiological Psychology*, 1975, 88:882-889.

Kruglanski, A. W. "The Endogenous-Eogenous Partition in Attribution Theory." *Psychological Review*, 1975, 82:387-406.

Kurtines, W., & Greif, E. B. "The Development of Moral Thought: Review and Evaluation of Kohlberg's Approach." *Psychological Bulletin*, 1974, 8:453-470.

Lefkowitz, M.; Blake, R. R.; & Mouton, J. S. "Status Factors in Pedestrian Violation of Traffic Signals." *Journal of Abnormal and Social Psychology*, 1955, 51:704-705.

Lepper, M. R., & Greene, D. "Turning Play into Work: Effects of Adult Surveillance and Extrinsic Rewards on Children's Intrinsic Motivation." *Journal of Personality and Social Psychology*, 1975, 31:479-486.

Lepper, M. R., Greene, D., & Nisbett, R. E. "Undermining Children's Intrinsic Interest with Extrinsic Reward: A Test of the 'Overjustification' Hypothesis." *Journal of Personality and Social Psychology*, 1973, 28:129-137.

Lepper, M. R., Sagotsky, J., & Mailer, J. "Generalization and Persistence of Effects of Exposure to Self-Reinforcement Models." *Child Development*, 1975, 46:618-630.

Leventhal, H. "Findings and Theory in the Study of Fear Communications." In L. Berkowitz (Ed.), *Advances in Experimental Social Psychology*. New York: Academic Press, 1970.

Lidz, T., Cornelison, A., Terry, D., & Fleck, S. "Intrafamilial Environment of the Schizophrenic Patient; VI: The Transmission of Irrationality." *AMA Archives of Neurology and Psychiatry*, 1958, 79:305-316.

Liebert, R. M., Neale, J. M., & Davidson, E. S. *The Early Window: Effects of Television on Children and Youth."* New York: Pergamon Press, 1973.

Lippitt, R. R., Polansky, N., & Rosen, S. "The Dynamics of Power." *Human Relations*, 1952, 5:37-64.

Locke, E. A. "Toward a Theory of Task Motivation and Incentives." *Organizational Behavior and Human Performance*, 1968, 3:157-189.

Locke, E. A., Cartledge, N., & Knerr, C. S. "Studies of the Relationship between Satisfaction, Goal Setting, and Performance." *Organizational Behavior and Human Performance*, 1970, 5:135-158.

Loeb, A., Beck, A. T., Diggory, J. C., & Tuthill, R. "Expectancy, Level of Aspiration, Performance, and Self-Evaluation in Depression." *Proceedings of the 75th Annual Convention of the American Psychological Association*, 1967, 2:193-194.

Lovaas, O. I. "A Behavior Therapy Approach to the Treatment of Childhood Schizophrenia." In J. P. Hill (Ed.), *Minnesota Symposia on Child Psychology* (Vol. 1). Minneapolis: University of Minnesota Press, 1967.

Luria, A. *The Role of Speech in the Regulation of Normal and Abnormal Behavior*. New York: Liveright, 1961.

McArthur, L. Z., & Eisen, S. V. "Achievements of Male and Female

Storybook Characters as Determinants of Achievement Behavior by Boys and Girls." *Journal of Personality and Social Psychology,* 1976, 33:476-473.

Mahoney, M. J. *Cognition and Behavior Modification.* Cambridge, Mass.: Ballinger, 1974.

Mahoney, M. J., & Bandura, A. "Self-Reinforcement in Pigeons." *Learning and Motivation,* 1972, 3:293-303.

Mahoney, M. J., & Thoresen, C. E. *Self-control: Power to the Person.* Monterey, Calif: Brooks/Cole, 1974.

Mann, M. E., & Van Wagenen, R. K. "Alteration of Joint Mother-Child Linguistic Styles, Involving Procedures of Extension, Elaboration, and Reinforcement." Paper presented at the biennial meeting of the Society for Research in Child Development, Denver, April 1975.

Marks, I. M., & Gelder, M. G. "Transvestism and Fetishism: Clinical and Psychological Changes during Faradic Aversion." *British Journal of Psychiatry,* 1967, 113:711-729.

Marmor, J. "Psychoanalytic Therapy as an Educational Process: Common Denominators in the Therapeutic Approaches of Different Psychoanalytic 'Schools.' " In J. H. Masserman (Ed.), *Science and Psychoanalysis* (Vol. 5, *Psychoanalytic Education*). New York: Grune & Stratton, 1962.

Marston, A. R. "Imitation, Self-Reinforcement, and Reinforcement of Another Person." *Journal of Personality and Social Psychology,* 1965, 2:255-261.

Martin, M., Burkholder, R., Rosenthal, T. L., Tharp, R. G.; & Thorne, G. L. "Programming Behavior Change and Reintegration into School Milieu of Extreme Adolescent Deviates," *Behaviour Research and Therapy,* 1968, 6:371-383.

McDavid, J. W. "Effects of Ambiguity of Imitative Cues upon Learning by Observation." *Journal of Social Psychology,* 1964, 62:-165-174.

McGuire, R. J., Carlisle, J. M., & Young, B. G. "Sexual Deviations as Conditioned Behavior: A Hypothesis." *Behaviour Research and Therapy,* 1965, 2:185-190.

McLaughlin, T. F., & Malaby, J. E. "Increasing and Maintaining Assignment Completion with Teacher and Pupil Controlled Individual Contingency Programs: Three Case Studies." *Psychology,* 1974, 2:1-7.

McMains, M. J., & Liebert, R. M. "Influence of Discrepancies between Successively Modeled Self-Reward Criteria on the Adoption of a Self-Imposed Standard." *Journal of Personality and Social Psychology,* 1968, 8:166-171.

Meichenbaum, D. H. "Examination of Model Characteristics in Reducing Avoidance Behavior." *Journal of Personality and Social Psychology,* 1971, 17:298-307.

Meichenbaum, D. H. *Cognitive Behavior Modification.* Morristown, N.J.: General Learning Press, 1974.

Michael, D. N., & Maccoby, N. "Factors Influencing the Effects of Student Participation on Verbal Learning from Films: Motivating versus Practice Effects, 'Feedback,' and Overt versus Covert Responding." In A. A. Lumsdaine (Ed.), *Student Response in Programmed Instruction.* Washington, D.C.: National Academy of Sciences—National Research Council, 1961.

Milgram, S. *Obedience to Authority: An Experimental View.* New York: Harper & Row, 1974.

Miller, N. E. "Learnable Drives and Rewards." In S. S. Stevens (Ed.), *Handbook of Experimental Psychology.* New York: Wiley, 1951.

Miller, N. E. "Learning of Visceral and Glandular Responses." *Science,* 1969, 163:434-445.

Miller, N. E., & Dollard, J. *Social Learning and Imitation.* New Haven: Yale University Press, 1941.

Mischel, W. *Personality and Assessment.* New York: Wiley, 1968.

Mischel, W. "Toward a Cognitive Social Learning Reconceptualization of Personality." *Psychological Review,* 1973, 80:252-283.

Mischel, W., & Liebert, R. M. "Effects of Discrepancies between Observed and Imposed Reward Criteria on Their Acquisition and Transmission." *Journal of Personality and Social Psychology,* 1966, 3:45-53.

Moerk, E. L. "Changes in Verbal Mother-Child Interactions with Increasing Language Skills of the Child." *Journal of Psycholinguistic Research,* 1974, 3:101-116.

Moerk, E. L. "Processes of Language Teaching and Language Learning in the Interactions of Mother-Child Dyads." *Child Development,* 1976, 47:1064-1078.

Moeser, S. D., & Bregman, A. S. "Imagery and Language Acquisition." *Journal of Verbal Learning and Verbal Behavior,* 1973, 12:91-98.

Moser, D. "Screams, Slaps, and Love." *Life,* May 7, 1965, 90A-101.

Murray, E. J. "A Content-analysis Method for Studying Psychotherapy." *Psychological Monographs*, 1956, 70(13), whole no. 420.

Nisbett, R. E., & Valins, S. *Perceiving the Causes of One's Own Behavior*. Morristown, N.J.: General Learning Press, 1971.

Olman, A., Erixon, G., & Lofberg, I. "Phobias and Preparedness: Phobic versus Neutral Pictures as Conditioned Stimuli for Human Autonomic Responses." *Journal of Abnormal Psychology*, 1975, 84:41-45.

Ormiston, L. H. "Factors Determining Response to Modeled Hypocrisy." Unpublished doctoral dissertation, Stanford University, 1972.

Packer, H. L. *The Limits of the Criminal Sanction*. Stanford, Calif: Stanford University Press, 1968.

Parker, E. P. "Information Utilities and Mass Communication." In H. Sackman & N. Nie (Eds.), *Information Utility and Social Choice*. AFIPS Press, Montvale, N.J., 1970.

Patterson, G. R. "The Aggressive Child: Victim and Architect of a Coercive System." In L. A. Hamerlynck, E. J. Mash, & L. C. Handy (Eds.), *Behavior Modification and Families*. New York: Brunner/Mazell, 1975.

Patterson, G. R., & Cobb, J. A. "A Dyadic Analysis of 'Aggressive' Behavior." In J. P. Hill (Ed.), *Minnesota Symposia on Child Psychology* (Vol. 5). Minneapolis: University of Minnesota Press, 1971.

Peterson, D. R. *The Clinical Study of Social Behavior*. Englewood Cliffs, N.J.: Prentice-Hall, Inc., 1968.

Piaget, J. *The Moral Judgment of the Child*. Glencoe, Ill.: Free Press, 1948.

Piaget, J. *Play, Dreams, and Imitation in Childhood*. New York: Norton, 1951.

Piaget, J. "Equilibration and the Development of Logical Structures." In J. M. Tanner & B. Inhelder (Eds.), *Discussions on Child Development* (Vol. 4). New York: International Universities Press, 1960.

Porro, C. R. "Effects of the Observation of a Model's Affective Responses to Her Own Transgression on Resistance to Temptation in Children." *Dissertation Abstracts*, 1968, 28:3064.

Postman, L., & Sassenrath, J. "The Automatic Action of Verbal Rewards and Punishments." *Journal of General Psychology*, 1961, 65:109-136.

Premack, D. "Reinforcement Theory." In D. Levine (Ed.), *Nebraska Symposium on Motivation*. Lincoln: University of Nebraska Press, 1965.

Rachlin, H. "Self-control." *Behaviorism*, 1974, 2:94-107.

Rachman, S. "Sexual Fetishism: An Experimental Analogue." *Psychological Record*, 1966, 16:293-296.

Rachman, S. *The Effects of Psychotherapy*. Oxford: Pergamon, 1971.

Rachman, S. "Clinical Applications of Observational Learning, Imitation, and Modeling." *Behavior Therapy*, 1972, 3:379-397.

Raush, H. L. "Interaction Sequences." *Journal of Personality and Social Psychology*, 1965, 2:487-499.

Raush, H. L., Barry, W. A., Hertel, R. K., & Swain, M. A. *Communication Conflict and Marriage*. San Francisco: Jossey-Bass, 1974.

Redd, W. J., & Birnbrauer, J. S. "Adults as Discriminative Stimuli for Different Reinforcement Contingencies with Retarded Children." *Journal of Experimental Child Psychology*, 1969, 7:440-447.

Reiss, S., & Sushinsky, L. W. "Overjustification, Competing Responses, and the Acquisition of Intrinsic Interest." *Journal of Personality and Social Psychology*, 1975, 31:1116-1125.

Rescorla, R. A. "Informational Variables in Pavlovian Conditioning." In G. H. Bower (Ed.), *The Psychology of Learning and Motivation* (Vol. 6). New York: Academic Press, 1972.

Rescorla, R. A., & Solomon, R. L. "Two-Process Learning Theory: Relationships between Pavlovian Conditioning and Instrumental Learning." *Psychological Review*, 1967, 74:151-182.

Rest, J., Turiel, E., & Kohlberg, L. "Level of Moral Development as a Determinant of Preference and Comprehension of Moral Judgments Made by Others." *Journal of Personality*, 1969, 37:225-252.

Revusky, S. H., & Garcia, J. "Learned Associations over Long Delays." In G. H. Bower (Ed.), *The Psychology of Learning and Motivation* (Vol. 4). New York: Academic Press, 1970.

Riesman, D. *The Lonely Crowd*. New Haven: Yale University Press, 1950.

Robertson, T. S. *Innovative Behavior and Communication*. New York: Holt, Rinehart & Winston, 1971.

Rogers, E. M., & Shoemaker, F. *Communication of Innovations: A Cross-cultural Approach* (2nd. ed.). New York: Free Press, 1971.

Rosekrans, M. A., & Hartup, W. W. "Imitative Influences of Consistent and Inconsistent Response Consequences to a Model on Aggressive Behavior in Children." *Journal of Personality and Social Psychology*, 1967, 7:429-434.

Rosenbaum, M. E. "The Effect of Stimulus and Background Factors on the Volunteering Response." *Journal of Abnormal and Social Psychology*, 1956, 53:118-121.

Rosenbaum, M. E., & Hewitt, O. J. "The Effect of Electric Shock on Learning by Performers and Observers." *Psychonomic Science*, 1966, 5:81-82.

Rosenhan, D., Frederick, F., & Burrowes, A. "Preaching and Practicing: Effects of Channel Discrepancy on Norm Internalization." *Child Development*, 1968, 39:291-301.

Rosenthal, T. L., & Zimmerman, B. J. *Social Learning and Cognition.* New York: Academic Press, 1977, in press.

Ross, M. "Salience of Reward and Intrinsic Motivation." *Journal of Personality and Social Psychology*, 1975, 32:245-254.

Ross, M. "The Self Perception of Intrinsic Motivation." In J. H. Harvey, W. J. Ickes, & R. F. Kidd (Eds.), *New Directions in Attribution Research*. Hillsdale, N.J.: Erlbaum, 1976.

Sandler, J., & Quagliano, J. "Punishment In a Signal Avoidance Situation." Paper read at Southeastern Psychological meeting, Gatlinburg, Tenn., 1964.

Schwartz, B. "On Going Back to Nature: A Review of Seligman and Hager's Biological Boundaries of Learning." *Journal of the Experimental Analysis of Behavior*, 1974, 21:183-198.

Schwartz, G. E. "Cardiac Responses to Self-Induced Thoughts." *Psychophysiology*, 1971, 8:462-467.

Seligman, M. E. P. "Phobias and Preparedness." *Behavior Therapy*, 1971, 2:307-320.

Seligman, M. E. P., & Hager, J. L. *Biological Boundaries of Learning*. New York: Appleton-Century-Crofts, 1972.

Shapiro, D., & Schwartz, G. E. "Biofeedback and Visceral Learning; Clinical Applications." *Seminars in Psychiatry*, 1972, 4:171-184.

Sherman, J. A. "Imitation and Language Development." In P. Lipsitt & C. C. Spiker (Eds.), *Advances in Child Development*. Vol. 6. New York: Academic Press, 1971.

Siegel, A. E. "The Influence of Violence in the Mass Media upon Children's Role Expectation." *Child Development* 1958, 29:35-56.

Skinner, B. F. *Walden Two*. New York: Macmillan, 1948.

Skinner, B. F. *Beyond Freedom and Dignity*. New York: Knopf, 1971.

Snow, C. E. "Mother's Speech to Children Learning Language." *Child Development*, 1972, 43:549-565.

Soule, J. C., & Firestone, I. J. "Model Choice and Achievement

Standards; Effects of Similarity in Locus of Control." Unpublished manuscript, University of Wisconsin (Milwaukee), 1976.

Spielberger, C. D., & De Nike, L. D. "Descriptive Behaviorism versus Cognitive Theory in Verbal Operant Conditioning." *Psychological Review*, 1966, 73:306-326.

Stone, L. J., & Hokanson, J. E. "Arousal Reduction via Self-punitive Behavior." *Journal of Personality and Social Psychology*, 1969, 12:72-79.

Stotland, E. "Exploratory Investigation of Empathy." In L. Berkowitz (Ed.), *Advances in Experimental Social Psychology* (Vol. 4). New York: Academic Press, 1969.

Stouwie, R. J., Hetherington, E. M.. & Parke, R. D. "Some Determinants of Children's Self-Reward Behavior after Exposure to Discrepant Reward Criteria." *Developmental Psychology*, 1970, 3:313-319.

Sullivan, E. V. "The Acquisition of Conservation of Substance through Film-Mediated Models." In D. W. Brison & E. V. Sullivan (Eds.), *Recent Research on the Acquisition of Conservation of Substance*. Education Monograph. Toronto: Ontario Institute for Studies in Education, 1967.

Testa, T. J. "Causal Relationships and the Acquisition of Avoidance Responses." *Psychological Review*, 1974, 81:491-505.

Thoresen, C. E., & Mahoney, M. J. *Behavioral Self-control*. New York: Holt, Rinehart & Winston, 1974.

Toch, H. *Violent Men*. Chicago: Aldine, 1969.

Truax, C. B. "Reinforcement and Nonreinforcement in Rogerian Psychotherapy." *Journal of Abnormal Psychology*, 1966, 71:1-9.

Turiel, E. "An Experimental Test of the Sequentiality of Development Stages in a Child's Moral Judgments." *Journal of Personality and Social Psychology*, 1966, 3:611-618.

Uzgiris, I. C. "Situational Generality of Conservation." *Child Development*, 1964, 35:831-841.

Valentine, C. W. "The Psychology of Imitation with Special Reference to Early Childhood." *British Journal of Psychology*, 1930, 21:105-132.

Valins, S., & Nisbett, R. E. *Attribution Processes in the Development and Treatment of Emotional Disorders*. Morristown, N.J.: General Learning Press, 1971.

Wallace, I. "Self-Control Techniques of Famous Novelists." *Journal of Applied Behavior Analysis*, 1976, in press.

Walters, R. H., & Parke, R. D. "Influence of Response Consequences to a Social Model on Resistance to Deviation." *Journal of Experimental Child Psychology*, 1964, 1:269-280.

Walters, R. H., Parke, R. D., & Cane, V. A. "Timing of Punishment and the Observation of Consequences to Others as Determinants of Response Inhibition." *Journal of Experimental Child Psychology*. 1965, 2:10-30.

Walton, D., & Mather, M. D. "The Application of Learning Principles to the Treatment of Obsessive-Compulsive States in the Acute and Chronic Phases of Illness." *Behavior Research and Therapy*, 1963, 1:163-174.

Watson, J. B., & Rayner, R. "Conditioned Emotional Reactions." *Journal of Experimental Psychology*, 1920, 3:1-14.

Weiner, H. "Real and Imagined Cost Effects upon Human Fixed-Interval Responding." *Psychological Reports*, 1965, 17:659-662.

Weisz, A. E., & Taylor, R. L. "American Presidential Assassinations." In D. N. Daniels, M. F. Gilula, & F. M. Ochberg (Eds.), *Violence and the Struggle for Existence*. Boston: Little, Brown, 1970.

White, R. W. "Motivation Reconsidered: The Concept of Competence." *Psychological Review*, 1959, 66:297-333.

Whitehurst, G. J., & Vasta, R. "Is Language Acquired through Imitation?" *Journal of Psycholinguistic Research*, 1975, 4:37-59.

Wilson, W. C. "Imitation and Learning of Incidental Cues by Preschool Children." *Child Development*, 1958, 29:393-397.

Yalom, I. D., & Yalom, M. "Ernest Hemingway—A Psychiatric View." *Archives of General Psychiatry*, 1971, 24:485-494.

Yussen, S. R. "Determinants of Visual Attention and Recall in Observational Learning by Preschoolers and Second Graders." *Developmental Psychology*, 1974, 10:93-100.

Zimbardo, P. G. "The Human Choice: Individuation, Reason, and Order versus Deindividuation, Impulse, and Chaos." In W. J. Arnold & D. Levine (Eds.), *Nebraska Symposium on Motivation*. Lincoln: University of Nebraska Press, 1969.

Zimmerman, B. J., & Rosenthal, T. L. "Observational Learning of Rule Governed Behavior by Children." *Psychological Bulletin*, 1974, 81:29-42.

Zimring, F. *Deterrence. The Legal Threat in Crime Control*. Chicago: Chicago University Press, 1973.

Author Index

Subject Index